A DELAYED
LIFE

A DELAYED LIFE

THE TRUE STORY OF THE LIBRARIAN OF AUSCHWITZ

DITA KRAUS

Feiwel and Friends
New York

A Feiwel and Friends Book
An imprint of Macmillan Publishing Group, LLC
120 Broadway, New York, NY 10271

Library of Congress Control Number: 2019949140

ISBN 978-1-250-76089-0

Our books may be purchased in bulk for promotional, educational, or business use. Please
contact your local bookseller or the Macmillan Corporate and Premium Sales Department at
(800) 221-7945 ext. 5442 or by email at MacmillanSpecialMarkets@macmillan.com.

Originally published by Ebury Publishing UK in 2020

First American edition, 2020

Designed by Kay Petronio

Printed in the United States of America

1 3 5 7 9 10 8 6 4 2

fiercereads.com

Contents

PART III: 1945–21ST CENTURY

Why Did I Call It a Delayed Life?

My life is not real life. It is something before the beginning of "real life," a kind of preface to the narrative. It's not yet what counts, merely a rehearsal. And someone is watching from behind, or perhaps from above, and passing judgment. There is a being that controls and judges my behavior. Perhaps it is not out there but inside me. Could it be my mother? Or my grandmother? Or something more internal . . . my id? I have no idea. But it is constantly present, holding an invisible mirror in front of me.

I can feel its approval or disapproval, the latter making me squirm inwardly, trying to suppress the nagging conscience or finding excuses for myself, although the negative feeling is extremely tenacious and cannot be shooed away. I make an effort to find reasons for having done or said what my controller finds unsatisfactory, but at the same time I know that I am only trying to justify my wrongdoing.

I don't yet know how this connects to me perceiving my life as being delayed. For as long as I can remember, I have been more focused on tomorrow than aware about what I am experiencing at that particular moment. Even now, when I am at a concert, my thoughts are on the return journey and on tomorrow's schedule and not on the music I came to listen to. When I eat, my mind is on washing the dishes, and when I lie down, I'm already planning what I must do when I get up. It's never on the here and now, and I sense that I'm missing the enjoyment of the present. There is too much control: never letting go, never totally relaxing. There's always the presence of the Watcher, forever passing judgment.

It must have been at a very early age that I began to delay my life. It was a way of indefinite postponement, a deferred satisfaction. How did I delay? I accepted the bitter fact that I would not get what I wanted, certainly not soon and probably never. I told myself I must wait patiently; perhaps fulfillment would come later. Or never. I thought that maybe if I put my hope on hold and didn't think about it, one day it may turn out right.

In some deep place, I kept believing that the circle would come around and things would rearrange themselves in their proper sequence, that everything would resume its normal place. I just had to delay.

But in a strange way, these delayed passages—these empty spaces—have created gaps, so that the mosaic of my life has spots where the picture is left unfinished.

There are so many of these gaps. How shall I fill them? Time is running out; who knows how long I have left to live. Already I am the grandmother of four grandchildren and four great-grandchildren. Most of the people from my earlier years are no longer alive and cannot answer my questions. I shall try to gather the fragments and write them down; perhaps a blueprint will emerge that might fill the blank spaces on the mosaic. . . .

A DELAYED
LIFE

Part I

1929–1942

CHAPTER ONE

Childhood

My earliest recollections emerge from the empty nothingness, which precedes conscious memory. They resemble a picture flickering for an instant on the screen and disappearing again into darkness. Yet each of these fleeting pictures is suffused with emotion.

I have been placed on the baby scale on the table covered with a white oil-cloth, in the doctor's office. I am naked, and the metal is hard and cold on my back. I may be two or two and a half years old. Mother and the doctor in a white coat are standing over me. I am not frightened, because they smile.

Dr. Desensy-Bill was our pediatrician. I remember later visits, when she put her palm on my chest, tapped it with her middle finger, and then listened, pressing her ear to my skin. Her office was connected to the private quarters by a brown leather-padded door with brass buttons.

Sometimes Mother stayed to talk to the doctor and I was sent through the thick door—which, although heavy, moved easily and noiselessly—to play with her daughter Lucy. Lucy was about my age, but I didn't take to her; she was boring.

Another memory. It is night and I am standing on my bed, crying and terrified. I must be still very small, as I am holding the cot's protective-netting bar with both hands. Mother and Mitzi, our household help, are with me, trying to calm me. But I cannot be pacified, because just a moment ago, a hand came through the wall and wanted to grab me. Mother lifts me out of the cot and takes me to the other side of the wall, which is the bathroom, to show me there is no hole in the wall. Both she and Mitzi are telling me that no hand can reach through a solid wall. But they don't know; they haven't seen the hand. I have. When I stop crying, they put me back to bed, believing that I have been convinced. They cover me and turn off the light. Yet the terror remains, and for many weeks afterward, I can only fall asleep when the cot is pushed away from the wall.

From the darkness of unknowing, another scene emerges. It is most disturbing. I am in the bathtub, and Mother is sitting on the rim. Suddenly I see tears flowing silently from her eyes. Mother is weeping soundlessly. It frightens me, and I start crying, too. "What have I done?" I ask. "What have I done?" But she only shakes her head and doesn't answer. I don't know why Mother cried. Had someone hurt her? Was it my fault? Did I misbehave? I have no clue, no idea. Even now, as I recall the event, I feel sorrow, guilt, and pain.

My mother's maiden name was Elisabeth "Liesl" Adler. She had a brother named Hugo, who was ten years older. Their mother died when Liesl was a baby, and her father, a judge, married again. Mother told me that her stepmother was fair and conscientious but lacked warmth and motherly love. I don't remember Grandfather Adler; he died soon after I was born. Hugo also became a judge. He married but didn't have children. I only saw him twice in my life.

Mother and I stopped over in Brno for two or three days on our way to a vacation in the Tatra Mountains when I was six or seven. I remember vividly two scenes from that visit. Mother broke into tears when we entered Uncle Hugo's flat. It was the same flat where Mother had grown up; when she had married, Hugo had remained living there. The same furniture was still there, which brought back old memories.

Wilhelm Adler with his daughter, Elisabeth Adler-Polach

The other scene I remember was from court. Hugo, wearing the violet judge's cape, presided over a trial while we sat at the back of the courtroom. When it was over, Mother commented that it was quiet and unexciting, and Hugo replied, "I don't do divorces. That's why my trials are boring."

My parents moved from their native Brno to Prague soon after they married. They rented a little flat on the ground floor of a villa. There was a garden with a lawn, flower beds, and gooseberry bushes around the fence. I was allowed to pick the berries but didn't like them because they were hairy and sour. Mr. Hackenberg, the owner, was a friend and party colleague of my grandfather Johann.

The Hackenbergs had a huge German shepherd called Putzi, who was so gentle that he let me ride on his back. A snapshot shows me naked, aged about two, standing next to the dog, and we are the same height.

A memory comes back to me: Mr. Hackenberg and my mother are sitting on a bench in the garden, while I am playing in the sandbox. I am digging with my bare hands, making a tunnel. Suddenly a horrifying pink slimy thing comes wriggling out of the hole toward me. I scream in terror and run into my mother's protective arms. When she understands what had frightened me, she bursts out laughing. Mr. Hackenberg also laughs. I feel ashamed, humiliated. How can they laugh when I was so frightened? My mother has formed a league with Mr. Hackenberg, and they mock me. She has let me down, betrayed me. How was I to know it was only an innocent earthworm? It was the first time in my life I had seen such a horrible creature.

I was three or four when we moved to another flat in Prague-Holešovice, and our household help, Mitzi, left us at that time. Nowadays only the rich have a live-in maid, but in prewar Europe, it was common practice. The young daughters of poor villagers came to the city to find employment, learn how to cook, learn good manners, and, if lucky, find a husband. They would occupy a tiny room provided for the servant in almost every flat, and they would receive a small wage and one free afternoon and free evening a week. Often they did not stay long with the family, either because they were too slow or were caught stealing; some became pregnant and had to be dismissed.

My mother was proud that the reason our Mitzi left us was because she was getting married. Her husband-to-be was a cobbler who had a shop around the corner on the main street, near the number six tram stop. Soon after she got married, Mitzi invited me for a Sunday breakfast. I was allowed to go alone; on Sunday morning the street was deserted, and I was very proud to walk unaccompanied. Mitzi and her husband lived behind the shop in a room that smelled of glue and leather. The shop was closed, and Mitzi made me feel like an honored guest. She served me a big slice of her *Gugelhupf,* the same as my mother used to bake, but hers tasted more festive, somehow. I was very happy and proud to be treated as an adult.

There were more such breakfasts, but they became rarer, and after some time, Mitzi and her cobbler moved away; I think he had to close the shop because it didn't provide them enough of a living. We never heard from Mitzi again.

While Mitzi was still with us, my mother and I went for a holiday to her native village. It was in the German-speaking region called Böhmerwald, also known as the Bohemian Forest. For a few days Mitzi stayed there with us, then she went back to Prague to oversee the housepainters, who were redecorating the flat during our absence. I remember it because when we came home, there was a smell of fresh paint and newly waxed floors.

There was a shallow river behind the farmhouse where we lodged. Another memory surfaces, of me, and several local children, standing knee-deep in the stream. The cascading water was crystal clear, and we were collecting gold. Yes, genuine gold. The grains were no bigger than poppy seeds, but they shone among the pebbles in the transparent water.

We held them in our palms and let the sun play on them. It was very exciting. Today when I see a film about the Gold Rush, I smile and remember how I too was a gold digger once upon a time.

It was in that village where I first learned about death.

There was a road running along the foot of the hill on the opposite bank of the river. A horse was lying on the road, its head and neck hanging over the sloping incline. Behind the horse was an overturned cart. The horse didn't move. I stood, watching, for a long time, waiting for the horse to get up. Several people stood around. They too waited. But the horse didn't move, and I began to realize the frightening, terrible fact that the animal would never rise again . . . that it was dead. I was very disturbed and scared. Yet as with other discoveries made later in life, it was not as if I was encountering a new phenomenon, but rather as if some knowledge, which had lain dormant within me, emerged into the light of consciousness. As Plato believed: "Much of our knowledge is inherent in the psyche in latent form." It was the first intimation that the world was not such a bright and happy place as it had been up to that point.

My next encounter with death occurred a few years later, when I was eight years old. One morning, near the school, I saw a bunch of children pressed to the fence that enclosed the schoolyard. Behind the fence was a steep slope, and at the bottom there was a railway. There, on the tracks, lay a figure: someone dead, looking more like a heap of clothes than a body. The children were staring down, hushed and immobile. It was a moment of profound sadness. I knew it was a suicide; someone who no longer wanted to live had jumped under a train. The place is forever associated in my memory with tragedy. Even when, after almost sixty years, I stood again near my old school, I was drawn to the same spot at the fence, as if the pitiful figure were still lying there.

A frequent visitor to our home was Aunt Lori (Grandmother's distant relative), whom I liked very much. She always brought me nice presents. She herself was not married and had no children, but she just knew what would please a little girl.

Once she brought me a stuffed toy dachshund. I called it Waldi. It was black, velvety soft, and cuddly and had a red leather collar and leash. I would "walk" it behind me as I saw people do with real dogs.

One day I was sitting with my dog in front of our building on a little stool when I needed to go upstairs. I tied the leash to the cellar window grille and told Waldi to be good and wait for me. I used to see dogs tied to a post in front of shops, waiting for their masters.

When I returned, the dog was gone. I was terribly unhappy. I couldn't grasp that someone was so bad and cruel that they would take my dog and that I would never see Waldi again. I cried bitterly with pain and disappointment.

While Mitzi came from the German-speaking border area, our second maid, Maria, was from a Czech village. My parents had been educated in the German language, as were most Jews in Brno of those times. They spoke Czech well enough, but my perfectionist father did not want me to pick up his occasional inaccuracies. So it was decided to engage a Czech girl, from whom I would learn the native accent.

I passed Marla on the stairs the day she came to introduce herse
flying downstairs with her open coat fluttering behind. Our eyes m_
in love with her. I didn't know she was coming from our flat, but when she came
back after a few days to live with us, I was very happy. She could have been about
sixteen, very pretty and full of life and laughter. She was also fond of me, and I
liked going for walks with her better than with my parents. I remember her telling me of her former employers, who were very stern with her. She pointed out
their house to me and told me about the dictatorial Mrs. Brod. I imagined her as
the witch stepmother from "Snow White."

Maria and I became conspirators. My mother would never buy me colored
lemonade or ice pops from street vendors, but Maria herself was crazy about
them and sometimes treated us both, paying with her own money and swearing
me to secrecy.

Our flat had two large rooms and a small one. The small room was mine,
and the others were my parents' bedroom and the living room with the round
dining table in the middle. Our Maria, therefore, spent her nights on a folding
bed in the kitchen, which she pulled upright every morning and hid beneath a
curtain. She had a private wardrobe for herself in the kitchen with a full-length
mirror inside. She used to stand behind the open door when she dressed, before
going out on her weekly free afternoon.

Once I sneaked behind her and saw her breasts. "Your *brunslíky* are bigger
than my mother's," I said. She burst out laughing and, when she repeated it to
my mother, she too joined in the merriment. *Brunslíky* was a meaningless word,
which I must have invented or jumbled from another, but since then it became
our family's official term for that part of the female anatomy.

Maria's work wasn't hard: the parquet floors were covered with carpets that
had to be vacuumed; once in a while the double-glazed windows needed washing; the stone floor in the kitchen needed to be polished. One of the features
that astonished visitors to our house was the automated laundry in the basement.
Since there were about sixteen flats in each of the two wings of the Electric House,
we had to book our washing day in advance at the janitor's.

I loved to accompany Maria as she took the two large baskets full of washing down in the lift. The air in the basement was dry and warm and smelled of soap and cleanness. The two huge drums of the washing machines rotated with a low hum. There were hot-air drying cabins. I liked to hear the bell that announced the end of drying, and then Maria would roll out the pulleys, take down the starched sheets, and run them through the ironing press. A few hours later we ascended to the fourth floor with the beautifully folded and scented linen.

I used to wake up to the sound of the coffee grinder. Mother bought one hundred grams of freshly roasted coffee every week. I also drank coffee for breakfast, but it was one part coffee and three parts milk. Maria would shake the pillows and quilts and place them into the open window for airing. When Mother and I went shopping, we would go to the butcher first and buy the meat for dinner, then to the dairy shop for milk and butter. I always begged Mother to take me to Pilař's Sweet Shop, but this happened only rarely because we had to economize. The shop was carpeted from wall to wall and smelled marvelously of vanilla and chocolate. I knew I could choose two pieces; usually I picked an *Indianerkrapfen* with a chocolate base and one meringue, both filled with whipped cream. Mr. Pilař had a brown triangular cloth bag with a white spout at the end, from which he squeezed a spiral of fresh cream. He placed the two delicate pieces on a cardboard plate and wrapped them carefully so as not to crush them. Mother let me carry the parcel, but I was allowed to eat them only after dinner because they would spoil my appetite.

I was a picky eater. What I disliked I just wouldn't eat, and because I was thin, the family was eager to get something wholesome into me. I became nauseous when the tiniest bit of milk skin floated on top of my coffee. Meat had to be absolutely lean, without a trace of fat; otherwise I left the whole meal on the plate, even after Mother had removed the repulsive bit. She tried several educational methods, telling me that millions of children all over the world were hungry and would be happy to get such nice food as I did. She invited a friend for dinner, so I should see how other children eat properly. Every day I had to swallow a spoonful of awful-smelling cod liver oil to prevent me from getting the rickets. Nothing helped. In the end Mother gave up and cooked for me separately, spaghetti with Parmesan cheese or schnitzel with French fries.

Once, my parents had a bright idea. The youth movement of the Social Democrats was sending its members' children on a winter vacation to the Iser Mountains. The trip was meant for children of school age, while I was only five and still in kindergarten. But one of the accompanying adults was Giesl, a friend and upstairs neighbor of ours, so I was accepted and put under her special care. All the children were older than me, but I didn't mind. We went sledding and skiing and had fun playing games in the rustic hostel where we lodged.

The staff must have been forewarned about my food problem.

I can still see myself sitting in the dining room, with a plate in front of me of something unidentifiable and suspicious. I didn't touch it. Nobody got angry, and I was allowed to leave the table with the others. But at the next meal, everyone got a different dish, while on my plate was the thing I had left at noon. Again I didn't touch it.

The next day we dressed warmly and went on an outing to the woods. We walked through high snow and came to a little brook, all frozen over with only a narrow opening in the middle, where we could see the cascading water. There was a wooden plank across the brook with a handrail on one side. We started crossing it one by one—then suddenly my memory goes blank.

I woke up in a big strange bed, covered by a huge eiderdown. Several adults were standing around, with Giesl bending over me. I didn't understand what was going on. Later the children excitedly told me that I fainted near the brook and was carried back unconscious. They gave me tea and good things to eat; I had become the center of everyone's attention.

For the rest of the wonderful holiday, no one tried to make me eat what I didn't like. My eating problem remained as before.

When we returned from shopping, Mother and Maria would start cooking. To this day I cannot understand what the two of them did in the kitchen for at least two hours every morning. There were always several pots steaming on the electric stove, both women with their aprons and flushed faces stirring, chopping, or peeling. Sometimes they made noodles, the dough rolled out into thin sheets that were put to dry on white tablecloths on every table and bed all over the flat. Later they cut them into thin strips for soup, broader ones, and also little squares for the wonderful *Schinkenfleckerln*. Mother used to make a dish from the broad noodles, sprinkled with sugar and poppy seeds or cinnamon.

In summer Mother made preserves and jams for the winter. Apricots, strawberries, or cherries were cooked with sugar and then put in glass jars with tight lids. The jars in turn were placed in an enormous pot with a thermometer in the middle. When they cooled, Mother wrote the dates on stickers and stored the jars in rows on the shelves in the pantry. In autumn, when the plums were ripe, she made a marvelous black jam called *powidel*, which was used as filling in dumplings or in *buchty*, a kind of baked pocket, so beloved by the Czechs.

On washing day, dinner was simple. Often it was *Wurstgoulash*, made of potatoes and cubes of salami with gravy. But the most common meal was stew, which my father was especially fond of. Mother always saved a portion for him, and in the evening he would dip pieces of bread in it to mop up the gravy. What I loved best was the dessert Mother sometimes made for Sundays, especially when Father's younger brother, Ernst-Benjamin, came for dinner. It was called *Dukatenbuchteln*, small square yeast cakes covered with a hot, delicious, sweet vanilla sauce.

The meals were served on the green oval table in my little room. The kitchen was too narrow for a table and chairs. It was most uncommon to have the servant share the table with the family, but when Maria brought the soup tureen, she would sit down and eat with us. My parents, being socialists, believed in doing away with class distinctions. Maria was an employee, but she was never treated as an inferior.

After dinner Maria washed the dishes, and Mother went to lie down on the sofa in the bedroom to smoke a cigarette. I usually knelt near her and begged her to "leave a long ash." She held the cigarette very carefully over the ashtray on her abdomen, not flicking the ash off, letting it grow longer and longer, until it almost burned her fingers. When it finally drooped and fell, I always let out a sigh of disappointment.

Mother would rest only for a short while, and then we would go to the park. There were two parks near where we lived: one called Stromovka, the other Letná. Letná was a bit farther away and smaller, while Stromovka was the former Royal Park, stretching all the way to the Vltava River. There was a kind of bridge, made of a number of flat-bottomed boats tied together, and I loved to walk on it because it rocked gently on the waves. On the other bank was Prague's zoo. In both parks there were children's playgrounds with sandpits, but I preferred the Letná, while Mother always wanted to go to the Stromovka. True, in Stromovka there were little ponds with ducks and fluffy ducklings paddling frantically behind their mothers and creating a V on the surface. One could feed them with pieces of stale rolls. There were also a great number of brown squirrels, hopping quite near our feet. For one koruna (the Czech money) Mother sometimes bought peanuts from a man who carried a tray on a strap around his neck, with cone-shaped cups fashioned from newspapers. I was allowed to share the peanuts with the squirrel. It would sit on its hind legs, holding the nut in its tiny paws and nibbling delicately with its two long front teeth. Sometimes it would scurry away and bury the nut for the winter. I loved to watch the little creatures with their bushy tails, which undulated like a double arch.

Mother liked the Stromovka because of its magnificent garden with rows of roses of all colors and sizes, some almost crawling on the ground, others in garlands or climbing on trellises, but I was bored with them. I wanted to go to the Letná, where I knew several children and where a man sold balloons. Mother sometimes gave in and bought me a balloon. Once, as I was transferring it to my other hand, it escaped and flew into the sky. I was expecting it to come down again, as did everything else one threw upward, and was distraught to the point of tears when my new balloon was lost.

The children who played in the Letná Park were well dressed; some were accompanied by governesses with dark-blue veils hanging down their backs. A few owned shiny metal scooters—or corquinets in Hebrew—with rubber tires, while mine was the cheap wooden kind with bumpy wheels. My mother had won it at the Konsum, where she did her shopping. Here and there I would be able to borrow such a marvel, especially from a little girl with corkscrew curls like those of Shirley Temple. She let me have two runs on the downhill path, which was the best, because I could just stand and steer as the scooter rolled by itself and I didn't have to propel it with my foot.

But often it was Maria who took me to the park, when Mother had other engagements. It was more fun. Maria didn't seem to educate me; she was like a big child herself.

On the way to the Stromovka, we often saw "Handless Frantík," an amputee who made a living by demonstrating his skill writing on a typewriter with his toes. Sitting on his low-wheel wagon, he was a familiar sight on the streets of Prague, and people would gather around him and throw coins in his hat. But the sight of suffering people or animals always caused me pangs of pity.

Once, as Maria and I were walking back from the park, we met a woman with a girl about my age whose arm was in a plaster cast. It seemed as if the girl's arm ended at her elbow and the white thing was attached to the stump, instead of to her hand. I had never seen such a thing before, and, horrified, I asked what it was. In a flash of inspiration, Maria said, "This happened to the girl because she picked her nose." I was terrified. I knew I had this ugly habit. I used to try hard not to do it but could not overcome the urge; my finger just went to my nostril against my will. But after that day, I at least managed to do it only when I thought no one could see me.

When I was small I was not aware of class distinctions. The families I knew lived much like ours. We were what is commonly considered middle class, but Father's salary wasn't large, and so we had to calculate expenses carefully. For example, my parents put aside a certain sum for the whole year to pay for our summer vacation.

Later, in first grade, I met a rich boy. His name was Fredy Petschek. Fredy was brought to school every morning by a chauffeur-driven car, and at noon the automobile was waiting for him again in front of the entrance. He lived in a large villa with a park, surrounded by a high wall. His father owned coal mines and banks. One bank was in a huge palace in the center of town; it later became notorious, when the German occupiers turned it into their Gestapo headquarters.

Fredy's mother was a fine lady, whom we sometimes saw in the car. I overheard some adults saying she was so afraid of microbes that, when she went to buy dress material, she always took a servant along to feel the fabrics, lest she catch some infection.

Little Fredy was a thin child, who held his head a bit sideways. He usually forgot to remove the satchel with his sandwich from around his neck and wore it there all morning. The children in class often mocked him; he had a funny walk with his knees close together. But somehow he didn't notice or care, as if he were absentminded. He was a habitual nose picker. Once, we first graders were told to give one another small gifts; I don't remember on what occasion. One of the boys gave Fredy a large box. We all watched eagerly to see the big gift. As he unwrapped it he found a smaller box and another, smaller again, until in the last one he discovered the tiny present. It was a toothpick with a cotton wool tip. "It is to help you pick your nose," the little joker explained.

The story about Fredy Petschek doesn't end here. When I was in the United States a few years ago, say in 2010, I met a lady named Nancy Petschek. *She must be a member of that family*, I thought. I asked her if she was related to Fredy Petschek. She thought for a while and then said, "That could be Uncle Alfred." *Funny!* I thought. *Little Fredy is now Uncle Alfred!* "I will ask him if he went to the same school as you," she said. But unfortunately before she had a chance to do so, Uncle Alfred Petschek died.

Another rich child was my classmate Annemarie Brösslerová. On her birthday there was a party with wonderful sweets and ice cream, and each of us little girls got a present. The party was presided over by a governess, and when we asked where her mother was, Annemarie said she was somewhere at home. That surprised me, but Annemarie told us that they had eight rooms and she often didn't know in which of them her mother was at the moment.

I envied Annemarie—not for the many rooms or the books and toys she had but because she had an older brother. Among my close childhood friends, she was the only one who had a sibling. The others—Raja, Gerta, and Anita—all came from one-child families like myself. Annemarie's brother was handsome; he collected stamps and rode a bicycle. I admired him so much! I wished I had such a big brother.

Poor Annemarie. When the Germans started to deport the Jews, she and her family were sent to the Łódź ghetto in one of the first transports from Prague. I never heard of her again. Before their departure, I went to say goodbye to her, and she pointed to her books, which I used to borrow from her, and said, "Take as many as you like. They will all be left behind."

I picked one I had read several times, a silly and sentimental girls' romance. But as I was taking it, I already knew that soon I too would leave it behind, together with my own books and toys, when our turn came to be deported.

CHAPTER TWO

Anita

W e had not lived long in the Electric House when one day I saw a big moving van in front of the entrance. Workmen were carrying furniture into the building, directed by a lady. When she saw me, she asked me if I lived here, what my name was, and how old I was. Then she said that she also had a girl my age and we must become friends.

Anita became my friend for many years, although our relationship was a strange and uneven one. Anita was much taller than me, even though she was

Anita Steiner

only six months older. It was always she who decided what we would play, and sometimes she had queer ideas.

The Steiners lived on the second floor, two stories below us. Anita's mother, Hilde, was fond of me and used to call me *Shpuntl*, a funny term of endearment for small beings. It was convenient that they lived in the same building; my other friends, Gerta and Raja, with whom I preferred to play, lived a few streets away.

Anita planned a grand project: we would prepare a puppet theater show. She owned a collapsible stage with a curtain in front and various backdrop sceneries, including a wood, a room in a castle with a throne for a king, and a village street. There were plenty of puppets on strings: a witch, a beautiful maiden, a clown, a knight, a queen, and a king. Anita decided that we must paint another scenery on cardboard for her show. What the story was, I never learned. She changed her mind every few days, and each time, we began to make a new set. For weeks we were busy painting, sewing clothes for the puppets, and preparing the stage. The show never materialized. When I asked her what the play was about, she just changed the subject. Anita was the leader, and I, the reluctant but obedient follower.

One day she made up her mind that I must stay with her overnight. She didn't ask permission and said it had to be kept secret; otherwise the mothers wouldn't allow it. She brought pillows and blankets into her room and spread them on the floor. Then she locked the door. When bedtime arrived, Maria came to fetch me, but Anita whispered that we should pretend to be asleep and not answer. Maria knocked on the door, then Anita's mother joined her, and when that didn't help, they called my mother. I felt terrible; I had no desire to sleep on the hard floor in Anita's room, and on my part, there just was no reason to behave so obstreperously. But I obeyed Anita's instructions and remained quiet. In the end, the three women somehow managed to enter the room, and Anita got into a fit of rage. I was led home, up the two floors, feeling guilt and shame, because I myself couldn't explain why we did it.

Yet apart from her strange conceptions of games, Anita was a loyal friend. She proved it later during the German occupation, when we already had to wear the yellow Star of David with the word *Jude* and the Aryan population was forbidden to have any contact with Jews. Since her father was a German and her mother Jewish, the parents thought it expedient to have Anita join the organization BDM—Bund Deutscher Mädel, or the League of German Girls—a section of the Hitler Youth. Mr. Steiner belonged to the three-million-strong German minority that had lived for centuries in Bohemia—a historical region in the present-day Czech Republic—most of them in the border area, the Sudeten. He worked in a bank and, as far as I know, was not politically engaged.

Anita often came to visit me in our cramped one room, where we lived before our deportation. She told me about the activities at the BDM meetings, which resembled those of Scouts. She always brought something that we Jews no longer could buy, such as a piece of fresh fruit or some honey.

When I came back from the camps after the war, I visited Anita several times. She told me how her mother was deported to Terezín during the last months of the occupation and her father, being the spouse of a Jewess, was interned in a labor camp. Anita was left alone in Prague and was extremely worried about her parents. When I visited her in July 1945, both parents were back, and Anita was solicitous of them like a mother hen. Mrs. Steiner saw that I had nothing to wear, having just returned from Bergen-Belsen, and she gave me a pair of stockings and a few other things she could spare.

One day I arrived to find the door of their apartment sealed by the police. I had no idea what had happened and went downstairs to the janitor; perhaps he could explain.

"Don't you see?" he said. "They were Germans, and they escaped before they would be expelled by the government."

The entire German minority of Czechoslovakia was expelled to Germany a few months after the end of the war. The Steiners, however, would not have been among them, since they themselves had been persecuted by the Germans. Nevertheless, Anita vanished from my life, and I never heard from her again.

CHAPTER THREE

Gerta

Of all my friends, my truly close one was Gerta Altschul.

I envied Gerta, too. She didn't have a brother, but she owned two skating dresses, which her mother had prepared for the day when she would be proficient enough to dance on ice. Both dresses had tiny skirts that swirled prettily when she pirouetted; one was made of dark-blue velvet, the other wine-colored.

We used to go skating together at the Winter Stadium, a few tram stops away from our street. I was obliged to wear thick trousers over my wool underwear, a knitted cap, and fur-lined gloves, which became caked with a crust of ice from the many falls. Gerta wasn't allowed to wear her flimsy dresses. She too was swathed like me in warm clothes, but hers were more elegant than mine.

Gerta took figure-skating lessons to become a second Sonja Henie, whom her mother admired. In the meantime, we put on the velvet dresses at her home, where we played almost every afternoon and danced on our tiptoes, humming waltzes in lieu of real music. Neither her family nor mine owned a radio or a gramophone. We sometimes also played in my home, but I liked it better to go to hers. Gerta's mother understood little girls' desires for fancy clothes, ribbons, shawls, and high-heeled shoes. And I loved the snack she used to make for us: a small bowl of homemade cottage cheese sprinkled with salt.

Gerta's father was Jewish, but her mother was not. At the time it was of no consequence, but later, when the Germans persecuted Jews, Gerta was spared because children of mixed marriages who were not registered as Jews were not deported. Her father, however, died in the Small Fortress of Terezín.

I wanted to be like Gerta in many respects. Not only did she learn figure skating; she also learned English with a lady who took her for walks in the park — Letná, of course—and talked to her only in English. When we met she wouldn't stop but walked on, conversing with her teacher.

Gerta and I decided to look like sisters. Her mother suggested to mine that her seamstress make identical dresses for us girls. I felt that my mother was not enthusiastic—perhaps she didn't share Mrs. Altschul's taste—but she agreed. We each got two dresses, one of which I especially loved. It was made of soft fire-engine red wool fabric, with a tight bodice, a wide skirt, and a white lace collar. What my mother couldn't understand was why such a warm dress had short sleeves: for summer too warm; for winter impractical. We also went together to the Bata shoe shop, where we got the same shoes, two pairs of them. Two pairs of shoes at once! I was so impressed by the unheard of extravagance that I never forgot it. But it didn't happen again; my sensible mother was unwilling to discard two pairs of shoes at once, which of course I had outgrown in less than a year.

We girls wanted our parents to become as good of friends as we were. The Altschuls were more than ready and invited my parents to celebrate Sylvester Eve at their home. Gerta and I prepared the entertainment. We were about eight years old. We rehearsed a ballet, and after the festive meal that Gerta's mother prepared, we performed it, clad in Gerta's skating dresses, accompanied by our own singing. The parents sat around the table and clapped, we bowed low and threw kisses like real ballerinas. Afterward, Mr. Altschul, who was a traveling salesman, told a few jokes, one of which was disgusting. It had to do with a man who slept in a strange house and didn't find the toilet, etc. The mothers were conversing together, but my father sat woodenly, and I sensed his uneasiness in this incompatible company. Midnight came at last, we cheered the New Year, and then we went home to my parents' relief. But I knew that the party had not been a success.

Every year on Saint Matthias's Day, there is a fair in Prague, called Matějská Pouť. It used to be held on a huge circular plot in Dejvice, one of the suburbs of the city. Maria and I went there by streetcar, and even from afar, we could hear the loud music. There were carousels with white horses standing on their hind legs, swings with boat-shaped cradles in which one could sit, but the more courageous youngsters stood and made the boat swing sky high, so that their bodies became horizontal. There were shooting booths, where one could win a stuffed animal or a plaster figure of Amor with red lips and blue wings, pushcarts with pink sugar foam or tough and sticky Turkish delight. However, most interesting of all was the tall carousel, with the seats hanging on chains.

The first round started slowly, the chairs swinging gently to and fro, but with each revolution the speed increased, and we were pushed outward by the centrifugal force and I felt my stomach heave. My fear turned to constricting terror and then to a state of abandonment. When we came to a halt, I slid from the metal seat on wobbling legs and tried to overcome my nausea. But I must have been so pale that Maria comforted me by saying, "This carousel is not as pleasant as I thought; we won't ride it again." I protested, because somehow I had enjoyed the scare; it had given me a sensual feeling in my underbelly.

My father's name was Hans—in Czech, Hanuš or Jan. He was well-proportioned, medium height, with straight shoulders and a lean body. He had short, wavy dark hair, a Jewish nose, and gray-green eyes, the same as mine, which Mother used to call "Daddy's eyes." He was always carefully dressed, his fingernails perfectly clean, and when he took off his clothes at bedtime, he folded everything neatly on a chair. He removed the keys, pocket comb, and wallet and placed them on the table. In the wardrobe there were the starched detachable collars, arranged in the same order as the stack of ironed shirts. The collar was changed daily, and the shirt every second day. I see my father standing in front of the mirror, deciding which tie would match the color of the shirt and putting a clean handkerchief in his breast pocket. The bed is still unmade, because only after breakfast would Maria enter the bedroom and air the quilts and pillows in the open window. When I returned from kindergarten, and later from school, the bed would be smooth and tidy, covered with the beige bedspread, and the bedroom would smell cool and fresh.

One day Mother and I went to see where Father was working. We took the tram to the outskirts of the city. There, on the slope over the Vltava, stood the impressive Social Security Institute, a huge building with a large cupola in the middle. Inside the grand entrance hall were two marvelous elevators without doors, moving slowly, one upward and the other down, without stopping. Mother said they were called Paternoster (the first word of the Catholic prayer), because people were afraid to ride in them and prayed to God for safety. I was scared, too, and asked her anxiously what would happen if we didn't get off on the top floor; would the lift turn over and go downward headfirst?

I was immensely impressed with Father's office and proud that he was such an important man. He was Dr. Hans Polach, a doctor of law. At the Social Security Institute, he defended the workers' interests, a task which was in keeping with his political views. He had done training at the law office of Dr. Ludwig Czech, who later became minister of welfare in the Czechoslovak government. Father had already decided then not to go into private practice, because it might have obligated him to defend criminals, knowing they were guilty, something his conscience couldn't bear. And so he chose to become a salaried state employee and never grew wealthy, like many other Jewish lawyers.

Not far from Father's office, on the banks of the Vltava, was a bathing area, where we often went swimming in summer. Mother and I arrived by tram, and Father would join us in the afternoon after work. There were lawns and changing cabins and wooden jetties from which the swimmers could jump into the river. For children and nonswimmers there were floating enclosures, with boardwalks and railings around. The lifeguard was also the swimming teacher. He held a long pole with a rope over the railing, and the learner was hooked to it with a canvas belt around his middle. The guard chanted, "And one and two, and one and two," while the spluttering victim tried to move his arms and legs in rhythm.

When we had changed into our swimsuits—wool, of course, because synthetic fabrics were not yet available—Mother would rub our backs and shoulders with cocoa butter, the suntan lotion of those times. It looked like a big cube of brown soap and had a very distinctive smell, which I remember to this day. Mother and Father usually swam to the opposite bank and back again, while I played in the shallow pool.

It was there where I—at the age of three or four—first became aware of my nakedness, like Adam and Eve after the Fall. Mother had taken off my clothes to put on my bathing suit, and suddenly I felt that my "popo" was exposed. Ashamed, I quickly sat down on the blanket and covered my crotch with my hands. I had made one of those inevitable transitions from innocence to knowledge. After that day, I did not let Mother undress me in public.

Father loved books. He read ancient Greek and Latin classics, German and French literature, but most of all he was fond of history and geography. He spent most of his free time reading, sitting on the green sofa under the reading lamp. There was a stillness about him, as if he were enclosed in a cocoon of tranquility. He moved silently and closed doors noiselessly; no click was heard when he put down the cup on the saucer. With the atlas of the world on his lap, he traveled with his finger over the continents.

Mother once told me that when they were traveling on their honeymoon in a train across Switzerland and Italy, Father pointed out every mountain they passed, noted its name and height, and knew the name and lengths of each river and the number of inhabitants of the cities where they stopped, until she became embarrassed in front of the other passengers, who must have thought him a show-off and a bore.

Father wanted to introduce me to good literature, and when I was about ten years old he decided I could read Ibsen's *Peer Gynt*. Of course it was far above my head and didn't interest me at all. After that, I avoided any book that my father recommended, believing they must all be boring. Thus I owned Selma Lagerlöf's *The Wonderful Adventures of Nils* for several years without reading it, because Father said it was a nice story. When I finally opened it one day, having run out of anything to read, I was so captivated that I didn't put it down until I finished and then immediately started again from the beginning.

My parents loved music and often went to the opera and to concerts. They both played the piano well enough, and sometimes they played four-handed, which I enjoyed. The pieces I liked best I marked in block letters in the little green music notebook, with lots of spelling mistakes in my preschool handwriting. My favorites were Schubert's "Serenade" and a song about a rose that a naughty boy wanted to pick, but the rose revenged herself and pricked his finger with her thorn.

My father had been a soldier in World War I. He was drafted toward the end of the war, just after his matriculation examinations when he was eighteen. He was wounded on the Italian front. I remember the four depressions, one on each side of his thighs. A single bullet had penetrated both legs, fortunately the first in front of the bone and the second behind the bone. I always begged Father to tell me again how he was rescued.

He was shot just as his unit was retreating and was left behind, lying on the ground bleeding, perhaps mistaken for dead. He must have been unconscious for a long time. When he opened his eyes, he saw two Italian soldiers standing above him. When they noticed that he was alive, they made to shoot him. At that moment he remembered his Latin from school and begged, "Aqua, aqua." The two soldiers took pity on him and gave him water from their canteens.

For many weeks and months, his parents had no news about him. He had been taken prisoner of war, lying in a military hospital in Napoli, where he could see Mount Vesuvius from a window. His parents were notified that Hans was missing, but only much later did they get a postcard from him.

I don't have that particular postcard, but I possess a number of other postcards that my father wrote from the front to his Uncle Adolf, who was also in the army. They are faded and written in pencil and bear the stamp FELDPOST, with the Kaiser's portrait. Only years later, when I was a mother myself, could I imagine the terrible anxiety my grandmother and grandfather must have endured when they did not know if their eldest son was alive or dead.

What a good-looking couple were my parents! A photo of Father in swimming trunks shows his well-proportioned body. Mother was not beautiful, but she had delicate skin, good proportions, and shapely legs. Her hair was light brown, and she wore it rolled up on her nape, as was the fashion of the time. Her eyes were light blue, her nose perhaps a bit too long. She was painfully aware of her protruding two front teeth, therefore she never smiled in photographs, except for one, when the photographer snapped her unawares.

Father and Mother were good at other sports besides swimming. They went ice skating with me at the Letná, where in winter the tennis courts were turned into ice rinks. Father wore his green knickerbockers, which ended with a buckle under the knee, as well as his Windjacke (windbreaker) and wool gloves. He skated slowly and regularly, with his hands behind his back, around and around the rink. Mother's ears were covered with a knitted headband. It was more fun when she came along; Father was always too serious and didactic.

Both were also good skiers, but what they especially loved was mountain climbing. In the storeroom in our apartment were shelves with the hobnailed boots, short pickaxes, and ropes they used on their climbing expeditions in the Alps or the Dolomites. They did quite strenuous trails with mountain guides. I have some photos showing them suntanned, sitting on a snowy peak in Switzerland, which I found out later was the Matterhorn.

Hans and Liesl Polach (right)
on the Matterhorn, 1933 or 1934

That storeroom, called *Kammer*, had another purpose. When I misbehaved (to this day I cannot believe I did; in my memory, I am an obedient little child . . .) they locked me up, until I repented and promised to be a good girl. In the dark I would find a hobnailed boot by touch. The inside of the door became pockmarked from the nails up to the height I could reach, as I banged on the door, screaming and howling.

What my wrongdoing was that necessitated such punishment, I don't recall. Once, perhaps, it was when I wet the floor. I had seen boys peeing standing up, and I also wanted to accomplish this feat. Time and again, I tried to stand with my legs apart over the toilet, but I was too short, and although I pushed my belly as far forward as I could, it still went all on the floor.

I have another recollection concerning the toilet. I was maybe three and a half years old, just graduated from the potty to the adult seat, when one evening I slipped into the bowl and jackknifed, and with my head touching my knees, I could not free myself. My mother was in the living room, entertaining some friends; I could hear their conversation. I called and called as loudly as I could.

"Mama," I begged as she lifted me out, "don't tell the guests that I fell into the toilet." She washed, dried, and carried me back to bed.

With bated breath I listened to the sounds from the living room. There was silence for a moment and then a loud burst of laughter. I knew she'd told them. Embarrassed, I cried myself to sleep.

The flat in the Electric House in Prague-Holešovice was our home from 1932 until the Germans evicted us at the beginning of the war in 1939. It was a new building with unheard-of innovations that were the talk of the town. I remember the flat exactly. In the entrance hall there were several doors: the glass door to the living room and plain ones to the bathroom and the utility balcony, which we called "gonk." We also had a refrigerator, which came with the flat. Refrigerators were still very rare; kitchens had pantries to store food in. And of course one door belonged to the notorious storeroom. From the hall, a small corridor led to the kitchen, my nursery, and the toilet. My parents' bedroom could be reached either through the bathroom or the living room. The rooms had large double-pane windows with pull-down black blinds called Rollo. The floors were wooden parquet, except for the kitchen, which had a reddish stone floor.

On one wall of the entrance hall there was a closet for coats and hats. On the upper shelves, Mother stored all our woolens in summer—pullovers, shawls,

Dita Polach with her parents, 1932

and mittens—each wrapped separately in newspaper with a few grains of naph-
thalene against moths. I was very excited when they were taken out and aired
at the beginning of winter, because I had forgotten them from the previous year
and welcomed each cap and sweater like a long-lost friend.

It was the same joy that I felt when I was allowed to wear knee socks on
the first warm day in spring. In winter I had worn long, thick stockings like
all the other children, along with my warm navy-blue coat and ankle-high boots,
and I was elated at the lightness of my bare knees and the ease of movement in
my thin shoes.

Oh, for the years of childhood, when there is no awareness of the passing of
time, when a day has no end and a summer seems to last forever. What joy to get
a new pair of sandals, because the old ones have grown too small. Suddenly my
flower-patterned, light dresses appeared in my wardrobe, together with one or
two new ones. Mother used to make them herself, often assisted by my grandmother. Then my nursery would be turned into a sewing room, and for the next
few days, the two women produced not only dresses for me but also aprons,

pajamas, and skirts. Mother cut the fabric from paper patterns, and Grandmother stitched the pieces together by hand. I had to stand on a chair, and their four hands would pull here, put a pin there, and make me lift my arms. They stepped back and told me to turn left and then right, and at last pulled the dress slowly over my head, taking care the pins wouldn't scratch me. The sewing machine stood near the window, and Mother sewed on it, moving the pedal with her feet; there was no motor.

Once I asked her to make me a tennis dress with a short skirt like those the young ladies who played tennis on the courts of Letná Park wore.

Mother bought the material, but it was not completely white; it had colored stripes, and I was disappointed. "This isn't a real tennis dress," I complained. But when it was finished, I liked it notwithstanding.

One did not buy readymade coats and suits in those years. They were considered to be of low quality and shoddy craftsmanship. One went to a tailor to have the garment made to measure. In our family we had a different procedure.

First a letter was sent to Brno to my uncle Hans Bass, who had a textile shop and would, of course, give us a discount. A few days later, a parcel would arrive with samples of the best-quality fabrics. Mother, Grandmother, and Father (Grandfather would never deign to deal with such mundane matters) sat around the dining room table, rubbing the brown, gray, and black samples between their fingers, deciding which was suitable for a new winter coat for Grandfather, a suit for Father, or a skirt and jacket for Mother.

When the heavy parcel with the material arrived from Brno, our tailor was summoned. He lived in Pilsen and came by train, bringing a stack of fashion journals. He took the measurements, made notes, sketched the models, and went back to Pilsen. He came a second time for the first fitting, full of smiles and politeness, carrying a suitcase. I loved to watch how he drew lines with white chalk directly onto the cloth. Sometimes a second fitting was necessary. And then at last the garments arrived, new and beautiful, meant to last if not a lifetime, at least for many, many seasons.

Ours was a very economical family. Nothing that could still be used was thrown out. Dresses were made for me with large hems to be let out as I grew, and shoes were usually one size bigger, so they could be worn the next year.

To this day I save remnants of material, bits of wool, and scraps of food. It was, and to a degree still is, the custom of Europeans not to be wasteful. It is part of a tradition and has nothing to do with poverty or affluence. My grandmother was the champion of frugality. She unraveled old sweaters, laundered and stretched the wool to make it smooth again, and knitted new ones. She cut spiral strips from old stockings that were beyond mending. With a huge crochet needle, she made mats from these strips, quite handsome ones, brown, beige, and black, pleasant and springy under the foot. Another habit of hers was to save used matches. She kept a box for them on the rim of her cooking range, using the burnt ones to transfer the flame from one ring to another.

When I was older, Grandmother explained to me the reason for her extreme frugality. They had a son born after my father, Hans, and before my uncle Ernst-Benjamin. His name was Fritz, and he died before I was born. He had to be kept in an institution for the mentally ill. What his ailment was I don't know. He was hospitalized as a child, and from that day, Grandmother began saving so that his two brothers would have money for his upkeep once the parents were dead. Fritz died at the age of twenty, but Grandmother could no longer change the economizing ways she had imposed on herself for so many years.

It is so strange that, years later, our daughter, Michaela, would also die at the age of twenty. She became ill when she was eight. Her disease was incurable, and we were told that she would not live long. No one could predict how long. We started to save strenuously, almost as extremely as my grandmother, to ensure that her brothers could afford her care if we died before her.

I loved my grandmother more than anybody else. Even now, almost seventy years after her death, a soothing warmth envelops me when I think of her. She was a small woman with a large nose and warm brown Semitic eyes. She wore dark, shapeless clothes that belonged to fashions of long ago. Her gray hair was collected into a bun and fastened with hairpins on the nape of her neck. I think she was never in her life in a hairdresser's salon. Her own person was of no interest to her; her attention centered entirely on other people. She was the most unselfish person I have ever known, and I wish I had inherited this quality from her. I try to be unselfish and struggle against my egotism, but my efforts are conscious, while for Grandmother it was her nature.

She was never angry with me; even when I misbehaved and she scolded me, I felt totally accepted. She would say, "*Das macht man nicht*"—you do not do that—and I'd protest cheekily, "*Das macht Frau ja*"—that's what women do. (It's a wordplay, because *man* = anyone, *Mann* = a man, and *Frau* = a woman.)

Grandmother never hugged or kissed, neither me nor other members of the family. She respected others, even if they were her sons or granddaughter. I never heard her giving an opinion or criticizing a person. She just accepted people as they were; everyone was treated with the same respect, whether minister or servant girl. She was the kindest and most loving person of my life. She called me Edithlein; nobody else ever called me by that name.

One day when I was in kindergarten, I got a severe bellyache. The janitor's wife was summoned to accompany me home. (No one had a car then, and few families had telephones.) On the way I insisted she take me to Grandmother, who lived much nearer. When Grandmother opened the door, the fat woman wanted to be quite sure she wasn't making a mistake and asked, "Are you really Mrs. Grandmother?" Grandmother had to answer her twice before she was reassured, and I laughed in spite of my aching belly.

Grandma took me into the living room, made me lie on the sofa, and went to the kitchen. After a while she returned with a cup of tea and a warm pot-lid wrapped in a towel. She placed it on my belly, and when it cooled, she changed it for a second one, which had meanwhile been warming on the stove in the kitchen. After several changes, the pain miraculously vanished.

We used to visit my grandparents quite often. They had moved to Prague from Brno in the thirties, when Grandfather became a member of Parliament. I remember the day they moved into their flat, when I was three and a half years

Johann and Katharina Polach, 1932

old. There was a great to-do, with the movers carrying big pieces of furniture held by straps over their shoulders. I saw two old people whom I didn't know, and Mother told me that these were my grandfather and grandmother.

I remember the flat in great detail. There was a tall, yellow tiled stove in the corner of the living room, and it was most pleasant to warm one's back against it in winter. During the night the fire went out, and, in the morning, Liesl the maid would scrape out the ashes and start a new one with thin sticks and newspaper. Bigger chunks of wood were added, and at last came the coal. The bedroom was cold, the stove unlit, and I rarely went there.

In the middle of the living room stood a large dining table covered with a rug, and when visitors came a white tablecloth would be spread over it. They would sit around the table, drinking tea and eating Grandmother's ginger cookies. These cookies had a strange property: when they were fresh, they were extremely tough—one could break a tooth on them—but after some weeks in a tin box, they became brittle and very tasty.

There was a black grand piano with shiny brass wheels, and I liked to "play" on it. It made Grandfather nervous. He used to say to Grandmother, "Kathi, don't let the child harass the instrument." So Grandmother would put her arm around my shoulders, which was easy for her because she was barely taller than me, and take me to the kitchen, where she would make me a *topinka*: She opened the cupboard, releasing the fragrance of the hundreds of loaves it had held in the course of a lifetime, cut a slice of bread, and put it in a blackened pan, where goose fat was sizzling. She fried it on both sides and then smeared it with garlic. My mother sometimes also made *topinkas*, but they were never so crisp and tasty like Grandmother's. Probably the pan had to have a black crust; ours was always spotless and shiny. Everybody was pleased when I finished the whole *topinka*, because I ate so little, and they were happy that I got something nourishing into my thin body.

Near the window there was Grandfather's writing desk. Sometimes, when the adults were sitting around the table and talking politics, Grandmother gave me a piece of paper and some crayons and I knelt at the desk and drew pictures. Grandfather didn't like it; he always thought I would ruin his blotting-paper mat.

On one side of the room stood the sofa, and on the opposite wall a huge bookcase almost touched the high ceiling, with decorative carvings and glass doors. It was crammed full of learned books, but some were books I could also enjoy. There were *Andersen's Fairy Tales* and Wilhelm Busch picture books that had belonged to my father and his brothers when they were children. I was allowed to take them out to look at, or Grandmother would read from them to me. She also knew lots of songs and poems by heart. One poem by Friedrich Rückert I liked above all others was about a young tree that wanted to dress in something grander than the needles that grew on its branches. Its wish was granted, and next morning it was covered in beautiful green leaves. But the goats came and ate the leaves. The little tree asked for new leaves, but this time the frost burnt them, and again it stood bare. Each time, something happened to the new leaves until the little tree asked humbly to get its old needles back and never complained again.

Grandmother recited the poem with emotion, changing her voice from loud to a whisper, and I sighed with relief at the end when everything turned out for the good.

Grandmother sang, in her somewhat quivery voice, songs that I thought were folk melodies. Only as an adult did I discover that one was a Brahms lullaby and another a Mozart lied. Grandmother had had very little formal schooling but knew a surprising amount about classical music. She was the eldest of four children and often had to take care of her siblings when her mother went to work. My great-grandmother's profession was something like a midwife's; she nursed young mothers who had given birth. At that time it was customary to engage an experienced woman to care for the baby because the mother was not supposed to get up from her bed for six weeks. My great-grandfather was abroad, trying to make his fortune in foreign lands. Grandmother, for example, was born in Hungary, where her father had worked for several years as manager of some nobleman's estate. Then they returned to Brno, where the family stayed while Great-Grandfather was off again. He went to America to work for Baron Hirsch, the builder of railways. In the end he disappeared altogether; no one knows where he is buried.

Grandmother Kathi grew up in poverty. When she was a teenager, she was acquainted with a certain Alfred Fröhlich, who played an instrument in the symphony orchestra, and she would often attend rehearsals. She told me how she sat on the balcony and listened to the conductor's instructions, thus becoming quite knowledgeable about classical music. I would have forgotten the man's name, of course, had she not given me a leather-bound diary with a little lock and key for my seventh birthday. It was a present Fröhlich had given her, and she'd kept it since her youth. She never wrote anything in it, but on the first page is her friend's dedication, dated October 27, 1892. Who knows what feelings there were between Kathi and Alfred? Perhaps she was in love with him? I will never know; more than 125 years have elapsed since then.

Miraculously, the diary is still in my possession, even though the key is long lost. A friend, Judith Lamplová, kept it for me, together with some photos and souvenirs when my family was deported to Terezín. Since one of her parents was not Jewish, Judith was not sent to the ghetto. When I came back from the camps after the war, she returned the diary to me. There are entries I wrote in 1941 and 1942, before our deportation, childish descriptions of what I did each day, but also names of those of my friends, who were in the next transport. One entry, however, contains the momentous information about my first kiss. I received it from a boy named Erik. It took place while we were sitting under a tree on the gravestone of some long-forgotten Jew in the Old Jewish Cemetery, on July 8, 1942. It was an awkward, wet, and lopsided kiss.

Dita Polach, 1942

But that was later. For now, my life was still following its regular course.

When I was small, I suffered recurrent inflammations of the ear. I remember how it hurt and how Mother held my head on her lap and administered warm ear drops.

One evening, my parents went out, and they put my bed in the living room so that Maria could sleep near me on the green sofa. My aching ear was padded with a big wad of cotton wool held in place by a knitted cap, and an electric pad was placed under my head.

In the middle of the night, Maria was awoken by an unfamiliar acrid smell. She rushed over to me and found the pillow smoldering; the cap had a burnt hole, and the cotton wool was beginning to catch fire. There must have been a short circuit, but I hadn't felt anything—I hadn't even woken up. It was a frightening event; I heard it told many times afterward. I must confess I have kept a certain dislike to electric pads and blankets to this day.

My ear inflammations stopped when Dr. Desensy-Bill, our pediatrician, decided to have my tonsils removed. This is one of my unforgettable childhood memories. Not because of the operation but because of the taxi. It was the first time in my life I'd ridden in a car. In Prague one took a tram, and when out of town, a train. No one owned a car; the only people I knew who had a car were our neighbors on the same floor, Mr. and Mrs. Moller. Mrs. Moller, who had a slight limp, was a young woman who'd had no children and often invited me over. Her name was also Edith, which made us namesakes. She had lots of picture magazines—something I never saw at home—with photos of beautiful film stars. She was a perfectionist housewife, always baking cookies and polishing the parquet floors. In the kitchen she wore red slippers, but when she went to the salon, she changed them at the door and put on blue ones. She went in and out, and every time, she took off and put on blue slippers and red slippers, blue slippers and red slippers. She did it to spare the carpets, Maria explained mockingly. But the Mollers never took me for a ride in their car.

I was so excited in anticipation of the taxi that I forgot it would take me to the doctor who was going to cut out my tonsils. I don't remember the operation, only the fact that I got a double portion of ice cream to cool my hurting throat. And Mother explained that the tonsils would grow back; they had only been clipped and not extracted.

It was a comforting thought. For the next few years, I believed that if somebody lost an organ it would grow back. When I saw an invalid in a wheelchair, it was a relief to know that he would grow a new leg instead of always missing one. It helped me to bear the pity for the suffering person.

I was in love with boys as far back as I can remember. In the Czech kindergarten, there was a pretty boy whose name I have forgotten. I had a crush on him, and I would feel my cheeks flush when I met him in the afternoon in the park, he with his mother and I with Maria or my mother. One day, when he had a nosebleed in kindergarten, I lent him my handkerchief. A few days later, his mother returned it, washed and ironed, and I felt proud and important as if I had saved his life.

In the first grade there was Helmut, again the best-looking boy in class. He was popular with other girls, too, but that didn't deter me from being in love with him. It was a German school, just around the corner from my home, which I attended from first to third grade. Helmut, like the rest of the pupils, belonged to the German minority who were citizens of Czechoslovakia.

Gerta and I were in love with the same boy when we were about nine. He lived on her street and would show us all kinds of stunts on his bicycle. He could make a U-turn on the back wheel only and jump from the road to the sidewalk and back again. We admired him immensely. We would stand in the doorway of Gerta's house and laugh and clap hands. Gerta and I were rivals for his attention, but I felt that he secretly preferred me because he once accompanied me on his bicycle all the way from Gerta's house to mine, three streets away.

Another crush we shared was a young circus performer of about fourteen or fifteen. The circus tent was on a vacant lot near Gerta's house. Twice we attended the show, properly with tickets, just to see the lithe athletic boy with his bare torso perform on a freestanding ladder. His number was accompanied by a certain waltz melody, which brings him back to memory whenever I hear it played. We loitered at the fence of the circus almost daily to catch a glimpse of him and then we would endlessly describe his features to each other. Yet when the circus folded its tent a few weeks later and moved on, our young athlete was forgotten without a tear.

CHAPTER FOUR

Grandfather

Grandfather Johann Polach was born in the small town Velké Bílovice in Moravia. He had three brothers, Adolf, Arnold, and Bernard, and two sisters, Johanna and Theresah. My grandfather was the only one whose name was mistakenly registered as Polach; his brothers' and their descendants' family name is Pollak.

Johann was sent to study at the Schottenring gymnasium in Vienna. There he came in contact with the Social Democrats and became an activist in the party.

My grandmother once told me that Johann's grandmother was very religious. She was known as the *Ofensetzerin*, the person to whom housewives brought their pots with the Shabbat *cholent* on Friday, because she had an enormous oven that would keep them warm till next day—Jews are not allowed to light a fire on the Shabbat. When Grandfather Johann was a young student, he once had a discussion with her about the existence of God. He was an unbeliever, an ardent socialist, and tried to convince her that there is no God. But she argued that she had absolute proof of God's existence.

She related what happened to her one Friday afternoon: "I was walking home from a distant village with a heavy basket on my back. It was getting dark, and I was so tired I could hardly walk. I was afraid I wouldn't be home in time before the beginning of the Shabbat. I sat down on the roadside and prayed to God to give me strength. And lo and behold, in that instant, I wasn't tired anymore and was back home before the first star appeared in the sky. Now, Mr. Student, isn't that proof enough for you?"

A few years ago I came across a passage about Grandfather in the autobiography of Friedrich Stampfer (1874–1957) one of the leaders of the Social Democratic Party and a well-known journalist. This is what he wrote:

In those days of my youthful enthusiasm, I met a strange schoolmate. Despite being in the same class as I, he was three years older, but judging from his appearance, he could have been ten years older. He was gaunt, poorly dressed, and had an interesting ugly face. His name was Johann Polach. I met his father, a porter at one of Vienna's railway stations, a few years later. It happened when I was changing one students' lodging for another and hired him through Johann—"to keep the money in the family"—to help me with the moving. But when the old man came and heaved my heavy trunk on his bent back, while I was walking beside him with a light suitcase, I had the feeling I was committing an injustice. And when he took off his red porter's cap to thank me for the meager fee—to pay him more than the standard, I didn't dare—I was deeply ashamed.

Johann came from Vienna, too. His abject poverty had forced him to earn a living; this was the reason he was three years behind. Like myself, he was an enthusiastic admirer of Greece; like myself, he was an ardent socialist, but he was also something more, namely a Marxist.

Until then I had never heard about Marx, and I must confess that the first encounter with him did not attract me in any way. The deprecating manner with which Johann regarded me as a mere "charity socialist" and "utopist" hurt me.

Soon Johann returned to Brno. Had our ways parted then forever, he would have remained in my memory as a presumptuous young man. However, our acquaintance later developed into friendship, and I came to know him as one of the kindest and most amiable persons I have met in my life. He became a professor of Greek and Latin and won great esteem from his students. He later became senator for the Social Democrats in Prague.

I was surprised to learn that Johann's father had been a porter in Vienna. Uncle Ernst-Benjamin, in an article for a German publication, wrote that "Johann was the eldest son of a poor farmer and carter in Velké Bílovice near Kostel (Moravia), the only Jew in the village."

Perhaps his poverty made him go to Vienna to try his luck?

Johann met Kathi when she was visiting her younger sister Sophie in Vienna. Sophie had to marry quickly when she was very young, perhaps sixteen. Her husband was a housepainter in Vienna and a distant cousin of Johann. Kathi had come to help her sister with the new baby. After some time of courtship, Johann and Kathi were married, and their firstborn was Hans, my father. By chance he was born in Vienna, when Grandfather and Grandmother were on a visit there. Their two other sons were born in Brno.

Grandfather was quite a tall man, a bit stooped when I knew him. He had a gray goatee, but his hair, although sparse, was still black. He wore spectacles called *Zwicker* in German, or pince-nez, which were fastened by pinching the nose.

Grandfather suffered from a strange disease. He would get seizures that resembled epilepsy but were diagnosed as something different. A few seconds before an attack, he would become suddenly rigid, stare fixedly ahead, and utter a cramped cry. I was sent out hurriedly while Grandmother and the maid Liesl, or my mother or father, laid him flat on his back. For a few minutes, his body shook and then he fell asleep. When he woke he knew nothing of the attack, and I was included in the conspiracy not to tell him what happened. Sometimes he didn't have an attack for months, then two or three in a row. Once when he was alone in the room, he fell from his chair and broke his collarbone. After that he was never left unattended.

Grandfather was a highly esteemed and respected man. His colleagues and friends were politicians of the first rank. The names I heard as a child were those of members of Parliament, of journalists and writers—for example, senators Holitscher and Jaksch; Erich Ollenhauer; Friedrich Stampfer, chief editor of *Vorwärts*; and Ludwig Czech, minister of social welfare. After World War II, when Grandfather was no longer alive, I came across the names of some of these men, who were now ministers and party leaders in Czechoslovakia, Austria, and Germany.

On one occasion I became the witness of the reverence accorded to my grandfather. The German Opera in Prague staged a gala performance of Mozart's *Marriage of Figaro* in honor of the Workers' Day on May 1. The entire theater was reserved for members of the Social Democratic Party and its leaders. My parents and I were invited to join my grandparents in a ground-level box, the choicest seats of the opera house.

I was still very small and had never been out at night. Mother made me take a nap in the afternoon, but I was unable to fall asleep, I was so excited. I pretended to be sleeping, afraid that they wouldn't take me with them in the evening. But although Mother knew I had been faking, she went ahead and told me the story of Figaro. It was too complicated for my understanding, but it didn't matter.

We took our places in the stall before the curtain went up, with Grandfather sitting in front and us behind him. And as the people came in, they stopped in front of Grandfather, greeted him reverently, some bowing low, others shaking his hand. He was treated with such respect that I could feel what a prominent personality he was. I still have in my possession two newspaper cuttings with his photo. The occasion was Senator Johann Polach's sixtieth birthday.

Every day my grandparents walked to the Café Continental on Příkopy Street. Grandfather sat at his customary table, and the waiters brought him all the newspapers of the day. Grandmother would knit or also read something, and Liesl would be released till their return. Anyone who wanted to meet Grandfather had only to come to the Café Continental in the afternoon.

When Mother had something to attend to "in town," we sometimes walked to the Continental to say hello. I liked to see how the waiters bowed deferentially, addressing the Herr Senator or Herr Professor, and then asked what madam and the young lady wished. I was allowed to choose a slice of cake from the glass bell. This was an ingenious contraption with six or eight compartments, in each a different kind of cake, one with fruit, another with chocolate icing or jelly, a *Mozartkugel*, a strudel, or a marzipan. You inserted one koruna coin and then you could turn the bell to the opening of the cake of your choice.

When the weather was nice, my grandparents would come to the garden café in the Stromovka. The waiters there also addressed my grandfather with reverence and brought him the day's newspapers attached to a bamboo frame with a handle, but they didn't have such a large choice as in the Continental. When Mother took me to the park in the afternoon, we would have a look if Grandfather and Grandmother were in the café. If they were, we joined them, and Mother would order strawberries with whipped cream for me. That was something I liked. It came in a tall long-stemmed glass, and both women watched me with satisfaction: I'm sure they were thinking, *At least the child is eating something nourishing to strengthen her.*

CHAPTER FIVE

The Operation

A n important event in my young life was my operation. I was in the second grade of elementary school, just after the half-term vacation, when I became ill. I had a bellyache, and Dr. Desensy-Bill, who came to our home, said I should stay in bed for a day or two. But it took longer, and I wasn't better. Finally I couldn't even sit up, and the adults looked worried. Another doctor was summoned for consultation: a specialist, Professor Růžička. His decision: I was to be rushed to hospital immediately.

That same afternoon he performed an appendectomy, but during the operation, my appendix burst and the pus spread into the abdominal cavity. The incision was therefore left open with a drain, which had to be cleaned and bandaged every morning. Days passed, and I wasn't better.

Mother was at my side all the time. She wet my lips with a damp cloth, which I sucked because I was terribly thirsty and wasn't allowed to drink. She told me stories and read from books. Sometimes she dozed on an armchair in the corner. Once, I remember, as she was reading from a fairy-tale book, I noticed that tears were running down her cheeks. I had no idea why she was crying, and I felt guilty, thinking that I was cruel, making her read to me for so long when she was probably too tired.

Something was wrong, but what? Anything I swallowed I vomited, even a spoonful of water. I grew thinner and weaker. They thought my mother made me nervous, being by my bed day and night. She was banished to the corridor, and only one nurse was allowed into my room. The hospital was staffed by nuns. They were nice, but I wanted my mother. I could see her face peeping in whenever the door was opened.

On the twelfth day after the operation, I vomited the contents of my bowels. Now they knew what was wrong: a stoppage in the intestines, or ileus. The second operation was more severe than the first; I was brought back to my bed in a state near death. Of course I remember nothing but heard about it all later. They placed eight hot-water bottles around my body and gave me oxygen. The entire family gathered in the corridor—parents, grandparents, our Maria, and Liesl, the grandparents' maid—fearing the worst.

Slowly I came back to life. Most of the time I slept; once when I woke, I saw a tube protruding from my arm leading to a bag with some liquid hanging above my head. I became stronger, could sit up for a while. Every day visitors came, each bringing some present. It seemed the whole world knew of my illness, all our relatives, all my friends and Grandfather's colleagues, neighbors. I got get-well letters from all my classmates and even the teacher and the headmaster. There were mountains of presents. My parents took them home every day: dolls and games and books; there was no room for them all.

But alas! The glucose they fed me through the infusion solidified and caused thrombosis. My arm became swollen and blue, and a third operation was necessary. How I hated the smell of ether, which they used to anesthetize me. Again this horrible feeling of falling into nothingness. . . . I opened my eyes and saw doctors and nurses pulling a long piece of gauze out of a cut in my arm. I heard someone say, "She woke up," and then nothing. . . .

There are two scars on my right upper arm. In the first incision, they did not find the clot, so they cut another higher up. The wounds on my belly healed very slowly, because of the drain, and left wide and ugly scars for life. But at the time my mother, happy to have me alive, said to me, "You just won't become a belly dancer."

When I was about twelve, I gave up children's literature and started reading adult books. In some of them I met the word *dowry* and understood that it was what the bride gets from her parents when she marries. One day I asked Mother, "Mama, when I marry will I also get a dowry?"

Mother sighed, but then she laughed and said, "Your dowry is in your belly."

During the school year in grade two, the pupils were urged to learn swimming. The daughter of our headmaster, a pretty young woman named Miss Scholz, taught us in the indoor pool, Axa on Na Poříčí Street. There were about ten lessons, all of which I attended. But at the end of the course, all the children could swim except me. I felt guilty because my parents had paid for nothing.

After my three operations, Professor Růžička forbade me from jumping, running, and, above all, swimming. (He didn't know that I couldn't swim.) He expected with certainty a hernia in my cut-up belly. That summer Mother and I, together with friends, a young mother and her little boy, went on vacation to Senohraby, near Prague. Father would join us later for two weeks, as he did every year. There was a river, Sázava, and when the weather was warm, we would go bathing. I was allowed to dip in the shallow water but could make only careful and slow movements. From time to time Mother went for a proper swim, and I used the time when I was alone to practice what Miss Scholz had taught us. Suddenly it was not difficult anymore, and I swam around happily.

But Mother saw me, and that was the end of happiness, because the next day she rushed me back to Prague to see the surgeon. He examined my belly, pressed his fingers all over it, and declared with surprise that he didn't find any hernia.

I was allowed to swim, and we returned to continue our vacation in Senohraby.

While we were staying in that holiday village, there was a festive event in which all the little local girls participated. They wore pretty new white dresses and flower wreaths on their heads. In their hands they carried baskets full of flower petals and, as they walked along the main street toward the church, they strewed them on the ground. I also wanted to become a *družička* like little Vera, the daughter of the people in whose villa we lodged for the summer, but Mother absolutely forbade it. I didn't know why, and it was not explained to me.

Similar restrictions had happened before. When other children hung an empty stocking out their windows on December 5 every year, expecting Saint Nicholas to fill it overnight with sweets and nuts, my stocking remained empty. We did have a decorated Christmas tree in our living room three or four times, when I was very small, but no longer when I started school. Mother told me that this was only for little children, and now I was big—a schoolgirl. But both Anita and Gerta were also big, and they always had a Christmas tree, and all my schoolmates, too. . . .

On our walks with Maria we often entered the church on Strossmayer Square, and she would put her finger in a marble basin at the entrance and make signs with it over her forehead and chest. I also wanted to do it, but she didn't let me.

"What is it in the basin?" I asked.

"It's holy water."

"Why is it holy?"

"Because the priest has blessed it."

"Why can't I also kneel and pray to Jesus?"

"It's not for you."

Yet there were also no other feasts or rituals in my family. My grandfather had resigned from the Jewish community as a young socialist, and his sons were *konfessionslos* (i.e. belonging to no faith), and so was I. At school I had a free lesson during religious instruction; I was neither Catholic nor Protestant, nor anything else. I had never seen a chanukiah nor heard the words *Pesach* or *Yom Kippur*.

I came across the word *Jew* for the first time when I was in grade three.

The year was 1938. Hitler had occupied the Sudeten. My parents were worried; I heard them discussing the possibility of emigrating. Names like Chile, Bolivia, and Brazil were mentioned. A busy correspondence started with my father's uncle, Adolf Pollak, in Tel Aviv, about moving to Palestine. What kept my father from making a decision was not only the difficulty of obtaining entry visas but also his doubts about his ability to provide for his family.

Many people began learning some handicraft or skill to make a living in another country. But my father was not a handy person, and he knew that he would not be permitted to work in his profession as a lawyer. While my parents were hesitating, developments soon made emigration impossible.

After the annexation of the Sudeten, the German minority of Czechoslovakia became overbearing and aggressive. In school one morning, I found a piece of paper on my desk with the words *You are a Jew*. I didn't know what it meant and took it home to show my parents. They became very serious, and I could tell that something important was going on.

"What is a Jew?" I asked.

"It's a special kind of people."

I kept asking more questions but was still not satisfied with the explanations.

"Are we Jews?"

"Yes, according to the Nuremberg Laws."

"What are these laws?"

Father told me that Jews were being harassed and abused; however, this was happening in Germany, not in our country. But I sensed ominous implications in what he said. Within a short time, I was transferred to a Czech school.

There were only girls in my class; boys learned in a separate wing. I disliked the teacher from the first moment. She was short, old, and dry. But I was not the only new girl; Annemarie was there, too. The transition was not too difficult, because I spoke Czech as well as anybody and only had to get a few private lessons in spelling. My teacher was a young woman whose name began with the letter *D*, which she wrote with a flourish, without lifting her pen. It impressed me so much that I adopted it for my signature and use it to this day. By the end of the school year, I was fully integrated and got top grades in all the subjects on my school report.

Gerta was also transferred to a Czech school but to a different one. However, we met almost every afternoon as before, either at her home or mine.

CHAPTER SIX

Žd'ár

The war broke out when I was ten years old. That summer, in 1939, my parents did not go on vacation as they had in past years. Czechoslovakia was now occupied by the Germans. As a Jew, my father was dismissed from his job. My parents worried about the dangers; they remembered World War I. They wanted me at least to have a vacation in the country, away from the city. And so I was sent to a friend of my father's, who lived with his family in a little market town named Žd'ár. He had two daughters who were a little younger than me, and both families hoped I would feel happy with them. In Prague there might be air raids; the child would certainly be safer in the country, my parents thought.

Mr. Weinreb came to our house to fetch me. We went by train, talking very little, and although I felt his kindness, I was shy. We arrived in the evening. Mrs. Weinreb had a meal ready, and we all sat around the large kitchen table. Their two little girls stared at me with their big, round brown eyes, and I felt awkward. But by the next day they'd already accepted me and excitedly showed me all their toys, took me out to meet their friends, and showed me off as their guest from Prague. Hanna, the younger, was six, about to start school at the end of vacation. She was the stronger personality, Eva, who was seven, was her follower; she never had ideas of her own. Eva hadn't mastered reading in the first grade, while Hanna read even before she entered school.

It was a truly marvelous summer. The two girls became my devoted companions. With their mother, we went bathing in the nearby lakes; we gathered hazelnuts from the bushes that lined the field paths. In the forests that surrounded the little town, we collected blueberries in cans and came home with our teeth and tongues all blue. We went to the country fair and won prizes: plaster angels with wings painted gold. We picked cherries in the landlord's garden, which he silently tolerated. We listened openmouthed to Mrs. Weinreb's tales about her adventures in the nursing school. She and her fellow student nurses would spy on the young doctors' activities from an opposite window. Some of the accounts must have been vastly exaggerated, but that made them only more fascinating. Most of the time I forgot about my home, my parents and grandparents, about the war and the danger.

Dita Polach (center) with the Weinreb sisters in Žd'ár, 1939

On the first day of the new school year, September 1, 1939, World War II broke out. In Prague, the Germans requisitioned my parents' flat; they had to move out quickly. Another apartment was found, but it was in Smíchov, too far from my grandparents. My parents decided they would move in with us. About all this I knew only from the letters they wrote me.

My parents made an agreement with the Weinrebs to keep me in Žd'ár for the time being, as a paying guest, I suppose. The first phase of my delayed life began. Instead of continuing school with my former classmates in Prague, I was temporarily removed from my accustomed world and put on hold until times were better again.

I began attending fifth grade at the local school. I liked the school. The girls in my class were nice, and a few of them became my good friends. In fact, I had become their model—I was the girl from the capital city Prague. If I tied a ribbon in my hair or combed a lock into the middle of my forehead, they would copy me, believing that it must be the latest fashion from the big city. The teacher was kind, and I felt accepted and well treated. They never made me feel that I was different because I was Jewish.

Once a week there was religious instruction. The priest, called *katecheta*, taught the New Testament and spoke about Jesus Christ. I was exempt, of course, but allowed to stay in class. I would sit in the back and draw in my notebook. But each time I lifted my eyes, I saw the priest looking at me, as if he were talking over the children's heads directly at me. I believe he wanted to convert me, to make me a Christian.

We had a drawing teacher, Mr. Večeřa. I liked him. Once he stood over me, giving some advice about my picture, and stroked my hair. It felt most pleasant. But at home I told Mrs. Weinreb that the teacher pulled my hair. She went to the headmistress to complain. I don't remember what the result was.

I remember the year in Žd'ár as a tranquil and lovely time. Yet in some way I could not have been entirely happy.

One night I woke up from a strange noise. I heard a thump on the flat roof over my head, as if some heavy object had fallen from the sky. An airplane, I decided.

I jumped out of my bed in the kitchen and crept to Mr. and Mrs Weinreb's bedroom, through the room where the two girls were peacefully sleeping. Breathlessly I whispered, "An airplane has fallen on our house."

"It's nothing," said Mrs. Weinreb, unperturbed. "Perhaps Mr. Marek downstairs slammed the door as he went to work."

But I didn't believe her. My heart was pounding in my throat; I was scared to return to my bed. I stood there, yet no help was offered. I felt that for her the matter was closed; she wanted to go back to sleep. I felt shamed, humiliated. Mr. Weinreb's back was turned to me; he was fast asleep. Clutching my blanket and expecting the ceiling to cave in on me, I lay awake till morning.

Soon after this incident, my mother came for a visit. To her I confided that I felt pains in my stomach; sometimes they became really bad cramps. With Mrs. Weinreb, who was an experienced nurse, they decided on a light diet for me, and after some time I was better. It was comforting to have my mother with me, but she stayed only a few days. She returned to Prague, and I was left in Žd'ár.

My stomach troubles returned sometimes, but I liked being in Žd'ár. I became accustomed to the pains and accepted them as an inevitable part of life. I had many friends, and as usual I was in love with one of the local boys, Pepík Pelikán. It didn't matter that he more or less ignored me. I wrote him little notes, which I pushed into a crack in the stone wall near our house. Sometimes I found an answer there, and that made me happy. Hanna and Eva knew of my infatuation and always reported to me when they met him, told me what he was wearing or whether he was kicking his football. However, they kept a secret from me, which they revealed only years later, when I came for a visit after the war.

"You know," they said, laughing, "who wrote you the little notes you found in the crack in the wall? Not Pepík Pelikán, but Zdeněk Šiler."

Zdeněk was the older brother of a girl on our street with whom we used to play. He secretly fancied me. His sister was a tomboy, extremely daring and fearless. There was a half-constructed house on our street; the owners, it was rumored, had run out of money. It was our favorite place for games of hide and seek. We ran up and down from the upper floor on wooden planks, as there was no stairway.

One day the girl stepped on a nail, which protruded from a plank, and it went all the way through, sticking out of her foot. She was literally nailed to the board. We were horrified and wanted to call her mother. But Zdeněk pulled her foot out and ordered her not to say a word at home. He knew their strict disciplinarian mother would punish them for playing where it was forbidden. He rinsed her bleeding foot with the watering hose, and she didn't even shed a tear.

In winter my father also came to visit me. He loved nature and took me for long walks. Once when it was snowing outside, he and I stood by the window. In the street below I saw Pepík walking along, and I told my father that I was mad about this boy. He inspected him as he passed and then said, "A sturdy fellow." And he was indeed—Pepík had broad shoulders and a wide chest at the advanced age of ten or eleven—but I sensed that my father did not really understand me, even though he tried.

One day in Žd'ár, I had a wonderful experience that I have never forgotten. On my way to school I had stopped near a flower bed. The sun was shining, nobody was around, and I was alone with all this marvelous glory. Suddenly I was overcome by a feeling that the world was absolutely perfect; it was pure bliss. I was surrounded by beauty that filled my whole being with happiness. It was a moment of grace, of indescribable joy.

There was a second such moment, later, when I was back in Prague. But this time it was not so profound. I was standing near the window in our living room. It was winter, the street outside was covered with fresh virgin snow, the room was pleasantly warm and smelled of the wood burning in the stove. The glass in the window was half covered with beautiful intricate star patterns made by the frost, and no sound could be heard; all around was silence. And I felt happy, just happy.

These two moments lasted only seconds, but they had a special quality. They were like drops separated from the stream of life, permanently fixed outside time, unforgettable.

Žd'ár was a very small market town, surrounded by farmland and villages scattered on the hilly plateau, called Českomoravská Vysočina. In the center of the town was a large square, with the church at its lower end and in the middle a fountain with stone figures, blackened by age, commemorating the Great Plague of the seventeenth century. Three sides of the square were formed by old, one-story houses of the well-to-do. But if you passed through any of the wide entrances, you were suddenly in a yard full of geese and chickens and a pig in a pen, and beyond them, fields and meadows stretched into the distance.

I became friendly with several of my schoolmates and played with them in the afternoons. One was Věra Šlerková, whose widowed mother owned a shop just off the square, where she sold household utensils and farm tools. Věra and I liked to climb through their loft onto the roof and watch the people below. Her mother kept goats in a pen in the yard and often sent Věra to their meadow to cut fresh grass for them. The path led across the railway tracks and through the fields. When Věra finished cutting the grass with her sickle, we lay down among the daisies and poppies and watched the clouds float by in the sky. Sometimes the train passed, and we waved to the passengers in the windows. Then I helped her heave the basket with the shoulder straps onto her back and we walked home.

Another friend lived quite a long way from the town. Such pupils were called *přespolní*, meaning they lived beyond the fields. She was so poor that she had no shoes and walked to school barefoot, always wearing the same old, loose dress. Once she invited me to her home. It was a long walk, perhaps three quarters of an hour. The small house stood alone and consisted of only one room. Nobody was at home. The girl was very excited at my visit and wanted to make me feel like an honored guest. On a shelf above the bare table was a loaf of bread wrapped in a white cloth. She cut a big slice and served it to me on a plate. They had no butter, no jam, just the bread. For the first time I understood the meaning of the word *poverty*. I felt guilty and wanted to apologize.

But in Žd'ár I also saw a rich farm. One day our class went with our botany teacher to collect herbs along the field paths. She showed us how to pick chamomile, wild thyme, lavender, and other plants, which we dried in class, and then we learned about their medicinal properties. When we were already quite far from the town, we saw dark clouds rising from the horizon. In a field nearby, several people were hurrying to load bundles of dried hay onto their horse-drawn cart. We called out to them the local blessing—"May the Lord help you"—and they answered, "May the Lord grant it." The clouds were approaching fast, and we saw that they wouldn't finish before the rain started and they would lose the fodder for their animals for the next year. The entire class of forty-two girls with the teacher joined the workers, and we were just entering the large farmyard when the first drops began to fall. There was a main building with a spacious kitchen downstairs and several rooms upstairs, flanked by a barn and cowshed and many storerooms. The grateful farmer's wife invited us to the huge kitchen table, poured each of us a mug with cool buttermilk, and put before us dishes piled high with *koláče*, the round, flat yeast cakes filled with poppy seeds and raisins. Outside the storm was raging with lightning, and at each roar of thunder, the girls ducked their heads and crossed themselves. But it was soon over, and we took our leave. The entire episode was probably nothing significant for the local children, but for me it has remained an indelible memory.

A year later the war had not ended and the situation was deteriorating. I had to return to Prague, to the unknown section and unfamiliar streets of Smíchov, to the strange and much older apartment house where my parents had moved during my absence. We now had a large flat with high stucco ceilings. Two rooms were occupied by my grandparents, and two rooms were ours. The building did not have central heating, and we had to use the tall tiled stoves in every room, filling them with coal and scraping out the ashes every morning. The coal was stored in the cellar, and we fetched it in pails, bringing it up in the lift. The grandparents still employed a maid, Bláža, who did the heavy chores. Since Grandfather's accident a few years earlier, he was never left alone. However, the Germans soon forbade the gentiles to work for Jews, and Bláža had to leave.

I missed Žd'ár terribly. I was so homesick for Žd'ár that I would often have dreams in which I was back there, and a wave of happiness would fill my whole being. Then I would wake and find I was in my bed in the living room next to my parents' bedroom, staring at the stucco flower pattern on the ceiling above me. The disappointment would make me cry. Again and again the dream returned, each time a little differently, and each awakening sharpened the longing. And then one day I dreamed again and awoke, and it was true: I was in Žd'ár! I was so happy, so happy; at long last it was not only a dream, I was really in Žd'ár. But then I opened my eyes and understood that the first awakening had been only a part of the first dream, which came in answer to my fervent wish not to awake to another disappointment. I was not to see Žd'ár again until after the war.

CHAPTER SEVEN

Maturing

I was now eleven years old, and I began to sense stirrings in my body. Gerta was developing tiny hillocks in front, and I was watching my chest for similar signs. I thought there were two swellings, but Gerta dismissed them as invisible. We met less frequently now because it was quite a long way to her place. Formerly we had met almost every afternoon, as she lived just around the corner. Now I lived in Smíchov, and she too had moved to another suburb, called Břevnov. It was an hour away by tram. At that time Jews were still allowed to use public transportation.

Our games changed, too. We no longer pretended to be dancing on ice or to be ballerinas on the stage. Gerta now loved to put on her mother's silk stockings and high heels, to powder her face and paint her lips red, and she talked a lot about boys. Many older boys followed her and wanted to date her, she said. When she accompanied me to the tram stop, she would point out one or another, riding a bicycle and glancing in her direction. I couldn't be sure if some of her claims weren't only fantasies; still, I was always a bit jealous.

I am incredulous myself when I remember how ignorant I was. I knew that women gave birth to babies, but I had no idea how they became pregnant. A few years previously, my mother had told me that if a man and a woman loved each other very, very much, they would have a child if they wanted it. Up to now I had been satisfied with this rather vague knowledge.

One Sunday morning, when my parents were still in bed reading the newspaper, I came into their bedroom and said, "Mama, how does a woman become pregnant, and from where exactly does the baby emerge?"

My mother glanced at my father, then said to me, "Go back to your bed, and I'll come over to explain it to you."

"But why can't you tell me here?"

"It will take a while, and it is better if we women speak about it alone."

And so I heard how a man's organ becomes stiff and enters into the woman's vagina to leave a seed inside, which combines with a tiny egg in the womb. The egg then starts growing inside the woman's womb for nine months and then the baby is ready to be born. It sounded rather disgusting that the male appendage with which he urinated should come into such intimate contact with this most private woman's part. I don't remember if my mother mentioned an element of pleasure in this act. At least, for a long time I believed that making babies was a one-time affair, just for the purpose of getting the woman pregnant. It never occurred to me that I must have come into being in the same way. I lay in my bed for a long time, thinking about the newly acquired information. I had the notion that somewhere deep inside I had always known it.

That afternoon Gerta came to see me. I was excited and eager to share my new knowledge. All the time one sentence kept repeating itself in my head: *I know the world's secret. I know the world's secret.*

I told Gerta everything my mother had said. I was sure she would be surprised and astonished, but she remained unperturbed and said, "You didn't know this until now? I have known it for ages."

CHAPTER EIGHT

Ludvík and Manya

While we were living in Smíchov, a previously unknown uncle and aunt appeared on the scene. Uncle Ludvík, a cousin of my father, was a high school teacher, and Aunt Manya a qualified teacher for children with hearing problems.

I loved both of them instantly. Uncle Ludvík wore thick glasses and had a nose like a small potato. He was definitely ugly, but his was a lovely personality. He was always in good spirits, cracking witty jokes, full of kindness. I am sure he must have been beloved by all his pupils. Manya, who was not Jewish, was quite a pretty blond woman. She was shy and talked little. She used to sit and quietly watch Ludvík, when we were gathered around the dining-room table, with an expression of love in her eyes. They both could have been in their early thirties at that time.

The reason I had not met them before was that they had lived in a remote area on the eastern border of Czechoslovakia, in a town called Užhorod. They'd had to flee from there when the area was ceded to Hungary at the beginning of the war, and they eventually settled in Prague. Ludvík and Manya were Communists, and there were heated discussions with my parents and grandparents, who were

Social Democrats. I wanted to understand what the arguments were about, since all of them wanted a more equal society and more justice for the working class. My father explained that the Communists wanted a revolution immediately, while the Social Democrats wanted to achieve the same but gradually. To me the socialist plan seemed more humane, but on the whole I disliked politics.

I remember the day when distraught Uncle Ludvík announced his and Manya's decision to get a divorce. They were both party members, he told us, and this in itself was dangerous: the Germans had outlawed the Communist Party and imprisoned many of the known members. His being a Jew made him doubly vulnerable, and Manya would be less endangered without a Jewish husband. What a fateful decision it was!

Ludvík moved in with us. There was a small room for the maid next to the kitchen, formerly occupied by my grandparents' household help. So Uncle Ludvík became a member of our household and Aunt Manya a very frequent visitor. She would peck a shy kiss on his cheek each time she arrived, and they would sit together holding hands.

Their precaution did not work. Someone denounced Manya to the Germans, and she was arrested. Ludvík was devastated. He no longer joked, was withdrawn, and hardly spoke. Manya was held in the notorious prison called Bartolomějská (number four) but she managed to send Ludvík messages. They kept her there for a few months, trying unsuccessfully to make her confess and to denounce her comrades. In the end she was released. She immediately moved away from her former address, where she suspected the neighbors of being informers. She rented a flat in Podolí at the other end of the town. I loved to visit her; she had one room and a cozy kitchen, which was furnished like a living room.

Aunt Manya had lots of books; many were about the lives of workers or miners, others about travels in foreign countries and poetry. She willingly lent them to me and then we would talk about them.

It was some time later that Manya began postponing my visits. She made excuses and actually barred me from coming to her place. Again and again I tried, and each time she had another reason for rejecting me. I did not understand it; in our home she was as nice as always, but she definitely didn't want me in hers. One day I just walked over and rang the bell. When she saw me she became very uneasy but let me in. There was another visitor, a man, sitting on the sofa, wearing slippers. I could see it was inconvenient and didn't stay long. I didn't speak about it, and it also didn't bother me. I was so unshakably positive of her affection for Ludvík that I had no hint of suspicion.

Years later I would learn that for many weeks Manya had been hiding a very prominent Communist leader, one of the Synek brothers, who was the Germans' number one wanted man, and for her courageous act she was awarded high honors after the war. The man was later caught at another refuge and executed.

Toward the winter of 1941, the Germans began sending Jews in transports "to the East." Five such transports, each with a thousand persons, were deported to the Łódź ghetto.

My uncle Ludvík was among the first to be deported. For a time we sent him food parcels and postcards. But one day a few months later, our postcard came back with the words printed across it: ADDRESSEE DECEASED.

Had Ludvík and Manya not divorced, he would have survived, because Jewish spouses of gentile partners were deported much later, just a few weeks before the end of the war, and all of them survived.

My beloved uncle Ludvík was the first of my painful losses.

CHAPTER NINE

Fear

One sign that I was maturing was my realization that not all adults are omniscient, wise, and infallible. I started being critical: one person was too talkative, another was stingy, one was greedy, and, worst of all, some were stupid. But most shocking of all was when I became aware that my own father was not all-powerful and that he was unable to protect me when I needed him.

Many years before, when I was perhaps five or six, I already had my first disconcerting intimation of this. One late afternoon, Father and I were returning from the Letná Park. It must have been autumn; darkness was falling early, and I was wearing long stockings and a coat. As we were walking, I suddenly felt something wet and warm on the back of my legs. I jumped, and we both turned around. Two boys, slightly bigger than myself, were walking behind us and peeing on me. They laughed loudly and ran away. Father stood there, undecided and helpless, while I cried with frustration and shame. He didn't run after the boys, didn't catch and punish them; he didn't even shout at them. He just let them escape, and I was embarrassed and humiliated. That was long before the Nazi occupation.

One day, when I was about eleven and we were already living in Smíchov, Father and I were walking home from somewhere. As we crossed a street, I was knocked down by a bicycle. Father helped me stand up; my knee was bruised and bloody, and the stocking had a big hole. People gathered around, and the cyclist stopped and started apologizing, but Father took my hand and rushed me away from the commotion in long strides. He didn't even accuse the man or show anger; he just wanted to escape from the crowd. Perhaps he felt that it was unwise for a Jew to become the center of attention. Perhaps the police would be called, involving us in interrogations and protocols. Better to get lost. My painful knee was less important.

At the beginning of the occupation, I did not feel the persecution of the Jews so much. Yes, we had been evicted from the flat in the Electric House and Father had lost his job. Food was disappearing from the shops, and we were given ration cards. One had to stand in queues at the butcher's and fishmonger's, but the food shortage was shared also by the non-Jews.

But then began all kinds of anti-Jewish restrictions; every few weeks, new regulations were enforced. We gradually had to hand over our radios and jewelry to the Germans. I remember my mother saying that this was one thing she did not mind: she owned no gold nor diamonds.

Then came the order that Jews must hand over bicycles, sports equipment, musical instruments, cameras, pet animals, and fur coats. We were not allowed to go to theaters, cinemas, cafés, restaurants, parks, concerts, sport events, or any kind of entertainment. Jews were forbidden to be treated by gentile doctors or to travel outside the city limits. Our identity cards were stamped with a *J*, and a curfew was imposed from eight o'clock in the evening.

Yet the harshest blow for me was when Jewish children were no longer permitted to go to school.

On September 1, 1940, the school year began as usual. It began for all the pupils and students in Czechoslovakia, but not for me, nor for all other Jewish children.

I had been happily looking forward to starting high school, having finished the fifth grade of elementary school in Žďár. In high school, teachers addressed students with the more respectful *vy* instead of the familiar *ty*, and classes had Latin names: Prima, Secunda, Tertia. At the end of grade Octava, students got a matriculation certificate and were allowed to go to university. But by order of the Nazi rulers of Czechoslovakia, now called Protektorat Böhmen und Mähren, Jews were forbidden to attend schools.

On that day I stood at the window of our Smíchov apartment and enviously watched the children with their schoolbags walking to school. Like every pupil, I had been happy when the summer vacation started. But now the vacation didn't end; it became permanent. I wasn't pleased at all. I felt lost, excluded. What would I do all day long?

My parents also worried, of course. A child must continue her education; she cannot stay at home, perhaps helping with household chores[1] but remaining ignorant. They asked beloved Uncle Ludvík and Aunt Manya for help. Uncle Ludvík taught me Czech grammar, I think, and Aunt Manya math and biology, while my father tutored me in history and geography. Manya was able to provide the textbooks for my grade from her school, and I got proper lessons, including homework. I was also sent across the street to learn English with a Miss Pollak, who loved irregular verbs. I had to recite "do-did-done, go-went-gone, have-had-had, sing-sang-sung." Theirs was a household of three old spinsters, dry, proper, and humorless: the two Misses Pollak and their mother. I hated to go there, but I did learn English.

I had started learning English once before, when I was ten years old. My parents intended to send me to England with a group of Jewish children. They bought a beginners' English textbook and started to teach me. Only decades later did the world learn about Nicholas Winton and his heroic project of saving Jewish children from Hitler's murderous claws. Why I wasn't sent in the end I never heard, but I think it was because Mother was unable to part with me.

---

1 Now and again I stood in the queue at the grocer's instead of Mother. There was a pub in our building; as Jews were not allowed to be outdoors after eight o'clock, I could go through the cellar to fetch a beer for Grandfather's evening meal.

Yet the arrangement with my private tutors was soon disrupted. After Manya's arrest, Uncle Ludvík was so shaken and worried, he was unable to continue teaching me.

Another solution had to be found. My parents heard that some families engaged unemployed Jewish teachers, who arranged study circles for several children in private homes. After a short time I started attending such a circle, together with my best friend, Raja Engländer, my former schoolmate Annemarie Brösslerová, and a few other children.

Raja Engländer, 1941

For our study circle we used each pupil's home in prearranged rotation. The four, five, or six children would arrive one by one, a few minutes apart, because assembly of more than three persons was forbidden. We had to be as inconspicuous as possible, careful not to make much noise on the stairs. When the teacher arrived, we sat around the table in our crammed room and teaching began. Of course there was no blackboard, but that didn't matter; we learned willingly and gladly. We had quite a good time and often laughed.

We had another teacher, who we nicknamed Jinovatka (which means "hoarfrost"), as he seemed so cold and distant. But the other subjects were taught by Dr. Lichtigová, a pediatrician by profession. She was small, shorter than her pupils, and had a pronounced hunchback. But she was so kind and warmhearted that we all just loved her. Sometimes we were invited to her flat for the lessons, where she lived with her mother. Strangely, I have no idea how the parents paid our tutors. It must have been done delicately and discreetly behind our backs.

Gathering for classes was a dangerous enterprise. We had to be careful not to arouse the suspicion of neighbors, who might report the clandestine schooling of Jewish children to the Nazi authorities. At that time many families had already been evicted from their flats, which were expropriated by Germans. We had also had to move again. A German officer ordered us to vacate our Smíchov apartment because he wanted it for himself. We hadn't lived in Smíchov for very long, only one or perhaps one and a half years.

Jews were no longer allowed to reside in all parts of the city. They were limited to Staré Město and Josefov, which, in past centuries, had been the location of the Jewish ghetto. Soon there were no more vacant flats, and people were forced to crowd together, one room per family. Most apartments had three or four rooms with a kitchen, one bathroom, and one toilet. Now such an apartment housed three or four families, who had to take turns at the facilities. This was a great problem and caused much anger and squabbling among the tenants.

Raja and her parents, for example, lived in a large flat on Pařížská Street, together with three other families. At the entrance door were their names and the code for the bell: Kaufmann, two short rings; Platschek, one long, one short; Lustig, one short, two long; Engländer, three long. For my grandparents a room was found near us, in Kostečná Street. They shared it with two other elderly couples.

My parents were more fortunate. My young piano teacher, Helena Hőlzlová, with whom I had just started to learn, knew of a vacant two-room flat in Waldhauserova Street and suggested we take it together. And so we came to live with Helena, her charming husband, Arnošt, and her mother, Mrs. Steiner.

Of course we couldn't fit most of the furniture into our single room. Just the double bed, my sofa, two wardrobes, a table, and chairs could be squeezed into it. The other pieces were given away, except for the dining room sideboard, the green couch, and my father's bookcase and writing desk. An acquaintance of Aunt Lori's was willing to take these and keep them for us till after the war.

I must pause here, to tell about an event concerning the sideboard. It was made of brown oak with a clock on top and several drawers and compartments. In the lower part Mother stored the crystal glasses and the porcelain set (the one I was to get when I married); in the center section she kept the cookies she always baked, to have something ready for unexpected guests. She used to make two kinds that lasted for months without becoming stale. Both were called "little kisses"—one was white and crunchy; the other brown, with chocolate and almonds.

When the war was over and I returned from the concentration camps, Lori's friend kept her word and returned the furniture. The old familiar sideboard brought back memories of the times when we were still all together, Mother and Father and me. When I opened the door of the middle compartment, it was empty. No longer were there any "little kisses." But their sweet fragrance lingered inside and wafted out at me, like a greeting from better times.

Starting in 1941, Father was employed once more. He worked at the offices of the Jewish Community, the so-called *kille* (that is, *kehila,* Hebrew for "community").

It was in Josefovská Street, near where we lived; today the street is named Široká. I often went to the *kille*, mainly because another uncle of mine also worked there. His name was Julius Tutsch, a distant cousin of my mother. He was a photographer, who for years made all our family photos. I had two reasons for visiting him: I always wanted to pose for more photos of myself, but, above all, I wanted to see Uncle Julius's assistant, the handsome Honza. Honza wasn't interested in me but was willing to make a pact with me: to pretend to be my brother. I always wished to have a brother, and I begged Mother to have a boy, if not an older brother like Annemarie's then at least a younger one. But she said that in such bad times it would be irresponsible to have a baby. Of course, I could not claim to have an older brother to people who knew me, but when I made new friends, I boasted of having a brother who worked in the photo department at the *kille*.

Dita Polach (left) and Raja Engländer in Hagibor, 1941

One day a new restriction was imposed on the Jews. We had to wear a yellow star with the word *Jude* on our outer garments. It had to be sewn on firmly, not only on its six tips, but all around. On the first day with the Magen David on our coats, Raja and I were riding the tram to one of our teachers—standing on the rear platform, the only place allowed to Jews. We were apprehensive of people's reactions and tried to be as inconspicuous as possible. But one tall man in a long coat looked at us and then said loudly, so everyone could hear, "These are two princesses with golden stars." We had to smile, and so did all the passengers. I felt a great relief.

One of my father's cousins was Uncle Leo. I admired his wife, Verica, who I thought was the most beautiful woman I knew. Like Uncle Ludvík, Uncle Leo also appeared in Prague in 1938, when he and his wife escaped from Berlin. He was a charming man, as handsome as a film star. When he and Verica walked down the street, people would stop and stare, they were so glamorous. Verica was always perfectly dressed and made up, her shiny black hair reaching her shoulders. She wore very high heels so as not to seem too short next to Leo. Because Verica was not Jewish, Leo was spared the transports until close to the end of the war. He didn't find work in Prague. In Berlin he used to be a bank clerk; however, he didn't speak a word of Czech, so he took the only work offered him and became a porter. He worked at a moving firm, wore dirty clothes, and hauled heavy furniture, all with a smile and good cheer, which made him eminently popular with his Czech non-Jewish coworkers. He was deported to Terezín as late as spring 1945 and came back to Prague after the war, hale and sound. He was also most kind to my grandmother; within days he went to fetch her from the ghetto and took her in.

I wanted to continue learning to play the piano after we were evicted from the Smíchov flat. The problem was that I had no piano now. Gerta's parents had kindly offered to keep it for us when we moved to the one room. Aunt Verica agreed, if not enthusiastically, to let me practice on her piano, every day for half an hour at noontime. Helena and I also could have a lesson there once a week. And so I progressed for a while and was lauded, perhaps exaggeratedly, for my musical talent.

All this time the deportations of Jews continued, no longer to the Łódź ghetto, but to Terezín. The transports caused constant upheavals in our lives. Friends were sent away; every few weeks, there were tearful partings. My study circle disintegrated, and again I had nothing to do.

While Jews were forbidden to attend the public schools, one Jewish school was allowed to function in Prague. Despite filling classes to capacity and teaching in two shifts, morning and afternoon, and even adding more classrooms in another building, the school could not absorb all the Jewish children. But when transports started in 1941 and the Jewish population dwindled, places became available and pupils were accepted according to a waiting list.

Meanwhile a welcome occupation was found for me. I was to become the assistant to the assistant of the dentist, Dr. Wantochová. Her clinic was in a building next to the Spanish synagogue on Dušní Street (nowadays the Jewish Museum). I was given a white smock, and my duty was to call in the next patient from the waiting room. On the patient's card was a picture of the upper and lower row of teeth, and I marked with a colored pencil the tooth that was treated and wrote the date of the patient's next appointment. After a few weeks I was promoted and permitted to prepare the amalgam for the fillings. This was a mixture of mercury and some silvery metal flakes, which had to be crushed vigorously with a pestle in a little glass container until it became a smooth paste. I handed tiny bits of it, poised on a ball-tipped tool like miniature pyramids, to the assistant, who conveyed them to the dentist. I liked the work and felt useful and important, even though the assistant was a gruff and bossy person.

Everybody was afraid to ignore the restrictions imposed on us Jews. We heard of people being stopped on the street by the German occupiers and being arrested when their ID card showed the large *J* and they didn't have the yellow star on their coat.

At the beginning of the war, before we had to wear the star, my father took Gerta and me to see a wonderful film called *Boys Town*, with Spencer Tracy and Mickey Rooney. Since then I hadn't been able to see another film, because on all cinemas, theaters, restaurants, or sports clubs hung posters with the words JUDEN UND HUNDEN EINTRITT VERBOTEN (no entry for Jews and dogs).

I longed to see a film that was the talk of the town, with a famous actress whom I admired. I collected her photos and cut them out of magazines. I didn't dare remove the yellow star from my coat and enter a cinema, but Zdenka, Aunt Manya's young sister, was daring and invited me to come with her. Despite my nagging worry of being discovered, I went. I was enchanted; it was such a romantic story! I was terribly romantic when I was twelve and thirteen. I dreamed of running through blooming meadows, my white dress fluttering behind and a handsome, tall man picking me up in his arms.

On my twelfth birthday I was promised a special treat. Gerta and her mother invited me to come bathing in the Vltava River. They picked a spot way beyond the public bathing places, where the open meadows reach the banks of the river. Gerta's mother was sure there would be no German controls to check the IDs of the handful of bathers.

I was excited before the outing, looking forward to it with elation. However, on the morning of July 12, something unexpected happened. I discovered blood on my nightgown, and it turned out to be my first menstruation. I was quite proud that from then on I would be an adult woman. Mother instructed me in what to do, but she said I must not go bathing.

What a disappointment! I wouldn't be able to go swimming! When Gerta and her mother arrived to fetch me, I was in tears. But her mother saved the situation. She declared I should come with them anyway; if I could not swim, I might just dip my legs in the water up to my knees. In my summer dress without the yellow Star of David, under it the bathing suit over the panties with the necessary padding inside, we three went by tram to the end station of Podolí. After a short walk, we chose a shady spot, spread a blanket, had a picnic, and spent a happy day in the sunshine. I didn't even envy Gerta, who could swim while I only waded in the shallow water at the edge of the river.

In spring 1942 a place became vacant in the Jewish school, and I began attending classes again. The main school building on Jáchymová Street was filled to capacity. More classrooms were rented on the first floor of a residential building on Havelská Street. Even that was not enough to hold all the pupils, and instruction took place in two shifts. I have several vivid memories of that time. There were real classrooms, with a blackboard and rows of tables and benches. A bell would announce the breaks, and the pupils would crowd in the corridor until it rang again for the next lesson. I made new friends, especially with some children from the Jewish orphanage. There was Lilly Flussová, who died of typhus in Terezín; Hana Radoková; Erik Polák, who in the 1990s became the first director of the Museum in Terezín; Zdeněk Ohrenstein (later Zdeněk Ornest), nicknamed Orče, who wrote poems in Terezín for *Vedem*; and many more.

Orče would go on to study acting after the war, and he, my husband, Otto, and I were good friends. Otto and Orče held animated discussions about politics. Like many youngsters who were influenced by their instructor Walter Eisinger in Terezín, Orče believed in the Marxist doctrine. Otto once described these fanatic Communists as people whose heads are encased in a cardboard box, with two holes for the eyes, which allow them to see in only one direction. Otto and I lost touch with Orče for about forty years. But when we met him again in 1989, he was a well-known actor, no longer the starry-eyed follower of Marx. Sadly, Orče died tragically under a train at the age of only sixty-one.

In the class I fancied a boy: Zdeněk Lederer. He sat in the rear of the class, didn't pay much attention to the lessons, and seemed always to be daydreaming. I was fascinated by his mouth. He had a permanent pout, and I imagined how it would feel to get a kiss from those lips. He lived at the Jewish orphanage. Although Zdeněk must have seen me staring at him, he was oblivious and remained detached.

I still have his photo, which I acquired by subterfuge from one of the orphanage girls. When I came to Terezín, the first thing I was told was that Zdeněk was no longer alive. He died of typhus, barely a few months after his arrival.

There was another boy in my class who in his turn wanted to become my "boyfriend." His name was Erik, and I didn't especially like him. But he was better than nothing. Erik carried my schoolbag as he walked me home. Sometimes we stopped at the Old Jewish Cemetery, a substitute for a park with tall green trees and quiet paths. Here and there we met a mother with a baby in the pram, but there were secluded corners where we could sit on an old gravestone and talk. I already mentioned the first kiss I got from him on the grave of some long-forgotten Jew.

We were both thirteen.

I liked the teachers and fondly remember pediatrician Dr. Reich, who taught us about the human body. We adored him for his marvelous sense of humor and his lovely attitude to us children. He perished, together with the Białystok children, in the gas chambers of Auschwitz.

At the end of the school year, we got a kind of school-end certificate with grades.

In autumn I did not go to school anymore. I don't know if it was because the school had closed down or because my parents expected us to be deported at any day.

Later, when my parents and I arrived in Terezín, I reunited with some of my schoolmates, but many had already been sent on to Auschwitz and other concentration camps. Only a handful of them survived and returned after the war.

During the summer of 1942, I had my first encounter with Zionism. I knew there was a land called Palestine—Uncle Ernst-Benjamin had emigrated there—but at home I never heard about Zionists, nor about Theodor Herzl, the Zionist visionary of the State of Israel.

That summer a kind of vacation camp was arranged on the Hagibor playgrounds, and I went there almost daily with my new friends from Bílkova Street (renamed by the Nazis Waldhauser Street), careful, of course, to return home before the eight o'clock curfew.

There was a football field with a racetrack around it, volleyball courts, lawns, and a changing room. At a small kiosk one could buy a lemonade or *grillage*—browned sugar with nuts. The disadvantage was the distance, because we were now no longer allowed to use the tram at all, not even standing on the rear platform as before. Hagibor was quite a distance from where I now lived. So we walked daily, a few boys and girls together, through the town, one hour each day. My new friends were Herbie (whose face was full of acne. He would whistle below our window for me to join them. Mother objected strongly: "You are not to respond when a boy whistles"), Bobby Jochovitz, Esther Wohlová, and a few others. From them I started learning about life in Palestine, about the settlements and kibbutzim.

I also became friendly with another boy, Štěpán, who was two years younger than me. I visited him at his home in Maiselova Street and often walked with him to Hagibor, preferring him to my older friends. The friendship puzzled both our mothers, a teenage girl with a small boy who didn't even know yet how children came into the world! Nobody guessed the real reason for my strange behavior. Štěpán was a lovely child, very talented and inventive, and it was interesting and amusing to talk with him. But he had an older brother, Peter, aged fifteen, and I used Štěpán as a kind of back door to get closer to my idol, Peter, who I thought would never deign to look at such a nobody as me.

Both boys perished together with their parents in the camps. All that is left of Štěpán is a crayon drawing of a country alley that he dedicated to me, together with his photo.

Hagibor was the only place where Jewish children were allowed to gather for games, competitions, sing-alongs, and all kinds of sport. I became quite good at several sports, short-distance races, and long jumps. There were *madrichim* and *madrichot* (Hebrew for instructors) for each group; they played with us, taught us, and coached us. One of them was Avi Fischer, who later became a lifelong friend.

The organizer and leader of the program was the sports teacher Fredy Hirsch, beloved by all the children. He was our idol and role model. There I learned some Hebrew songs, which we got mimeographed in phonetic spelling. We sang enthusiastically, "*Anu banu artza livnot ulehibanot ba*" (Hebrew for "we came to our land to build it and be rebuilt"), without understanding one word.

In summer there were tents, where we could take a nap in the afternoon or just sit and read. Many of the adults who worked with us were Zionists and spoke about the land of Palestine, which they would build up as soon as the war was over. They transferred their enthusiasm to us children, and we began wanting to know more about it. These were bright days we spent at Hagibor, despite the ominous gloom of the deportations, which awaited all of us.

I also remember several performances of a magician named Borghini with his assistant, Harry Kraus (I did not know then that one day I would marry Harry's older brother, Otto). Another show was *A Midsummer Night's Dream*, performed by the children of the Jewish orphanage, directed by a young man—Rudolf Freudenfeld—nicknamed Baštík. The role of Puck was acted marvelously by Zdeněk Ohrenstein.

While I spent such happy hours on the playground, momentous events took place all around. More and more people were deported in transports, and one day in July it was my grandparents' turn. We helped them pack their bags, which neither of the old people could carry anyway. Young Jewish volunteers came to help. Within two days, they were gone.

A magic show in Hagibor, August 1941—Harry Kraus, the magician Borghini, and Fredy Hirsch

Just a short while before, a letter sent from Palestine by Uncle Ernst-Benjamin had arrived in a circuitous manner via England. He'd written that he now lived in Kibbutz Ashdot Yaakov, that he had married a woman named Hadassa, and that he had become the father of a boy called Doron. That was wonderful news, and I was given the responsibility of conveying it to my grandparents. Mother told me how to do it gradually, so as not to overwhelm the old people. While I was walking the short distance from Waldhauser Street to Kostečná Street, I rehearsed how I would tell it: first I would tell them only about the letter itself; then, by and by, the rest of the happy news in installments. Grandmother was relieved to get the first sign of life from her son since his departure and was overjoyed to have another grandchild. But Grandfather remained apathetic; he didn't show any signs of joy.

The summer ended, and everything became darker. Not only were the days shorter and colder, but the world grew emptier, and there was nothing one could look forward to. There were fewer friends, all the time only transports and deportations.

In November it was our turn. There wasn't much to prepare, as my parents had sorted our belongings well in advance. My mother's brother, Hugo, had come from Brno a few weeks before and taken a shoebox full of photos and some other items for safekeeping. A few non-Jewish friends came to say goodbye. And of course Manya, who tried to help as best she could.

My parents and grandparents had been very fond of both Ludvík and Manya, and she visited us often, even after Ludvík's death. Christians were forbidden to have any contact with Jews, but she didn't mind. She always brought us something to eat; food was scarce and already rationed, and we Jews got even less than the rest of the population. Later, when we were already in Terezín, she sent us parcels with bread, artificial honey, or a jar of goose fat. Manya's parents were farmers who were able to conceal some of their produce from the German controllers.

The evening before our departure, Mother told me to give Manya my toys for her nieces, and I was glad that they would not remain behind to be given to some Nazi children. But as I was handing over my favorite doll, the one with the Shirley Temple ringlets, I couldn't hold back my tears and started crying bitterly. Manya and mother were somewhat taken aback. A big girl of thirteen and a half weeping for a doll? They did not know that it wasn't the doll I was mourning; I was grieving for my childhood and the end of life as I had known it.

Next morning we closed the door behind us, handed the key over to the janitor, took the tram for which we had received a special permit, and went to the collecting station at the exhibition grounds.

This was the most significant delay of my life.

Part II
– – – – –
1942–1945

The War Years

CHAPTER TEN

Terezín

After spending two days and nights on the floor in the Radio Exhibition Hall, we marched in a column in the early morning to the nearby Bubny train station. Our transport arrived in Terezín on November 20, 1942. I don't remember the journey itself, only the arrival at Bohušovice. The train ended there, and we had to walk the two and a half kilometers to Terezín. A few carts transported the luggage, along with the old and infirm. Walking was difficult, because we wore several layers of sweaters and coats. Each person was allowed just fifty kilograms of luggage, but no one controlled what we wore.

The streets in Terezín were empty; no one was allowed to be outside whenever a transport arrived. But at the windows people peered out to see who arrived, and they waved and gestured to those they recognized.

Our suitcases, marked with our names and transport numbers in white paint, were strewn in piles all over the yard. We had to search for ours in that jumble. We never found one bag, that which contained the preserved food my mother had so laboriously squirreled away for our deportation.

At first we were housed in the catacomb-like space inside the thick city wall, a kind of dark dungeon with slits for windows. All day long my father, my mother, and I sat on our rolled-up bedding on the stone floor, together with hundreds of people waiting for accommodation. It was November, and we suffered from cold.

First to come and see us was Grandmother. She had sad news: Grandfather had died just a short time before we arrived. Because he was a former senator in the Czechoslovak Parliament, he had been given better accommodation in the so-called "prominents' house." It was the policy of the ghetto leadership, or perhaps by order of the Germans, to keep people of renown in better conditions. The better housing had consisted of a room shared by another elderly couple, with a blanket hanging in the middle to create "privacy." Our modest grandmother, in typical style, gave up the privilege after Grandfather's death and moved to the barracks of the common prisoners, saying, "I am not entitled to get preferential treatment."

After some time, Mother and I were moved to a room in the Magdeburg barracks and Father to the Hanover barracks. In the Magdeburg barracks, we also didn't have beds. We shared the room with some twenty-five or thirty women.

One day we heard that a transport would be sent from Terezín, but that the sick would be exempt. A kind of commission came, perhaps a doctor, a nurse, and some others, and I was determined to get a fever. I know that I wasn't ill, and of course I couldn't have rubbed the thermometer in front of the commission. Yet I had willed myself to be ill, and it really happened. The thermometer showed a high temperature, and we were saved from the transport.

My friend Raja's mother became manageress of the girls' *Heim* L 410. I wanted very much to live in the *Heim* to be with Raja. I asked her mother to arrange it, but she either could not or did not want to give me special treatment just because I was her daughter's friend.

It was finally accomplished in a simple and official way. A bunk bed became available in room 23, and I moved in. It was a kind of anteroom, from which there was an entrance to both adjoining rooms, on the left to number 24 and on the right to 25. In order to leave passage space, there were fewer bunks in number

23, just for twelve girls. In each of the two other rooms lived some twenty-eight girls. One of the girls in my room was Lydia Holzner; she slept next to me. Another was poor Marta Pereles, who had no mother, only a father. Marta became sick, ran a high fever, and was taken to the hospital. No one was allowed to visit her. Just a few days later came the news that she had died. Her father, a hunchback, would come and visit our room even after her death. He would sit silently on the windowsill and mourn. We didn't dare disturb him. We stopped talking, respecting his sorrow.

My bunk was the middle one, the least desirable, because on the top one there was room enough even to stand up, and you could sit on the bottom one with your feet on the floor. The middle bunk was so low that you could sit only crouched, with your head between your shoulders. Moreover, I was unfortunate enough to have Kuni Kulka above me.

She was a tall, redheaded girl who enjoyed driving us mad. She especially singled me out, perhaps because I was new and dared not start a fight with her. She liked to sing in a high, shrill voice, and I remember one of her melodies, the Hebrew song *"Lecho Daudi Likras Kalo,"* which is the traditional Jewish song to welcome the Shabbat. I heard it there for the first time; at home we did not celebrate the Shabbat. The funny thing is that Kuni was not born a Jewess; she had only been adopted by a Jewish family.

I bore her irritating behavior for quite a long time, not reacting to her provocations. When we wanted quiet, she would purposefully start singing at the top of her voice. She rocked the wooden bunk and made mocking remarks.

One day my patience ran out and I did something that was completely out of my character, for which I am ashamed to this day. It happened when Kuni started pulling straws out of her mattress and dropping them one by one on my bed through the slits between the boards. They landed on my head, on my face, in my hair. Asking her to stop was of no use. The angrier she saw me getting, the faster Kuni rained her straws on me. And then I boiled over and started shouting at her, calling her a bastard and an illegitimate child. I no longer had control of what I was saying; I only wanted to really pay her back.

Kuni started shrieking and sobbing. I had managed to strike her where it hurt. But I was wounded no less. I felt terribly ashamed; I knew I had done something forbidden, crossed some boundary, which is taboo. I also felt the shock of the other girls, although at the same time they understood me. I wonder which of them is still alive and remembers the event.

Not long after that, I finally got a bed in room 25 with Raja, and from then on, I enjoyed being with the girls. They read a lot, mainly poetry. They loved František Halas, Jiří Wolker, and Jaroslav Seifert and recited their poems. They would read famous novels such as those by Romain Rolland or Thomas Mann and discuss them. Each of us girls had brought from home a favorite book or two in our backpack, and we exchanged them among us. One girl, Sonia Shultz, would amuse us with her pantomime performance of "Granny, blow out the candle," twisting her mouth in all directions.

Lessons took place after work with our teacher Magda Weiss. They consisted of most school subjects. We were not obliged to participate, but most girls were eager to learn. There was no prescribed curriculum. Specialists in various subjects, such as music, biology, or even astronomy, would also come to the *Heim* to lecture. Only a few girls had copybooks to write in. In our room there was one table and a bench for four. The others sat on their bunks. Of course no attendance list existed; teaching was strictly forbidden and had to be done clandestinely.

Friedl Brandeis, herself a well-known artist and designer, taught painting and drawing. Whoever liked could attend. Once, she invited a few girls who had showed an interest in art to her tiny room. The room was actually only the end of the corridor, partitioned off with an improvised door. She had a large book of reproductions, one of them Van Gogh's sunflowers. She made us notice the bold brushstrokes, suggesting the wildness of the flowers.

She asked us, "Which colors do you see?"

We answered, "Yellow, green, and brown."

Friedl said, "Look again, more closely."

To our surprise, we discovered that there were specks of blue, orange, and even red.

It was a revelation for me. She taught us what to look for in a painting. It was Friedl who taught me to appreciate art.

***

But the best times were the rehearsals for the children's opera *Brundibár*. At first I noticed that some girls would disappear from the room and when they returned, they would sing such unusual, attractive, modern melodies. When I asked what they sang, they said that they were rehearsing an opera. I also wanted to sing, and they said I could come with them to the next rehearsal. It took place in the cellar of our building. There was a harmonium played by Rudolf Freudenfeld, known to us as Baštík, the young man who had directed the summer performance of *A Midsummer Night's Dream*. He checked my voice; I had to sing scales as he played them. He told me that I could join the choir.

The performances took place in a large room in the Magdeburg barracks. The small stage was decorated with a backdrop of roofs, a school, and a wooden fence. The soloists sang in front of the fence, while the choir was hidden behind it. Three animals—a dog, a bird, and a cat—were painted like a poster on the fence. We sat on our heels quietly, waiting for our cue. When our heads and shoulders suddenly became visible, the audience let out a loud "Aah." How I loved that moment! Later, the face of the soloist, who acted the animal, suddenly appeared in the hole cut out in the picture on the fence, and again the audience reacted noisily. After the twenty-fifth reprise, all the singers, including the choir, received a special bonus: one hundred grams of sugar and margarine.

I loved to sing in *Brundibár*. Of course I soon knew all the solo roles—everybody did. One day Greta, who was the lead singer, was ill, and Baštík needed to replace her in the evening's performance. I offered myself, and he let me sing a few lines. "A pity," he said. "You can sing it, but you are too tall." The opening words of the opera are:

My name is Pepíček
Our father died long ago
I'm holding Aninka's hand
Our mother is sick

They are sung by a boy who is obviously the older brother, and I was much taller than the boy who sang the role of Pepíček. That was the reason I lost the only chance of my life to become a soloist in an opera (but being tall would save my life a few months later, when I passed the selection of Dr. Mengele in Auschwitz).

I still remember a few fragmentary scenes from the time in the ghetto. I remember Sonia's mother standing in her mud-caked work boots in the middle of our room, looking up and talking to her on the upper bunk.

Sonia was in love with a boy, puppy love. She knew him from the vegetable gardens, where she worked. I am not sure he was even aware that she fancied him. One day, as we were standing at the window looking into the street, Sonia pointed at a boy walking by and said, "Look, that's him, that's Harry Kraus."

Another scene. The well-known singer Karel Berman once came to our *Heim*. The piano was brought up from the cellar, and he played and sang parts from the opera *Rusalka* by Dvořák. He explained to us how each character in the opera is represented by a certain melody. It was an exhilarating experience, and I never forgot it.

Another memory: I am standing in the corridor with my mattress placed in the open window, trying to catch the fleas that are hiding in the seams. I also remember the woman who came to the *Heim* once a week to check our hair for lice.

In room 25 there was a small, round wood-burning stove on which we stuck potato peels, and when they were toasted, they fell off.

During the thirteen months I was in the ghetto, we got one wonderful treat. We received tickets for one hour's swimming in the only indoor pool of Terezín. That was a unique pleasure indeed.

My parents did not visit me in the girls' home, but I would see them at my grandmother's. She lived in one of the women's barracks, and it was there my parents and I would meet almost daily after work. She always managed to have some bit of food to give us, often saved from her own rations. Two or three times we received parcels from Manya. Grandma kept them for us; they were safer with her, because she did not have to work.

My father was an intellectual who was unable to manage everyday chores. He did not know what to do with his shaving utensils; he just wrapped them in his rolled-up wet towel. He never washed his mess bowl properly. I began feeling responsible for him and often went to put his things in order.

One day my cousin Pavel Uri Bass, who worked in the carpentry workshop, brought me a present he'd made. It was a double-level shelf and became the envy of all the girls. Now I could keep my toothbrush and a few other items on it and did not have to rummage through my suitcase, which was stashed with all the others under the bunk. Cupboards or other furniture did not exist in the room, apart from the one table and bench.

Food in Terezín was distributed from central kitchens. The inmates had to stand in line in the yard of the barracks with a mess bowl or any vessel they owned, and the kitchen people poured a ladleful of soup into them. It had a brownish-gray color from the main ingredient: the so-called lentil powder. The smell of lentils makes me nauseous to this day. On the top of the mess bowl came the main dish of the day. It was either a potato with gravy or a dumpling and sometimes a spoonful of goulash. There was never any vegetable or fruit. Sometimes there was a *buchta* (a Czech specialty, which was a kind of doughnut) with a sauce made of sweetened coffee and margarine.

Bread of poor quality was distributed in the living quarters. Each person received a sixth part of a loaf, together with a slice of salami, a bit of margarine or here and there a spoonful of beetroot jam.

People who did hard labor got some additional rations, and so did we children. We also didn't have to stand in line outdoors, and the midday meals were brought into the *Heim*. This and the morning coffee substitute, without sugar, was all the food we received.

It was too little to live on but too much to die. The worst sufferers of hunger were the old people. They neither had workers' supplements nor any means to get more food. Some inmates worked in the kitchen, the bakery, or the vegetable gardens, where they could steal provisions at the source. Lucky inmates could get food parcels, for which they sent a permit once every three months to relatives or friends outside the ghetto.

I remember my mother saying to someone, "We are suffering from hunger." I asked her, "Is this what hunger means?" Her answer was, "Yes, we are starving." Suddenly I felt great relief. If this was hunger, then I could bear it without problems. I could eat all the time if I'd had food. But I wasn't suffering.

That came later.

Everyone over fourteen years old was obliged to work. The Youth Department of the ghetto administration sent us to work in the vegetable gardens. There were several reasons for that decision. First of all, work in the open is healthy, but also the youths would learn to grow vegetables, which would be useful when they went to Palestine after the war. And perhaps they would also be able to eat some of the vegetables secretly, although the entire produce crop was meant for the Germans and not for the Jews. The gardens were located in the space between, or on top of, the wide ramparts.

I didn't like the work. It was early spring, and nothing was growing yet. All day long it meant only carrying buckets of water. It was hard work and boring. I asked to be transferred to some other place. The referent at the *Jugendeinsatz* was Honza Brammer, later in Israel called Dov Barnea. My father worked in another department on the same floor and knew him. He took me to Brammer and asked him to find some suitable work for me. He sent me to a workshop that produced fake-leather wallets for Germany. Working there proved to be even more boring than carrying cans of water. The workers sat at a long table, and each performed one single step in the production of the wallet. The person on my left folded the top flap and shoved the item to me, I folded the lower flap and slid it to the worker on my right, and so on and so on, all day long. All the people around me were adults; I was the only youth. I lasted for a few days, then I quit. Afterward I did only chores in the *Heim*.

We had a nice tradition in the *Heim*. When it was some girl's birthday, we gave her a present, mostly something made with our own hands, a stuffed little cloth heart with her initials stitched on it or a tiny notebook with a picture. Since there were so many girls, there was always something to prepare. Sometimes we made a gift for someone in the boys' *Heim*, too.

One such gift was saved by its recipient and is now on exhibit at Beit Terezín in Kibbutz Givat Chaim. On one of my visits there, it caught my eye. It looked somehow familiar, and I asked the curator to take it out from the glass vitrine. As I turned its pages, I found my signature. It was a gift for a boy named Honza Wurm. He had sent it to Beit Terezín from America. I don't remember him at all.

One day there was a frightening event in the ghetto. The entire population was sent to a field beyond the walls to be counted. Thousands of people stood there all day long in the cold drizzle, grouped by their "addresses." To relieve oneself, one had to crouch on the ground hidden by a blanket held up by friends. We did not know what the Germans wanted to do to us, and we were very frightened. It was late in the evening when they let us walk back. There was great confusion, people lost their way in the darkness, and it took many hours until we got to our *Heim*.

I remember Professor Edith Weiss, the sister of our teacher Magda. She volunteered, together with a number of other ghetto inmates, to work with the Białystok children. These starved and bedraggled children arrived one day in Terezín. They were housed in some huts outside the ghetto, and contact with them was strictly forbidden. It was rumored that they would be sent to Switzerland in exchange for trucks for the Germans. The plan failed when it turned out that the children knew of the gas chambers where their parents had been murdered. Therefore they couldn't be released to the world. They were sent to Auschwitz, where they perished, together with all the wonderful people who accompanied them.

Another person I remember from the *Heim* was Mrs. Mühlstein, the mother of the boy who sang the role of Pepíček in the opera. She was one of the matrons in the girls' home. Of course I also remember Willy Groag, the manager of our building. I was a little in love with him; he was young and handsome.

For us girls in the *Heim*, life was somewhat less detrimental than for the adults. However, for me that changed in December 1943—when we were sent to Auschwitz.

CHAPTER ELEVEN

Auschwitz-Birkenau, Camp BIIb

What everyone dreaded most in Terezín were the transports. From time to time the news spread: *a transport to the East is going soon.* Some people were lucky to be exempt, either because they were members of the management or because they were hard-to-replace specialists.

A messenger from the Jewish administration would hand the summons and a tag with a number to each person, usually a day or two before the transport. There wasn't much to prepare. Our baggage had stayed packed anyhow since our arrival, as there was nowhere to store things. Some of the clothes we had brought had been lost in the laundry, despite the names we had stitched on every item. After thirteen months in the ghetto, I had outgrown some of my clothes and shoes. Thus I just had a backpack to carry.

Our turn came on December 18, 1943. We had to wait for the train in one of the barracks. Sonia, with her mother and sister, was also in the transport. People were milling around in the yard. Sonia pointed out a young man in knee-high boots, which were very fashionable at the time; his name was Otto Kraus, and he was Harry's older brother. We were fourteen; he was twenty-two. For us, he was an old, uninteresting person. Next morning, as we were brushing our teeth in the washroom, we saw an elderly gentleman in an undershirt who was shaving. Sonia whispered, "He is Harry's father." However, Sonia, her sister, and her mother were recalled from the transport and went back to the ghetto.

Next morning Mother, Father, and I were pushed into a boxcar with dozens of people, until there was no more room. The sliding door was slammed shut. There was no window, just a narrow slit under the roof. There was no possibility to sit, and we stood squeezed together. During the journey, we arranged the baggage one on top of the other to make some space for a few persons to sit on the floor. For our needs there was one pail, which we used in view of everyone. It was soon full, but there was no way to empty it. It is simply impossible to describe the stench . . . the lack of air. There was silence; stunned by the horror of our reality, no one spoke.

I don't remember how long we were on the way. Perhaps two days and a night, or two nights and a day. The train often stopped for hours. We took turns to sit on the floorboards. One girl sat on top of the luggage pile, where she could look out and read the names of the stations we passed. We realized that we were on the way to Poland.

The train, with more than two thousand five hundred passengers, reached its destination at night. Amidst blinding lights, strange men in striped prison uniforms shouted, "*Raus, raus, schneller, schneller.* Leave the bags." They beat us with short sticks. On the ramp stood SS men with barking German shepherd dogs—shouts, screams, pandemonium. "Men here! Women here! Five abreast! Form a column!" We heard the word *Auschwitz.*

This is where we are now, I realized. In the notorious concentration camp Auschwitz.

In the wagons our belongings remained, along with a few corpses.

Looking around us, we saw rows of wooden, windowless huts surrounded by barbed-wire fences attached to concrete poles, which bowed inward like the stems of some giant flowers. At each corner stood a watchtower with a guard.

Mother somehow managed to hold on to one of the bags. Stunned and disoriented, blinded by the searchlights, we marched along the fences toward one of the barracks. We huddled on the bare floor, trying to sleep in the freezing cold. The men had been separated from us; here we were just women and children. Mother's bag contained some food, painstakingly saved in the ghetto for the journey to the unknown. We knew that the bag would be taken from us. Mother and I ate all we could and shared the rest with the women around.

In another hut we had to strip and take a cold shower while SS men watched on the side, snickering, pointing, and making remarks. No clothes, no towels. In the freezing cold we ran wet to another barrack. Miraculously, I was still wearing my boots. Women prisoners flung us pieces of civilian rags from a heap. Another prisoner threw old shoes of various shapes, disregarding sizes, from a separate heap. Among ourselves, we tried to exchange small items for bigger ones and vice versa. Then we stood for long hours in line to have a number tattooed on our forearms. I got a *7* and then there was no more ink in the syringe. The digit *3* was barely visible. With fresh ink I received the last three digits to complete the number: *73305*. My mother was next.

Hopelessness and desperation overcame us. At this point Mother and I decided to die. We had reached total despair. There was no spark of hope left, and we didn't want to live. Yet there was no practical way to commit suicide; we had no weapon, no rope, no knife. We had to go on.

In the morning they began hauling us to some distant compound. The women stood squeezed on top of the open truck. The last to be pushed up was a tall, white-haired old woman in a black cape. Mother and I were waiting for the next truck with the remaining women.

The full truck started with a sudden jerk. The back flap had not been secured and hung open. The old woman lost her balance, toppled over, and fell from the truck. As she was falling, her white hair spread around her head like a halo, and she seemed not to fall but to fly. Her long black cape opened like a sail and descended slowly over her body on the ground.

She stayed sprawled on the frozen earth, and no one came. She might not have been dead; perhaps she could have been saved. But the truck had driven off, and we, standing there, didn't dare move because of the *Kapos* with their sticks. Yet she was perhaps the lucky one, spared the long suffering and a more horrible death.

But for me, a girl of fourteen, the memory of the old, nameless woman has become the quintessence of the Shoah that was Auschwitz.

We marched the final stretch along the fence to Camp BIIb. This was the so-called "family camp." Our men had arrived before us; they were unrecognizable. I didn't even recognize my own father.

In the camp we met the people from the previous transport, which had come from Terezín in September. We met friends, relatives, former neighbors. They looked weird; they said strange things such as "we will go up the chimney" or "we will end in the gas chambers." Their eyes had no expression, as if their light had been turned off.

I thought they were crazy, that they had lost their senses. But they pointed to the tall chimneys beyond the fence, which exuded dark smoke; the air smelled of burned flesh, and thin gray ash filled the air. At last I could do nothing but accept the truth. Yet an inner voice kept repeating: *I will not die, I will not die.*

In our compound, BIIb, there were thirty-two identical wooden huts without windows, each about seventy-five meters long. Sixteen sat on each side of the middle road, the roofs covered with tar paper. They were called blocks and had numbers. Inside there was a horizontal chimney with an oven at each end, but they were not lit. Some blocks were workshops; one was a clothes store, another a kitchen; there was a latrine, a washroom, and a *Kommandatur* (the commander's headquarters); and the rest served as the prisoners' sleeping quarters. Men and women were in separate blocks, boys with men, girls with women.

Mother and I were housed together in Block 6, a women's barrack. On the upper bunk next to me on each side lay the twins Annetta and Stěpa, and next to them Eva Weissová, one of our instructors in the *Heim* in Terezín.

Six people on narrow bunks meant for four, a thin blanket and a straw mattress, the clothes on our bodies, a spoon and a mess bowl—that was all we had. From then on we lived without a change of clothes, without a comb, toothbrush, towel, needle, scissors or knife, or pencil, not to mention toilet paper or sanitary pads. We kept the spoon stuck in a length of string that served as a belt, for fear it might be stolen or lost.

CHAPTER TWELVE

Latrine

I don't remember when we used the latrine or the washroom, which contained a metal trough and a line of faucets that trickled cold, brownish water.

I think that not many people in the world have seen anything like the latrine of the family camp. It was used by the thousands of inmates, males on the right and females on the left. It had six concrete rows with round holes running from one end of the "block" to the other. Under them was a deep pit. Every day, some disinfectant was strewn into the pit. The pungent, acidic stink made our eyes water.

The central double row was divided by a screen made of jute sacks, which hid the middle section of a standing person. The head and shoulders were exposed, and so were the knees. When the person sat down, however, his head was hidden by the screen, but his or her naked behind became visible in the gap.

The great majority of the prisoners suffered from incessant diarrhea due to starvation, so the latrine was constantly crowded. At night we were locked in the blocks and had to relieve ourselves in pails near the back entrance. During the day there were many hours when we stood in formation in front of the block for roll call—*Appell*—to be counted by the SS men. The time left to use the latrine was therefore limited.

You knew exactly whose behind was at your back, because you saw him walk in. If he sat down over the hole, you didn't see his anus, only heard the *plop, plop*. But many couldn't bear to sit on the concrete—even if not soiled, it was cold and scratchy—and they did their business bending forward with their hands on their knees. It was horrible but unavoidable to see the feces bursting out from the poor wretches' backsides, often with blood, a sight one had to bear several times a day. We saw the men, and the men saw us women, and so did the children. . . .

A very, very unpleasant memory—one I wish I could erase.

CHAPTER THIRTEEN

Life in the Camp

A day in the family camp started with the *Kapo* shouting to get up. From a barrel we got brown, warm water called tea. Some we drank, the rest we used to wash our face and hands. Then came the *Zählappell*, everyone out into the freezing cold, standing in a column of five in a row. This was the standard in all the camps—five, ten, fifteen, twenty—it makes the counting easier. When the numbers didn't tally—because there was now a corpse behind the barrack or a sick prisoner unable to get up was not counted—we stood for hours.

All the adults had to work. I don't remember what my parents did. The men carried stones in an attempt to pave the *Lagerstrasse*. When the stones sank in the soft mud or snow, the men were forced to carry the stones from one pile to another and back again. Women worked in several workshops or carried the soup barrels. Soup at noon contained mostly pieces of *Dorschen* (a kind of cattle-feed turnip), some potato, and other unidentifiable stuff. In the afternoon was another *Zählappell* and then free time. Since it was forbidden for women to enter the men's barracks and for men to enter the women's, I met with Mother and Father on the *Lagerstrasse*.

One late afternoon in January or February, a boy called Pavel Glaser invited me for supper in the men's Block 8. The *Blockältester* there was Jenda Hutter, a young man, who drilled his fellow prisoners. At the twice-daily *Zählappell* he would yell orders: *"Mützen ab! Mützen auf!"* The men had to snatch off their caps and put them on again. And again, five times, ten times, without end. Each of the survivors remembers it and wonders how their decent, nice friend from Terezín could have turned into such a beast.

Pavel was a few years older than me. We knew each other from Terezín but were barely acquainted. How he managed to get me into the men's block, I'll never know. We sat cross-legged on his upper bunk and ate a sausage, cut into little cubes, sprinkled with vinegar. Unbelievable! Where did it come from? Had he received it in a parcel? But why would he share such a delicacy with an almost stranger? We were not friends, nor did he expect anything from me in return. To give up even a mouthful of food, when we were so terribly hungry, was almost inhuman. Perhaps mothers or loving wives were able to do it.

But Pavel Glaser did it. He died only a few weeks later in the gas chamber. I wonder if anyone remembers him. I do, because of the sausage.

***

Within a short time the prisoners lost weight, looked shrunken, dragged their feet, had runny noses, and suffered from diarrhea. One could hardly think of anything else but food. The craving for food was overpowering.

My father soon succumbed. The soft-spoken, gentle intellectual perished in Auschwitz only a few weeks after our arrival. He just wasted away until he couldn't get up from his bunk. I noticed that he wasn't standing in front of the men's barracks at *Zählappell*. When it became dark, I sneaked into his barrack and saw him on the bunk. His eyes were closed, his unshaved face sunken. He did not move or react to my voice. Next to his head stood his bowl with the gray soup. I wondered at the fact that no one had stolen it.

He lay there for another day. At night I suddenly woke as if someone had called me. I knew that my father was dead. Next morning I found it was true. The day was February 5; Father was forty-four years old.

At the time, Mother was ill with diphtheria and was in the isolation ward. No one was allowed to enter, but I had to tell her about Father. I walked along the wall, knocked on the wood, and called, "Mama? Mama?" until I heard her answer. Through a slit between the planks I said, *"Maminko, tatínek umřel. . . ."* (Mama, Daddy died. . . .)

During the day, children were in Block 31, the *Kinderblock*. I don't recall when I started to work there. That was thanks to Fredy Hirsch. He managed to make the SS commander agree to keep the children in the empty block during the day. Youngsters of fourteen to sixteen were not considered children but were employed as assistants. Fredy was *Blockältester* of this incongruous facility: a day-care home for children who were destined to die in the gas chambers a few months later.

I was fourteen and a half. Fredy Hirsch appointed me to be the librarian of the smallest library in the world. My role was to watch over the twelve or so books that constituted the library. The books were a random collection. On the ramp, thousands of Jews arrived daily. They were led away, but their luggage remained behind. A number of lucky prisoners had the task of sorting their contents. When they found a book, they would somehow get it to the *Kinderblock*. I remember that one book was called *A Short History of the World* by H. G. Wells. Another was an atlas. One book had no cover, just loose pages. I have forgotten the other titles, but Ruth Bondy, who was an instructor, claims there was a Russian grammar book. Eva Merová, who also assisted in Block 31, remembers a book by Karel Čapek.

Among the activities on the *Kinderblock* were "the talking books." Instructors who remembered a particular book would walk from one group to another, recounting the narratives in installments. For instance, Ruth told Čapek's *The Gardener's Year.*

Fredy! How we loved and admired him! All the children wanted to be like him. Not only in Auschwitz but also back in Prague on Hagibor sports field and in Terezín. He was a wonderful athlete, good-looking, dependable, and honest. Even the SS men had a certain respect for him.[2]

The children would come to the *Kinderblock* in the morning, *Appell* was held indoors, and then the groups, according to age, sat on small stools in a circle with their instructor. There were no partitions and no floor, just packed earth. The horizontal brick chimney was warm because, unlike in the other blocks, here it was lit. I don't remember with what fuel, but I enjoyed leaning my back on the warm bricks with my books in front of me.

Otto Kraus was one of the educators. His group of twelve-year-old boys was in the same corner at the far end of the block, where I sat with the books. One of the boys was Arieh, the son of Jakob Edelstein, the former elder of the Jews in Terezín. I could watch Otto and the boys all day long. They learned a bit and played guessing games or held discussions. But Otto and I never spoke.

Discipline on the block was not strict. Some children didn't participate in the activities; they were free to leave or do what they wanted, except disturb the others.

There was no equipment, such as blackboards, chalk, pencils, or paper.

---

2   Fredy Hirsch did not die by suicide as is commonly believed but was given an overdose of sleeping pills by our physicians and died in the gas chambers together with the September transport on March 8, 1944. There was an underground movement in Auschwitz. It was decided that if the September transport was indeed going to be murdered in the gas chambers, the barracks would be set on fire and the prisoners would try to break through the fences and escape. Fredy Hirsch was to give the signal to start the uprising with his sport teacher's whistle. He was extremely perturbed, knowing that the children had no chance of survival. He asked the doctors for something to steady his nerves. The doctors had been promised by Dr. Mengele that they would be recalled to the hospital barracks, where he needed them. They therefore did not want the uprising to take place and gave Fredy a stronger dose of sleeping pills, so he could not be wakened to give the signal. He was taken in his sleep to the gas chambers together with the entire September transport. Several doctors and the pharmacist Dr. Sand survived. Otto Kraus personally heard this explanation from their mouths in March 1989 in Terezín.

Instruction was clandestine and only oral. The official version was that the children were learning German orders, or singing songs and playing games. We improvised. Some of the children "wrote" poems. We shaved a splinter of wood from our bunks and blackened the sharp end in the fire. A few words could be written with the tip and then it was singed again, until it became too short. Some paper could be salvaged from discarded pages behind the camp's administration office, or from parcels, which some prisoners received from friends. (They would arrive half empty, robbed by the many hands through which they passed.)

One day two prisoners managed to escape, and as a penalty, the SS ordered the heads of all the men in the camp to be shaved. We girls then decided to knit caps for the men on the *Kinderblock*. We got discarded sweaters from the clothes store, unraveled them, and made knitting needles from splinters of wood, which we rubbed on stones to make smooth.

There's one activity I remember well and with pleasure. It happened occasionally that Avi Fischer, one of the instructors (and, later in Israel, a neighbor and friend), spontaneously started a song with a few children. He would stand on the horizontal chimney and conduct, waving his arms. He sang the first stanza, and the children repeated the words in chorus. The song was in French—"Alouette, I will pluck the feathers from your head, from your wings, from your neck"—and Avi got carried away and added other parts of the bird which we would pluck. The children got more and more excited, other groups joining the chorus, until the whole block was filled with their voices. These were moments that raised our spirits.

In spring, when it became warmer, the educators took the children outside to walk around the block or do exercises. But, at the same time, they could see the ramp beyond the fence, where thousands of Hungarian Jews were arriving daily in trains. They were led directly to the gas chambers. Their luggage remained behind and was sorted by a team of prisoners. Mountains of bread lay almost within reach, divided by the rail and the electrified fence.

Most of the staff on the *Kinderblock* were men and women barely twenty years old. They were aware of their approaching deaths and must have been terrified. Yet they spent their remaining days with the children, creating for them a kind of haven in this hell. They are, in my eyes, the real heroes of Auschwitz.

One of the instructors on the *Kinderblock* was Mausi, aged about twenty-two. Her name was Marianne Hermann, but she was known as Mausi, because that's what her mother had called her since childhood. Most people didn't even know her real name.

She was one of the two young women who painted the pictures on the wall in the *Kinderblock*. I don't recall exactly what they depicted, except for the seven dwarfs from Disney's *Snow White*, but these were painted by the other girl, Dina Gottliebová.

In later life, Mausi drew the pictures again from memory, but I am not sure she recollected them correctly. They were an approximate replica that she made for the Yad Vashem museum in Jerusalem. But I, who had seen them every day, remember them differently. Some of the figures were perhaps the same, but others were definitely missing. It is too late now to discover what was painted on the wall. Many of the survivors of the *Kinderblock* are no longer alive, and we, the living, have mostly forgotten. But I think that it is not important whether there were Snow White and the seven dwarfs, Eskimos and igloos, Indians with arrows and bows, or a window with flowerpots that opened on a Swiss landscape. What matters is the story of the children and their dedicated educators, who were lost and have no graves.

In March 1944, half of our campmates, who had come three months before us, were loaded on trucks and taken away. The guards told them that they were going to another camp, but we soon learned the truth. They all died in the gas chambers. From that moment on, we knew that we would follow them in June.

The remaining inmates of camp BIIb were stunned. The previous day, March 7, 1944, the blocks were still crowded with people, but on March 8 there was only the frightening silence. Many blocks were completely empty. Even the two small rooms at the entrance of each block, where the privileged *Blockältesters* had enjoyed their much-envied privacy, were now unoccupied.

The *Kinderblock* was suddenly half empty. A new *Blockältester*, Seppl Lichtenstern, was appointed, and a new set of instructors. Jiří Frenkl, Avi Fischer, Otto Kraus, Hanka Fischl, Ruth Bondy, and Rejšík were some of them. They were among the survivors, and our friendship lasted all our lives.

People began wandering along the muddy camp road and into the vacant blocks. The bunks were empty. But in the right corner of each row, the blankets were still folded in orderly stacks as the drill prescribed. I saw that they were wonderful, warm blankets, each as thick as three of ours.

To own such a blanket would change my nights; I could wrap myself in it and be warm and able to sleep. But what if the owner returned? It would be theft; I could not do it. Yet it was certain that they were all dead. Can I take the blanket of a dead person? There were so many soft blankets, all neatly piled up on the bunks.

A few people came into the empty block. Without any hesitation, they started to take blankets and anything else they could find. My dilemma was solved. I took a blanket for myself and one for Mother and returned to my own block.

Yet the thought of the dead person under whose blanket I slept every night haunted me. Who was she? I knew she was a female, because it came from a women's block. I didn't speak about it with anyone. Many inmates now owned the blankets and other things that used to belong to the murdered people. The thought weighed heavily on my conscience. Sometimes I still feel guilty.

One day I perceived a young Polish prisoner between the barracks of the neighboring compound, which at the time was uninhabited. His striped uniform was of good quality, and he wore the beret that showed his rank as repairman. These prisoners had privileged status and could move freely between the compounds.

They patched the roofs with tar paper and did other maintenance jobs. They also got more food and looked healthy and strong.

The space between the wooden barracks and the electrically charged fence was carefully guarded by soldiers on the watchtowers. If one dared to get closer to the fence, they would shoot. I don't remember why I went there, perhaps just to be away from the crowd, just to be by myself for a while.

As I was walking on my side of the dividing fence, so did the repairman on the other, and at each gap between the barracks he smiled at me and made friendly gestures. The same happened a few days later and then again. Once he called out something in Polish, but I did not understand. The only word I made out was *yayko*, and he also showed something round with his hands.

"Ah," I said, "*jabko*" (which in Czech means apple).

"No, no"—he waved his hand—"*nie jabko, jajko!*"

I understood that he wanted to give me something. Of course he could not hand it to me; it was much too dangerous to get near the fence. A prisoner who touched the wires was electrocuted; some had chosen to end their lives this way. Nevertheless, I was eager to get whatever it was he wanted to give me. Next time, instead of walking between the barracks, I walked through the latrine, which had a back door facing the fence. I stood there hidden from view of the watchman, and when the Pole saw me, he motioned for me to wait.

The space behind the row of barracks was empty now; the corpses laid out there every day had been collected early in the morning. The only person in view was an old Jewish prisoner, who was squatting near a low fire in which he burned old rags; perhaps because they were lice-infested. He might not have been old; in the camp even forty-year-old men looked ancient, unshaven, pale, and bent. He had quite an easy job compared to the work of the majority of men, who carried heavy stones to build the camp road.

I was watching him while I waited when all of a sudden an SS guard stood opposite me. It was the one we called the Priest, because he walked with his hands hidden crosswise in the sleeves of his long military coat. He was particularly feared by us; there was something terrifying in his seemingly gentle behavior and stealthy, slow walk, while we knew of his cold-hearted cruelty.

He came so close to me that his face was just a few centimeters from mine, and I could smell his breath.

"*Was machst du hier?*" he demanded, almost in a whisper.

I did not dare step back, so I just lowered my eyes and pointed to the man at the fire.

"*Ich wollte mit dem Mann dort sprechen.*" This meant: I wanted to speak to the squatting man.

"*Und warum wolltest du mit ihm sprechen?*" Why did you want to speak with him?

"*Er ist ein Freund von meinem Vater,*" I blurted out. He is a friend of my father.

The SS man turned around, looked first at the prisoner tending the fire, then over the fence where no one was in sight, turned back to me, and stared into my face. I stood frozen, for what to me seemed like infinity, waiting for him to take out his gun and kill me.

Then, without another word, he stepped aside and walked on along the fence, from time to time glancing over the fence at the neighboring compound. My Polish friend cleverly stayed hidden.

A few days later, hunger made me overcome my fear, and I again stood at the back door of the latrine. The Pole noticed me and motioned for me to wait. He went into one of the barracks and reappeared, holding something in his hand. He looked around to make sure no one was watching; that day even the rag-burning man was not there. He stretched out his arm like a sportsman and threw something, and the white, round thing landed at my feet.

I picked it up hurriedly and stared in amazement. It was a hardboiled egg. The last time I had seen an egg was before we were deported from home, two years before. An egg!

In the following days, I was very nervous. I was afraid the man would come to our camp and demand payment for his generosity. It was common in the world of Auschwitz to buy the favor of a woman for bread or a few cigarettes. In my case however, the egg remained a free gift.

I have never forgotten that in Polish an egg is called *jajko*.

<hr>

We were expecting to be sent to the gas chambers in June, six months after our arrival in Auschwitz. Our names were marked 6 SB. That meant *Sonderbehandlung* after six months: "special treatment," a euphemism for death by gas.

But in May the Germans changed their plan. They decided it would be cheaper and more profitable if the prisoners were sent to work in Germany, where they would ultimately die from hunger and exhaustion. Dr. Mengele had to decide which of the prisoners seemed still able to do physical work.

The selections were held in the *Kinderblock*, which was vacated for the purpose. Only persons aged sixteen to forty were allowed to undergo the selection, but since no one had any documents, a few managed to cheat. With exposed upper bodies, we had to line up single file along the horizontal chimney, step forward, and say just three words: our number, age, and profession, and Dr. Mengele pointed his finger either left or right.

Most women named professions that they believed would be needed in Germany, such as gardener, cook, or nurse. When my turn came, I said three things: "73305, sixteen, painter." In fact, I was just fifteen.

Instead of pointing his finger, Mengele halted and asked, "Portrait painter or housepainter?"

"Portrait painter."

Mengele: "Could you paint my portrait?"

My heart stopped, but I managed to answer, "*Jawohl.*" Yes.

He smiled with one corner of his mouth and pointed to the group of younger and stronger-looking women.

Mother's turn came a few women later. Alas, she was sent to the other group! She couldn't bear to be separated from me, even though we didn't know for certain which group had the better chance of survival. Imperceptibly she sneaked back to the end of the line, chose two thin elderly women, and stood between them. Mengele never noticed, of course—he didn't look at the faces—and pointed her to my group.

My mother, Liesl, and I were among those destined to live. Some fifteen hundred women were sent from Auschwitz to work in Hamburg, Christianstadt, and Stutthof. About seven thousand people, the old, the weak, and all the children who remained, were murdered in July 1944 in the gas chambers.

The women who were selected for work were kept for a few days in the horrible *Frauenlager*. Before departure we stood in a queue on the platform to have our hair cut. Two prisoners from the *Frauenlager* in striped uniforms were performing that chore, while each of us tried to postpone the dreaded ordeal for as long as possible. I sneaked out and rushed to the end of the line several times to avoid the scissors. Suddenly the command was given: "All aboard!" The train was ready to go.

It was my good fortune, together with a few others, to be left with my hair intact. We received a ration of bread before being shoved into the cattle wagons and dispatched to an unknown destination.

CHAPTER FOURTEEN

Hamburg

T he ride from Auschwitz to Hamburg lasted several days. The conditions in the boxcars were somewhat better than on our journey from Terezín to Auschwitz. This time there was room enough to sit, even lie down and stretch our legs; the floor was covered with fresh straw; and, most important, the pail that served as our latrine could be emptied during stops.

Whenever the train halted, the girls near the narrow window slit tried to make out the name of the station, to guess where we were going. But although we understood that we were traveling across Germany, none of the place names were familiar, and so we had no idea what our destination might be. What raised our spirits, however, was the fact that we had received food for the journey. The reasoning was that if the Germans wanted to kill us, it would have been simpler to put us into the gas chambers at Auschwitz.

When the sliding doors of the boxcars were opened, a most surprising and wondrous sight met our eyes. There was a long row of red-brick warehouses in front of us, and in the windows dozens of young, healthy-looking, dark-haired men peered out eagerly, to see what the train had brought. When they saw us women, they started smiling and waving, calling "*bella signorina*," shouting compliments and marriage propositions in Italian. Immediately there was a sense of relief, of hope for some better conditions under which we could survive the imprisonment and the war. Even the most skeptical and cautious among our women agreed that this didn't seem like a place where they wanted to exterminate us.

When we got off the train, sentries herded us toward one of the small entrances, making us form the eternal *Fünferreihen*—columns of five in a row. The guards who had accompanied our train handed us over to a group of elderly men in uniform—not the SS, but we did not know who they were. Later we learned that they were customs clerks who had been recalled from retirement to serve as prison guards, because all the able-bodied men were in the Wehrmacht. They did not get the indoctrination like the SS; therefore, on the whole, they were not sadistic. They treated us rather leniently, but not in front of their commander, whom they feared because he was cruel and aggressive.

The warehouse buildings were in Freihafen, a section of Hamburg. They formed a row with several entrances—actually a whole street, called Dessauer Ufer. But the street with the rail for the train was actually the back of the warehouses; the front faced the river Elbe and was partly immersed in the water. The narrow stairs to the first floor led into a huge, cavernous hall, with rows upon rows of two-tiered wooden bunks, each with a straw mattress and a blanket.

But before ascending, at the foot of the stairs there was the distribution of a most sumptuous meal, such as we hadn't eaten since our deportation from home. To this day I remember the taste of the fried fish and boiled potatoes, which we got on a plate!

Unfortunately, this wasn't a foretaste of what the future held in store for us; it was just a one-time bonus, given to us by some error. Starting the next day, our meals consisted of soup, as they had in Auschwitz. At first, however, the soup was quite satisfying, with pieces of vegetables, potatoes, or beans, but in the following weeks it became thinner and more watery, as the raw materials were stolen by the camp commander and his helpers.

Within a short time new clothes arrived. I mean really new. They were over-alls that looked quite smart and had the smell of jute sacks, being made of some paperlike fiber. It was still summer—July—so we didn't mind the thinness. I was happy to be wearing a new item and not something that had belonged to some unknown person before. Moreover, each of us got an identical light-blue handkerchief—though for wiping one's nose, it was too nonabsorbing, and it was too small to be tied like a head scarf. But with feminine ingenuity, everyone managed to make some decorative use of it.

One of our tasks in Freihafen consisted of clearing rubble and debris after the air raids. There were huge oil refineries along the river that were the main target of the Allies' bombs. They sought to destroy the German fuel reservoirs. We also had to fill the craters made by the bombs. Sometimes we came across one that lay in the ground, unexploded. The Germans exerted great efforts to repair the damage as quickly as possible.

When we arrived at the work site, groups of ten, fifteen, twenty, each with two or three sentries, or *Posten* as they were called in German, were directed in-side the refinery compound. The refineries had names such as Rhenania-Ossag and Eurotank. A *Vorarbeiter* (foreman) handed us shovels and pickaxes and showed us what to do. Most of the ground on which we stood was soaked with spilled fuel; some formed large puddles of sticky goo, which exuded a strong smell of tar. To this day when I catch a whiff of tar, at a road or roofing repair, the smell immediately brings up the oppressive memories.

We had to work without pausing, and when one of us straightened her back for a moment, the *Posten* would shout, "*Los, los, arbeiten, sneller, sneller!*"[3] The only respite was when we had to *austreten*, usually behind a pile of debris, but never far, always under the watchful eye of the guard. He himself was from time to time replaced by another, since other groups were working nearby and the guards kept contact with one another. At noon we could stop and receive our

---

3   "Come on, come on, get working, faster, faster!" In Hamburg *schneller* is pronounced *sneller*.

soup, which arrived in a barrel. We ate sitting on a stone or squatting, holding the tin bowls on our knees with the spoon that each of us kept tucked under a makeshift belt. In some places the conditions were better, and whoever was lucky enough to be assigned there was the subject of our envy. But since the teams were chosen randomly, being counted off from the column every morning, everyone hoped to be fortunate next time. In those more humane workplaces, we women were allowed to get our soup in the workers' canteen, after the regular workers finished their meal. We sat on benches at proper tables, while the kitchen staff ogled us from a distance.

A few times, I was one of the fortunate ones. I noticed a tall blond boy, who idled so as to be among the last to leave the canteen and pass near me. He looked at me, and our eyes met. Later he also strolled by close to where I was shoveling sand into a bomb crater. At last he had the courage to leave something for me, motioning with his head discreetly so that our *Posten* wouldn't notice. The next girl who went *austreten* picked it up and brought it to me. It contained his lunch and a small gift, a fake silver ring. I hung it on my neck together with the metal tag with my number, which we all had to wear.

Both the tag and the ring were still on my neck when I returned to Prague. I have forgotten the name of the boy long ago, or perhaps I never knew it, but I keep his ring as a token, a reminder that there were also decent Germans.

Among the elderly customs officers was Robert, who was younger than the others. He actually took the youngest girls under his protection and tried to steer us to easier jobs. His unsuitable behavior must have been noticed by the head of the guards, Spiess, because he was soon sent away and the other guards were ordered to be more severe. Spiess, a brawny, large man, was much feared. He always held a short rubber hose, which he let fly frequently, whether it was to make us form the *Fünferreihen* faster or to get us out of our bunks, not to mention the twenty or twenty-five lashes meted out as punishment to some poor wretch for any transgression. (I am not sure whether Spiess was his name or a word denoting commander or some rank.)

Another of the sentries was a rather senile old man, who had the puerile habit of barging into the latrine (in some places there was a kind of field latrine) on the pretext that we stayed there too long. No one was afraid of him, and we would shove him out, where he went around the corner to peep at us through the slits in the planks, to watch us at our intimate activities. We mocked him, and he would laugh along with us.

It was a part of the Germans' policy not to let the prisoners get used to their guards. Therefore every few months, the whole squad was replaced, and each new contingent was more abusive and merciless.

It was July 12, a few days after our arrival in Freihafen. I was standing on the deck of the boat, which ferried us to our workplace, crying bitterly.

One of the guards noticed and asked me, "What happened?"

"It's my birthday today," I said.

He put his hand in his pocket, handed me a candy wrapped in red paper, and quickly turned away so that no one should notice.

I remember also another very unusual event from the first weeks in Freihafen.

We were a group of six or seven girls aged fifteen and sixteen, with Margit; the inseparable friends Dáša and Danka; a Viennese girl by the name of Fini, only fourteen, the youngest in the camp; and one or two others. Thanks to the *Posten*, Robert, we were allocated that day to the boiler building of one of the refineries. It was a tall, narrow structure, built around the huge three-story-high boiler. Our work was easy, just sweeping the floor, and the *Meister*, the boiler man, a smallish man of medium age, didn't press us hard. That day my mother was with us; she had just stood in a row with us girls when we were counted off.

During the noon break, the boiler man got into conversation with Mother. That was not so simple; his German was the Hamburg dialect, which to our ears sounded like a foreign language. He asked where we came from, for how long we were imprisoned and for what transgression did we have to do slave labor. Many German civilians who saw a gang of prisoner women assumed they must

Dita Polach and Margit Barnai, 1945

be criminals.[4] My mother answered all his questions, and he became more interested and involved. When my mother mentioned our family name, the man was flabbergasted.

"Are you telling me that you are related to Professor Johann Polach, the well-known Social Democratic Party leader?"

When Mother told him that she was his daughter-in-law, the man was beside himself with concern and pity. It emerged that he himself was a social democrat, a well-read and informed man. Our sentry was sitting in a corner, eating his lunch and not paying attention. Otherwise I am sure such a conversation

---

4   I remember a conversation from a later time, when we were working in a street, stapling bricks from a bombed building. A passing woman stopped and asked me, "What crime have you committed?" I said, "We are Jewish." She continued, "All right, but what crime have you committed?"

could never have taken place, since, in the Nazi regime, to be a leftist meant the concentration camp.

The next day he brought us gifts, things he had taken from his own family, a sweater for each of us, warm socks and some food. We could wear the sweaters only under our overalls of course, so they wouldn't be noticed. It raised our spirits tremendously. Not so much the gifts as the fact that in his eyes we were now individuals with names and identities. My mother considered the possibility of asking him to send a letter to Prague on our behalf, telling Aunt Manya where we were and perhaps to receive a food parcel. But while she was hesitating, not wanting the man to get into trouble, we were assigned to another workplace, and we never saw him again. We were constantly being rotated from one site to another, following the same policy as with our guards. They also never told us the truth about anything, and we learned always to disbelieve any information they gave us.

CHAPTER FIFTEEN

Air Raids

There were air raids both at night and during the day. If the alarm sounded during the day, important targets such as factories or refineries were concealed by an ingenious method. Around these sites were placed huge drums, which created a smoke-like fog, concealing entire factory plants in an impenetrable white cloud. This was called *Vernebelung* (*Nebel* in German is fog).

One late afternoon we were shuffling in our wooden clogs from the Eurotank refinery back to the camp when the sirens started wailing. The fog machines immediately started spouting the white cloud, but we were already some distance from the factory, and there was no shelter anywhere near. The sentries knew that a column of people on a road constituted a target for the bombers, and they rushed us to a little wood nearby, shouting, "*Sneller, sneller!*"

We had barely reached the wood when the whine of an approaching plane was heard. It was descending rapidly, having been hit by flak, and was dropping its load of bombs in its path. We had scattered under the trees, several women under each tree, seeking protection. We heard the thud of the impacts, the earth trembling beneath us. Nearer and nearer it came, and then a bomb hit the ground a short distance away on my left. The explosion threw up a mass of soil, which fell in a heap over us. It was fortunate that it was just loose soil and no rocks. We were able to crawl out from under it and shake the earth from our hair, eyes, and nostrils. We looked at one another, and to our relief no one was hurt.

A few minutes later, however, one of the guards walked toward us, and in his arms was a girl. He had found her wounded under a tree deeper in the wood. Her clothes were torn and hung in strips. But one of the strips was not cloth; it was her leg dangling from her knee by a piece of skin. Her head lolled backward, and terrible groans came out of her throat. The guard, visibly shaken, put her carefully on the ground nearby and went off to search for other victims.

The dying girl trembled, and her arms twitched, convulsing upward and sideways. She was all bloody but apparently unconscious. I cried, "We must help her, bandage the wound, stop the bleeding!" But the women around me shook their heads and said, "She can't be helped any longer."

I don't remember her name; I did not really know her. We were five hundred women and had not been together long enough to know one another. I knew nothing about her, how old she was, where she came from, who were her friends, what were her hopes.

There were other casualties, other losses. But it is she, the nameless victim, who visits me all these years in my bad dreams.

The nights were the worst. Every night, almost without exception, there were two or three *Fliegerangriffe*, air raids. The first wave of the British Allied bombers would come after midnight, an hour or two later there was a second wave, and sometimes, just before dawn, there was even a third one.

The sirens started howling and woke us from our sleep, and the next moment the camp commander, Spiess, burst into the hall, whacking his short rubber hose on the bunks, shouting, "*Sweinehunde aufstehen.*" The sentries themselves wanted to go into the shelter, and they yelled, "*Raus, raus, sneller, sneller!*" No lights were allowed, and we stumbled blindly down the narrow stairs. It was not a proper shelter, and neither was it a cellar. Beneath the building was the earthen bank of the river, sloping toward the water. Wide arches at the base of the warehouse allowed access for boats to load and unload cargo. But now, in the war, there were no cargo ships. As the waters rose with the tide, there was progressively less dry ground to sit on, and sometimes we were forced to squeeze, hunched, at the very top, right under the ceiling. When the tide was low, we could look out through the arches and see the streaks of light that illuminated the sky, the so-called Christmas trees, which the bomber planes dropped to pinpoint their targets. The impact of the many bombs made the earth tremble. First you heard the screeching whine of the falling bomb, then a moment's silence, then came the roar of the explosion accompanied by the tremor, and if the impact was nearby, it was followed by the crash of falling debris. The sentries, who had longer experience of the raids on Hamburg, told us, "When you hear the whistle of the bomb, that's all right. It's the one overhead, the one that's going to hit you, that you cannot hear."

I was paralyzed with fear. I crouched with knees under my chin, eyes shut, leaning on whoever was next to me—in the darkness I could never locate my mother—hands clamped together, unable to think of anything but my terrible fright. Others around me conversed, counted the bombs, commented how near or far each of them fell and even guessed by the thud if it was a fifty-kilo or a hundred-kilo bomb. I was terrified. Every night for an hour or two I huddled there, while rats scurried between or over my feet.

When the all-clear was sounded, we climbed wearily back into our bunks, hoping to continue our sleep. Most nights, however, there was a second raid and then it was morning and we were hunted out to work.

When the command was given—"*In Fünferreihen auftreten!*"—to form rows of five abreast, it was important to stand next to your mother or sister or friend, because as they counted us—five, ten, fifteen—the sentries separated us into teams. We were allocated to the various factories and refineries that had asked for prisoner-workers, and if you were in a different group, you were all alone the whole day among less-familiar faces. Actually, no one was a stranger, we all knew one another, but we had formed units of friends who kept together and helped one another.

It was an arrangement of utmost importance. The support of a friend was often the only way to overcome a black mood, some pain or illness, homesickness, and loneliness. There were a few mothers with daughters among us, which of course was the best. Some had a sister, and the rest formed fast friendships, usually two girls, but there were also some threesomes, who held together and shared whatever they had. If a girl acquired some extra food, she would divide it into equal parts and share it with her friend. This may sound a little too noble, but it really was so, and I believe it was necessity that caused such behavior. You needed someone to listen to you, someone to whom you could talk about your home and family, about your fears and anxieties. We came to know our friend's innermost world, the intimate details of her past, all her secrets. We were totally exposed to each other. You couldn't let her down when she needed encouragement, when she lost her will to struggle on and survive. It helped you to overcome your own depression when you had the responsibility to boost her morale. You talked yourself into new hope and made both of you believe it, for the next time, it would be her turn to do the same for you. None of us was immune against loss of heart; when everything seemed hopeless, the care of your friend saved you from desperation. In winter we lay close together under both our blankets for warmth, and when one turned over in her sleep, the other had to follow and wedge her knees again into the proper shape in order not to leave openings for the cold air to come between us.

CHAPTER SIXTEEN

My Italian Boyfriend

n Dessauer Ufer we had to rise when it was still dark. We stood *Appell* in the street to be counted, weary from lack of sleep. I actually learned to fall asleep standing up, leaning my forehead on the woman in front. The guards needed a long time to count us, and we had to be on the landing dock in time for the steamer that ferried us to our workplaces.

We boarded the regular ferry that served the civilian population, but there were special precautions to prevent any contact between us prisoners and the other passengers. We climbed the stairs to the upper deck, then the doors were locked and our neighbors, the Italians, were allowed to board. Only when they had been separated on the lower deck could the civilian commuters enter. Most of them were housewives, with kerchiefs knotted on their foreheads, as was the fashion of the time, carrying shopping bags, or they were elderly men. No able-bodied German men were seen; they were all "on the front."

While we were separated from the people below, there was no way to keep us from looking over the rails. And there just below us stood our neighbors, the handsome Italian prisoners of war who, like us, were on their way to work. They looked up at us, and we looked down at them. Relationships were spun, smiles exchanged, conversations went on in pantomime, and gestures conveyed feelings between the men and the women. Some were faked and exaggerated, but others turned into more.

The Italians—they were commonly called Macaronis—were POWs, prisoners of war, all in their early twenties or younger. Although they had to work, their conditions were much better than ours; they received Red Cross relief parcels, could write home, did not suffer from hunger, and were not treated cruelly.

For us women, contact with the Macaronis was beneficial. They would find ways to smuggle food to us; they wrote funny love letters in broken German, in which they swore eternal love.[5] They could laugh and joke without punishment, and they raised our spirits with their jollity and vitality.

One of the Italians, Bruno by name, started an affair with one of our young women. The Italians resided right next door, and it was possible to talk from window to window if you leaned out far enough. In this manner Bruno and the girl held long conversations in French and in time even discovered a way to meet.

When the tide was low, the cellars became interconnected, and if one had the courage, or the passions were stronger than the fear, one could crawl in the wet darkness through the openings to the neighboring cellar and find the lover, while outside the bombs were falling. Next morning however, there were telltale marks on her neck and cheeks, which earned her mocking remarks from the women. She was not the only one, but the others managed to keep their affairs more discreet.

I also had a boyfriend. His name was Franco, and he was less daring than his boisterous friends. At first he looked up at me admiringly from the lower deck, waved shyly, and then lowered his eyes. He became bolder the next time, placed his hand over his heart, and formed my name with his lips. I smiled in return. He was very young, perhaps nineteen, rather short, but very handsome with a dark complexion and black hair.

---

5 Written messages were on tiny pieces of paper wrapped around a stone and thrown up or down.

One morning he motioned to me to look at his hand; he was holding an apple. After two or three failed attempts, the apple did land on the upper deck, but another girl deftly picked it up and immediately proceeded to eat it. All the men below waved their arms frantically in protest and gestured—no, no—and a few girls also admonished her, saying, "That's not fair, it belongs to Dita." Grudgingly she gave up the rare delicacy and handed me what was left of it. Franco watched it all with dismay, and the next day, as we were disembarking, someone unobtrusively pressed a little folded note into my palm. A proper love letter it was, probably penned by one of his mates, who must have learned some German at school.

That evening I produced a small souvenir. With a borrowed needle and some snippets of cloth, I sewed two hearts and embroidered Franco's initials on one and mine on the other. I tied them together with a piece of braided colored string. Next morning I dropped him this present, together with a little note, over the rail. He beamed with joy at this token, and in the next exchange of notes, he wrote me his address, told me about his parents and his home in Milano. I learned the address by heart and of course threw the paper away. We might be stripped again of everything, as had happened before, and I would lose the note. I was also afraid of a search by the guards.

In fact, I learned the address so well that I can recite it to this very day: *Franco Z., Piazza Santa Maria del Suffragio, numero tre, Milano.* I also gave him an address, that of my Aunt Manya. If we returned to Prague, she would know where I was. I had no home address of my own in Prague, of course.

We never came close enough even to shake hands, but from then on, Franco considered me his girlfriend. Yet we didn't see each other often, because the Italians also worked in other parts of the city.

At the beginning of autumn, we were moved from Freihafen to another suburb called Neugraben. On a cold, gray day, as we were digging a narrow, deep trench, which stretched from horizon to horizon, the woman next to me nudged me with her elbow and pointed with her chin toward a cluster of trees in the distance. There, half hidden behind a trunk, stood Franco, waving cautiously so as not to attract the attention of the guards who were stationed along the trench. I also waved unobtrusively, but I don't know if he could see my smile; we were too far apart.

It was the last time I saw Franco.

When I returned to Prague after the war, Manya said, "There is a letter for you, it was sent from Italy." I knew immediately that it was from Franco. It was an extremely polite epistle, written in German with many mistakes, probably by some friend of his. He described what happened to him until the end of the war. He had also suffered much, but he returned to his family. He inquired about my esteemed mother and invited me to come to Milano, because he still loved me. He wrote that the little hearts helped him to overcome the bad times and that he still treasured them.

We wrote each other a few more times. In one of his letters he sent me two photos of himself, playing tennis. He wrote that he told his parents about me. He wanted me to come to Italy and become his wife. But I was only sixteen and was being urged to go back to school. We both realized that his dream was not realistic. By that time I had already met Otto, and we stopped writing each other. But I never forgot Franco, my Italian boyfriend.

Not only did I not forget him, but some years ago, I searched the Internet to find a trace of him. And to my surprise and joy, there was his name! But how sad! It was in an article about a tennis tournament, which was dedicated to his memory for the tenth time that year.

But in the article that described the tennis champion Franco Z., there was mention of Franco's son. I wrote him and received a warm reply. He asked me to let him, his mother, and his brother have as much information about Franco as I could remember from those tragic days.

I did that with all my heart.

CHAPTER SEVENTEEN

Neugraben

Our next location, Neugraben—a satellite camp of the Stammlager Neuengamme—was small, just three wooden barracks or perhaps four. It was located at the foot of a modest hill, called Falkenberg, enclosed by a regular wire fence without electric charge and surrounded on three sides by a leafy forest. A short footpath led to a road, which connected a number of villages.

A few meters below us, there was another camp with a collection of men from all over Nazi-occupied Europe, who had been coerced to work in Germany. They were free to move in and out of their camp and to write and receive letters and parcels from home. Of course we were forbidden to have any contact with them, but as in every prison the world over, some of us managed to find a way to communicate with them.

One day one of our girls was summoned to the *Lagerkommandant*. She was arrested and sent to the Gestapo headquarters. A letter had been captured; she had written to a Czech man in the neighboring camp. The two apparently planned to escape together. We were distressed, believing she would be killed. It was incredible, but two days later, she was brought back to the camp, unharmed but crestfallen. As a punishment they had shaved her head. She was so unhappy! She lay on her bunk with her face to the wall, with arms crossing her head. But we laughed with relief. What is a bald head when we feared for her life?

Our wooden barracks had a central corridor with three or four rooms on each side. The rooms were furnished with two-tiered bunks for about twenty women. There was a tiny oven in the corner, and when it became extremely cold that winter, a group of women, accompanied by a guard, were allowed to collect firewood in the forest.

When we arrived in Neugraben, it was still quite warm, but with the coming of autumn, the weather changed. The only clothes we had were the paperlike overalls, and the women suffered bitterly from cold. Mother and I were lucky to have the sweater and socks given to us by the kind boiler man, but our footwear consisted of a kind of clogs: a slab of wood for soles and some hard leather substitute as the upper part. Walking in them was difficult, and our feet were covered with abrasions and blisters. On the way to work we collected old newspapers or occasional rags to wrap around our feet. But the wounds did not heal, and many became infected. Of course there was no medication, no gauze or dressing. One just had to bear it.

We did have a kind of clinic and even a doctor, a fellow prisoner. There were a few beds for the very sick women, but Dr. Goldová was allowed to keep them just for two days at the most. She had nothing to cure them with anyway.

There was a rumor that we would get warmer clothes, though no one believed it. But for a change, this time it was true. One day a truck arrived with a mountain of coats of all colors. They were secondhand, but some still very pretty, even fashionable. Who knows what happened to the poor wretches who had owned them?

We could pull out of the heap what we fancied; the guards did not interfere. What a delight! Margit, who became my close friend since her mother and sister remained in Auschwitz and her father was sent to Schwarzheide, picked a navy-blue one. Mine was wine-colored with a princess-cut—both were lightweight and thin. Silly girls! Mother sensibly chose a long dark coat with good lining, shapeless but warm.

Our joy was short-lived. Soon came the order: exchange the left sleeve with one of a contrasting color. They even provided needle and thread. So now I had a blue sleeve and Margit a wine-colored one. Then we had to line up in the yard and our *Blockälteste* applied a stripe with a thick brush from a pail full of yellow paint on the back of each coat. This would make us easily recognizable when we worked near civilians.

Our work here was different from that in the Freihafen. We had to dig the foundation for a large air-raid shelter, which was to serve the new settlement of prefabricated cottages, where the German families were relocated when they lost their homes to the bombs. Another project was to scoop out a narrow, one-meter-deep ditch that snaked for a long stretch across fields between distant settlements. Whether they were for water pipes or some other purpose, we were not told.

When our work was rubble-clearing of the demolished houses in the city, we formed a human chain. The woman on top picked up the unbroken brick, threw it to the next in the row and she to the next until the last woman on the sidewalk laid the bricks in tidy stacks, each layer crosswise. The bricks had mortar sticking to them, and we had nothing to protect our hands, which were soon scratched and bleeding.

Yet there are also memories of a more cheerful nature. After I stitched those two cloth hearts for Franco, other girls asked me to make them similar items, and sometimes I even sewed little stuffed animals. Before Christmas, one of the guards asked me to make a gift for his little granddaughter. He brought me small colored pieces of fabric, scissors, and thread. In the morning when we arrived at our workplace, he pulled me aside and led me to a cabin that served as the workers' changing room. There I sat the whole day out of the cold and produced a doll dressed like a rococo lady. I wanted to give her a parasol, too, but had nothing for the stick. I went out to look for a twig, yet couldn't find one. At last I pulled from the earth a weed with a quite stiff root, and it made an adequate handle for the parasol. The man was very pleased with my creation. I only wondered what the little girl would say when the root withered or perhaps started sprouting leaves.

I became the *Puppenmacherin* (doll maker) for other guards, too. It was convenient for them to save the expense and trouble of buying Christmas presents. And I could sit sheltered among the laborers' street clothes and do something I loved.

Yet there was also a problem. Not only the workers' coats hung in the cabin; so did their lunchboxes. All around me there was plenty of food, and I was so hungry, so hungry! If I took anything, I might lose my comfortable job. I had to fight the urge to help myself from their lunches and the struggle was enormous, almost unbearable.

Of course in the end I was unable to resist.

I opened a few boxes to see what I could snitch without leaving a trace and hoped the workers didn't know exactly what their wives had prepared for them. I was frightened that at any moment one of them might come in for some reason and catch me stealing. But hunger is stronger than fear.

The idyll lasted only a few days, then it was back to the hard work in the cold outside.

Mother was not always on the same team with me. For several days she was working with her group near the houses of the evacuated German families. She told me about a young man who watched her. Another time he managed to have a short conversation with her, unnoticed by the guard. He was a foreigner, drafted to slave labor in Germany, and was employed at a butcher's. One day he brought her several sausages. Mother was extremely upset because he wanted to kiss her. She was crying when she told me. It was just eight months since my father had died. I was also shocked, but for another reason. I couldn't grasp that my mother was a woman who could be desired by a strange man.

One pleasant occasion in Neugraben was the Sylvester show produced by our women. I don't know whether the commander knew about our preparations for the party. The fact is, however, that he and the guards attended the show and applauded enthusiastically. I am trying to remember where the show took place.

Probably it was in the washroom, the only barrack with some empty space. The program consisted of several numbers, but I remember just two of them. On the makeshift stage, three girls appeared—Nanne Duxová and Gerti Hartmannová were two; the name of the third escapes me—clad in identical dresses, with crinoline skirts fashioned from dozens of those impractical sky-blue handkerchiefs we had been given in Dessauer Ufer. They sang Strauss's "Geschichten aus dem Wiener Wald" in three voices, while moving their arms and gyrating in rhythm. It was a well-rehearsed performance, quite professional. Someone remarked that it was a good idea their dresses were floor length, so Gerti's thick ankles were hidden underneath.

But the highlight of the evening was Lilly. Lilly belted out "The Donkey Serenade" (by the Czech composer Rudolf Friml for a film with Allan Jones and Jeanette MacDonald) in her deep, strong voice, wearing the brim of an old hat with scraggly strands of straw hanging over her face. It was wonderful! We didn't stop clapping until she sang it once more. All this, of course, without musical accompaniment, as there were no instruments in the camp.

We returned to our rooms after midnight. It was a freezing night with the clear sky full of stars. The windowpanes were covered with pretty patterns made by the frost. I was suddenly overcome by a strong conviction that this year—1945—would be the last of our imprisonment. I felt certain that the coming year would bring the end of the war and the end of our suffering.

Indeed it was the last year of the war, but until our liberation, we had to live through more horrors, worse than all that had already happened to us.

CHAPTER EIGHTEEN

Tiefstack

In the early spring of 1945, they moved us again to another camp in Tiefstack, a suburb of the city of Hamburg. The camp was located in the compound of a cinder-block factory, where the majority of us worked. We found that the name Tiefstack was quite apt, given our situation: *tief* means "deep" in German, and *stack* sounds like the English *stuck*, and we were truly stuck deep.

For a time I worked in the factory, actually producing the blocks. This is done as follows: A mixture of wet cement with gravel is poured into a wooden mold with detachable sides and pressed down with force. The heavy mold is then carried out to dry in the yard. In a day or two the blocks are dry. The molds are removed to be reused, and the blocks are stacked into huge cubes, about two meters high. The yard becomes a veritable maze until trucks haul them away. The work was hard and dirty, but the stacking was done by male workers.

Some women were sent to various other places, mainly to clear the debris of the bombed houses that blocked the streets. Sometimes I too worked outside.

I remember the bleak gray houses, the empty streets with the bomb craters and no greenery. There was also a high-rise air-raid shelter. Once or twice we were taken into this huge, windowless concrete building during an air raid. They herded us to the top floor, the least safe one, while the civil population used the floors below. Suddenly there was the thud of a bomb landing on top of the shelter. Fortunately, it did not penetrate the flat roof, but the entire building shook like a tree swaying in the wind. Our heroic SS guards had stayed downstairs, of course. They knew there was no way we could have escaped. After the all-clear was sounded, the civilians dispersed, and at last we too were allowed to descend.

On a certain day, our column of female prisoners was marching, or rather dragging our feet, back to the camp toward evening. As we were walking along a gray wall, which surrounded a huge gasworks, we saw one of our SS guards coming toward us on a bicycle. He had a bloodstained white bandage around his head. He came to tell our guards that the camp had suffered a few direct hits and there were casualties. We were gripped by great anguish; each of us had a friend or sister who worked on another team, and as it was the hour of our return from the various workplaces, they might be among the victims.

The rest of the way we ran as fast as we could in our clogs, whipped up by our fear. In the camp we found utter chaos and pandemonium. Two of the three wooden barracks had collapsed and turned into heaps of beams, planks, and roof tiles sticking out haphazardly. The women rushed around, screaming and calling the names of their friends. It was getting dark, which made the search even more difficult.

"Mama, Mama," I cried, pleading with anyone I saw, "Have you seen my mother?"

I dashed to the site where our hut had stood. Several women were trying to get under the collapsed woodwork, searching for trapped friends.

"Your mother is inside. . . . She is all right," one of them told me.

Relieved but not yet quite sure, until I had seen her with my own eyes, I too crawled under the beams. There she was, my mother, on the spot where our bunks had stood, great disappointment showing on her face. She had been looking for the bread we had hidden under her mattress, but it was already gone. Someone quicker had preceded her.

Saving bread was a constant struggle. We were permanently hungry, in fact starving. The rations were much too small to fill our stomachs. Yet we wanted to have some bread reserved for an emergency. The system was this: When you got your ration, you left a thin slice for the next day. On the morrow, you ate yesterday's slice and saved a thicker piece. And the next day, again. On the day of the bombing, we had already saved half a loaf. It required enormous self-denial to maintain this regime, and now it had all been in vain.

One of the destroyed barracks was the sick ward, and there were casualties among the patients; even our doctor was injured. Dr. Goldová was one of us but had been allowed to care for the sick. Of course, she enjoyed a privileged status since the guards also made use of her services. She and a few others were sent to a regular hospital in Hamburg. I heard later that she recovered.

Among the victims of the bombing was one of our guards. His body lay for several hours near the entrance of the last remaining barracks, with his fat belly sticking upward and his rifle beside him. We were obliged to step over him going in and out, which I found both disturbing but also somehow exhilarating.[6]

The day after the raid, no one went to work. It was necessary to find alternative accommodation for the women. One hall of the factory was turned into a sleeping quarter; we carried planks and put them on blocks and spread some straw mattresses over them. In the single remaining barrack more women had to squeeze in.

While Margit and I were rummaging among the ruins, collecting material for the makeshift beds, she suddenly stopped and stared at the ground. There were three packets of cigarettes half buried in the sand. Since we were on the site of the former sick ward, we concluded they must have belonged to Dr. Goldová.

---

6   I later learned that the date of the bombardment was March 21, 1945, and the name of the killed guard: Paul Gustav Karl Freyer.

Only she could have owned such a treasure. This was like a miracle. Three packets, that was sixty cigarettes!

After bread, cigarettes were the most important items in the world of the camps. They actually served as currency. Even among the civilian population of war-torn Europe, cigarettes could buy almost everything. In the camp, the lucky ones who had access to food were always eager to exchange bread or soup for cigarettes. You could approach any *Kapo* or *Blockältester* and make a deal. A double ration of soup for one cigarette was the norm, but one could even get triple rations when there was a shortage. Moreover, cigarettes didn't get stale or moldy like our substandard bread.

If we keep the cigarettes, it is not really stealing, we reasoned. Our poor doctor was taken away to a hospital; we could not return them to her, could we? No one had seen us, so what? Finders keepers.

Margit, Mother, and I each wrapped a packet in a rag, tied it around our necks, and hid it under our clothes. We felt that nothing could happen to us; our wealth protected us.

Who were the rich persons who could afford to give up their bread and soup rations for a cigarette? From the top down: the *Blockältester*, the labor *Kapo*, the kitchen staff, and anyone who had access to the provisions—after they had already been raided at the source by the SS men, of course.

Soon after the air raid we were evacuated from Tiefstack. There was a change in the air; we sensed tension, perhaps fear, among our guards. Several SS women had been added to the guards, who had become a bit relaxed toward us. The SS women were vicious and coarse; they lashed out with their whips to beat us into straight rows, each trying to outdo her colleagues in inventing more cruel punishments.

It was through an SS woman that I experienced the most degrading and embarrassing humiliation of all my years in the camps. The train that was taking us to an unknown destination often stopped for hours on the tracks. Other trains passed us, some transporting wounded soldiers. We had no idea where we were; hours passed, a day, and another. There was no toilet in the cattle wagons, and we had to relieve ourselves next to the tracks in full view when the train was stalled. As I was squatting to urinate, an SS woman came from behind and kicked me over with her boot, and I fell with my face into the puddle. I can still feel the shame and the rage as I am writing about it. Even animals refrain from attacking their rivals while they are relieving themselves.

CHAPTER NINETEEN

Bergen-Belsen, Close to Starvation

I n Bergen-Belsen, unlike Auschwitz, the fences were not electrically charged. The barracks were made of wood, the interior without bunks or any other furniture, just straw mattresses on the concrete floor.

In the beginning the routine was a familiar one: *Zählappell*, the twice-daily counting of prisoners, who had to line up in rows of five, the living standing upright, the dead spread out on the ground. There was food distribution once a day, food consisting of a ladleful of soup.

In each of the concentration camps I knew, soup was the only cooked food the prisoners received. In some of the camps, there was also a piece of bread, but

ALLIED EXPEDITIONARY FORCE
D. P. INDEX CARD
G01524723

1. (Registration number) 16—35306-1
POLACHOVA   Edita
2. (Family name)   (Other given names)
Polachová Edita
3. (Signature of holder)   D.P.1

Register card from Bergen-Belsen, 1945

gradually even that disappeared. In the family camp at Auschwitz, at noontime, a large barrel lugged by two inmates was placed in front of the barracks, and we lined up with our bowls or whatever receptacle we had. Each of us also carried a spoon, either tucked into the string that served as a belt or hidden inside the clothes. Everyone sought to stand toward the end of the queue, but not the very end, because then one could be left without any soup at all, if it ran out before your turn came. Yet being at the beginning was also bad. Then you would get only the liquid from the top, without any solid pieces in it. The inmates who carried the barrel to the barracks were allowed to scrape off the remnants of soup that adhered to the inside of the barrels when they were empty. To do that they laid it on its side and crawled inside with their spoon and mess bowl.

At Auschwitz, children had received better soup from the Gypsy camp (like us Jews, they were persecuted by the Nazis.) But Fredy forbade the educators to touch it, even if some child wanted to give his teacher a spoonful. The adults and assistants got the soup of the camp.

You could find all kinds of treasures in your soup. There could be a piece of potato or turnip and here and there even a sliver of stringy meat. A greater part of what was meant for the prisoners went into the bellies of the camp commander and his family, and our guards and their families, and only the rest reached the kitchen. Then there were of course the kitchen staff and their friends, who also skimmed their share. At the end, we, the lowly prisoners, got our daily soup, which became thinner and thinner.

Margit, Mother, and I still had our secret treasure—cigarettes. We took care that no one should know about them, to make sure not to be robbed in our sleep. The knowledge that we were in possession of such a treasure gave us a feeling of security. We would not suffer hunger; we could always buy another soup. It was as if we had a bank account in Switzerland.

When we arrived at Bergen-Belsen, we did not immediately make use of our wealth. We asked ourselves if we could bear the hunger yet another day, when the need might become even more acute. After the first two or three days, a strange change came over the camp. The guards stopped counting us, and the watery soup came irregularly. Now Margit and I were in the position to barter.

Once or twice we were successful and got an additional portion of soup in exchange for a few cigarettes. But then the soup distribution stopped altogether and no one wanted our cigarettes. Everybody was hungry, no one had food, not even the *Kapos*. The whole structure of camp life was collapsing.

After several days at Bergen-Belsen, we were commanded to carry things from a supply store to the railway station of the town. Each of us had to shoulder a bundle, but Mother was unable to carry anything and could hardly walk.

At night we could see bursts of explosions over the horizon and hear the thuds of artillery rockets. They seemed to come nearer; the front was coming closer. We dared not hope that liberation would reach us in time. In the neighboring compounds all around us, the dead lay everywhere.

I became aware of the imminence of our death when one girl, lying only three paces away from me, couldn't get up in the morning. Her legs were swollen; we all had edemas, but we were still able to stand up. She lay on her back moaning, her eyes closed, breathing with difficulty. Some of the women gathered around, talking and encouraging her, saying it would pass and she would soon feel better. But I overheard what one of them said out of earshot: "This is the end."

So this is the way one dies of hunger, I thought. And I knew that this was what would happen to all of us.

It wasn't as if I hadn't seen dying before. There was a certain point at which the downward slide started. I had seen it in Auschwitz many, many times. It was as if the person suddenly became marked for death. Their eyes became vacant, expressionless. They might still have been functioning, even working, but in a kind of shuffling manner. Their shoulders slumped as if their backbone had been removed. They hardly spoke, took no interest in anything, not even food. At their nose hung a permanent drop, which they never bothered to wipe off. They had given up and stopped fighting for survival. These people always died very quickly.

Yet now it was happening close to me. Now they were not the old, not even the middle-aged; now they were the young women around me, and soon it would be me. In the camps the concept of age changed. Anyone over forty-five was old. They did not pass the selections of Dr. Mengele in Auschwitz. Women of thirty were the middle-aged. The young ones were eighteen or twenty. I was just short of sixteen and believed that I was among the few with the best chances to remain alive.

One morning, some four or five days after our arrival in Bergen-Belsen, Mother did not want to get up. She sat on the floor, her face unwashed, her hair uncombed. It made me feel miserable; I wanted to cry. I started pleading with her, coaxing her. "How you look! You haven't washed your face. Comb your hair, don't let yourself go like this." I knew that she was at the point of giving up, and I couldn't bear it.

I succeeded that time. She pulled herself together, and with my and Margit's support, she kept on. For the time being, I felt relieved.

Then came the morning when there was no *Zählappell*, no guard was seen, nothing was as usual. Only at the four corners of the compound the soldiers in the watchtowers stood with their machine guns. They were rumored to be *Volksdeutsche*, recruits from occupied countries who had volunteered to serve in the German army. They were crueler than the Germans themselves.

At first no one realized what was happening. We thought maybe the SS men would come later. But hours passed, and no guard appeared. It became clear that they had taken to their heels, locked us up and run for their lives. So it was true, the Allies were coming closer. It was now a question of days, perhaps even hours, until they arrived.

What happened next cannot be described; human words fail to convey such hell. Yet I will try to speak about it because I must.

On the day the guards left us, the water supply broke down. Whether they had closed the main deliberately I don't know, but I suspect they did. There was no water at all. Then we noticed that some women were gathered at the latrine, clustering at the entrance, jostling to get in. Someone had discovered a leaking pipe from which water was dripping. The pipe ran along the far wall beyond the pit, which was full of stinking excrement of the camp inmates, who were all suffering from diarrhea. To reach the dripping water, if one was lucky enough to own some vessel in which to collect it, one had to swing a leg over the cesspit, brace it against the wall, and hold the pot for a while to collect a few drops. And so we formed a line and waited for our turn all the hours of the day and night, because we realized that fighting would do no good.

I don't know how many people there were in the camp. It was partitioned into several enclosures, with a road running through the middle. In our enclosure there were perhaps eight or ten barracks. When we women arrived from Hamburg, we found in the camp inmates of many nationalities. Our contingent was perhaps the last to be added.

One of the prisoners we met there was a Czech girl, Eva Kraus, whose deportation route was different from ours. She had been sent from Prague directly to the Łódź ghetto in Poland. From her we heard what happened to the Czech Jews, who were the first to be transported eastward, back in 1941. Most of them had died. She was also in other camps, tried to escape once but was caught, and ended up in Bergen-Belsen. To her surprise and delight, she found among our women her aunt, Marie Kraus, who by chance was the mother of my future husband.

Again, as always, I find myself digressing, turning away from the sights I don't want to remember, or rather, something in me, some defense mechanism, diverts my thoughts to other channels. Every time I start speaking of the Holocaust, I seem to be drifting to those postwar experiences. Although they are directly connected to our suffering, they are still peripheral, as if I could relate only to the edges, but not to the wound itself. The more bearable experiences, the humorous incidents and scenes of friendship come to mind, trying to eclipse those that I cannot bear to face. But I feel I must come to grips with them, too. They are also true, those darkest pictures that exist in the hidden crevasses of memory. I must plunge beyond the barrier and bring them into the light of conscious reality.

No water and no food. We were locked in and left to die. Near the fence there was a pile of white turnips, the kind that farmers use to feed their cattle. It must have been there for a long time, because the rotting stench permeated the surrounding area. But there might be some pieces that were still firm. We dared not come nearer because of the guards in the tower. But hunger made the women more daring, and some tried to creep closer. They succeeded in remaining unnoticed and started rummaging in the smelly heap.

I pulled Margit's hand. "Come, we can also try it," I whispered. A few others also advanced cautiously, step by step. We came nearer. Nothing happened; it seemed safe. The stink was awful, but the women were pulling out turnips that were only partly rotten.

Suddenly we heard shots. The guard had seen us. Perhaps he was watching us all the time and was only waiting until the targets came closer. Margit and I started running, but, as we had no strength, we fell and lay sprawled on the ground. Others had also fallen, but some of them never got up again, while Margit and I finally crawled away. The woman just in front of me was killed. I didn't look; there were already so many corpses lying everywhere. It was impossible to know who was already dead and who had been shot now.

The dead lay everywhere. There was no one to bury them. At first the corpses were collected and piled one on top of the other. Some were dressed, most were naked. But their nakedness was as inoffensive as that of small children, the genitals aroused no shame, the dead bodies had lost all sexuality. The limbs were just bones, fleshless, covered in skin, the knees and elbows like knots of ropes sticking out of the heap at incongruous angles. Most faces had open eyes, vacant and empty; one could not imagine that these eyes could once see. The chins hung unhinged, showing the cave-like interior of the blackened throats. Some of the dead had become so small that their clothes looked empty and only the shrunken head was proof that there was a body inside those rags.

In the course of the day or two between the disappearance of the guards and the arrival of the British army, the camp grounds became covered with excrement and corpses. The weakened inmates had no strength to walk to the latrine and just relieved themselves wherever they sat. They also died there. In a short time there was no way to get around without stepping over the dead and it was almost impossible to avoid the patches of bloody shit.

You who read this must be asking yourself: How is it possible to live through such horrors and not become insane? It is. Nature, it seems, has a way to protect man even from the ultimate of hells.

I felt no sorrow, no pity. I felt nothing at all. I understood that what I saw was horrible beyond human understanding, but I felt no emotion. I moved about, stepped over bodies, sat with Margit and Mother and talked, saw women fall and die or heard a last sigh of the dying. But I felt no pain and no sorrow, not even for myself. I existed on the biological level only, devoid of any humanity.

But no, I am wrong. There still remained friendship. Margit and I stuck together; we were a support for each other. And I still cared for my mother and tried to perk up her morale. I don't remember it, but we probably still held some hope for rescue, as we heard the front coming closer.

The emotions were not entirely dead; they were encased in some frozen place inside me, unreachable now, but somehow protected from total loss. I retained the knowledge of feelings like a past memory. An experience once lived recedes into a store of reminiscences but becomes dull, without taste and color. I was aware of the fact that what I saw was unspeakable horror, yet the knowledge failed to be accompanied by any vestige of emotion.

On the last day, Margit and I were sitting at the far end of the enclosure, some distance from the watchtowers and barracks. The sun was shining, and it was warm. Around us there were no corpses, and we sat on the sandy ground soaking up the balmy warmth on our skin. There were other little groups of women, squatting here and there, but not close together, and I felt a rare awareness of privacy, unknown for years.

We took off our clothes and checked them for lice. We did this slowly, following the inner seams where the lice usually hid. As we found them we squeezed them to death between the nails of both thumbs, a practice learned in the camps. When we finished delousing one piece of clothing, we spread it out in the sun and removed the next layer, again turning it inside out. We did this until we both sat baring our torsos to the sun, feeling a kind of bliss at the lightness of the naked body, at the contact with the clean sand, relieved that when we put our clothes on again there wouldn't be any lice in them.

We were awfully skinny. Not yet like the *Muselmänner*, but almost. Our breasts had vanished completely. How interesting is the economy of our bodies. First, back in the ghetto, we stopped menstruating, as if the body had decided that it was wasteful to lose blood when replenishment is uncertain. Then the layers of fat go, and when all of it is absorbed, the roundness of the belly disappears until it caves in and looks like a bowl with the hip bones for handles. After that the flesh itself starts vanishing, from the cheeks, from the arms, and from the legs. When I stood with my feet together I could insert my open palm horizontally between my thighs.

No longer did we feel hunger. Instead there was a kind of weightlessness. Our thoughts were no longer concentrated solely on food. We hadn't put anything in our mouths for a long time, two days, three days, I can't remember. I felt somehow relieved, even elated. The sun was wonderful.

There was a group huddled together some distance from us. Margit got up to see what they were doing. Something had drawn her attention and she became curious. The group consisted of Gypsy women. We had encountered them in Auschwitz; they were also here in Bergen-Belsen. The four or five women sat in a circle, and in the middle there was a depression in the sand, and from it there arose a wisp of steam.

When Margit came nearer, they waved her away. She stopped a few paces from them, but they started shouting and made threatening gestures. They were guarding something in that hole and did not let her approach. Margit came back and sat down quietly. We looked at the Gypsies, and they too threw glances in our direction.

And now we discerned also a smell coming from there. There was a fire and they were cooking something. It smelled good, it must be some soup. I felt drawn to it but was scared to get closer.

We got up and started moving back toward the barracks. We made a wide berth around the Gypsies to show them we were no longer interested in them. But then we turned and walked past the group to get a glimpse of their food. Yes, there was a can serving as a pot, and inside something was cooking. We didn't speak when we passed them, and they didn't shout when they saw that we were not stopping.

Margit didn't say anything. After a while she asked, "Did you see it?" I said that I couldn't make out what they were cooking in that can. She repeated, "You didn't see what it was?" After a long while she said, "It was a liver."

I had forgotten the scene. The details begin coming into focus while I am writing this. What is prominent again is the absence of any reaction. There was no revulsion or horror, although the implication of what I had seen did register in my brain: I had witnessed cannibalism.

I don't know what I would have done if the Gypsies had invited me to join them. Today I hope I would have refused, but I am not certain. Margit and I never spoke about it again.

CHAPTER TWENTY

Liberation

It must have been the next day that the British arrived, because if it were later, I wouldn't have been able to walk any longer. At first we heard a voice over a loudspeaker, somewhere from the direction of the camp entrance. Although this was something new, no one showed any curiosity; it was too much of an effort to get up from the ground. The voice came closer, repeating some announcement. There was a stirring in the neighboring compounds. The lying figures that were not yet dead raised their heads and listened. Some stood up and went to the fence, where they could see the central road. We heard shouts from the other compounds; something unusual was going on.

And then I could see it, too. It was a green military vehicle with a white symbol on its door, but it was not the *Hakenkreuz* (swastika). A loudspeaker was mounted on the roof, and inside the car were soldiers in unfamiliar uniforms. The car was moving slowly along the road, and the voice repeated in several languages, "You are liberated, you are free. We are the British army, and we have come to liberate you."

Maybe they said it differently. My memory has blanks, especially of things that were spoken; I remember much better the sights than the words. I can see the women clustered at the fence, those who still had the strength to become enthusiastic. The majority, however, lay apathetically, a few smiled weakly, understanding that this was something good.

I did understand, but I didn't rejoice. What I felt was a kind of relief: *From now on all will be better; we will get food.* But in the camps one didn't raise high hopes. We had learned that the expectations of something positive had never been fulfilled. Each day, each month, each year brought only worse suffering. One just suspended any hope of improvement, the expectation of anything good had long ago been suppressed. It wasn't only foolish but harmful. Because each new disappointment was harder to bear, the lower one's spirit sank, the more effort was needed to raise oneself up and go on. It sapped your strength to be optimistic.

Some women tried to open the gates to get to the road, but found them locked as before. Freedom was still something abstract, distant. We would have to wait patiently. This was also announced through the loudspeakers. "Remain calm. You will receive food, and the sick will be treated. We have to keep you in quarantine to prevent an epidemic. You will be sent back to your homes as soon as you are free of contamination."

Yet despite their goodwill, the British made fatal mistakes, which caused the deaths of many more victims before things began to improve. On the very first day they began distributing the food from their army supplies. They did not realize what their tinned meat and beans would do to the emaciated, starving bodies. The sudden glut was devastating, and those that vomited immediately were the lucky ones.

My sensible, level-headed mother declared resolutely, "You two will not eat anything unless I approve of it." Of the available tinned food, she allowed us to take two tins. One was dry powdered milk, and the other sugar. She explained to me and Margit that we must be extremely careful and eat only a spoonful from each tin with long intervals in between, to let our digestive systems learn to function again.

So the three of us sat on the ground and licked the delicious mixture of sugar and milk powder, keeping it long in our mouths to let it dissolve slowly.

We promised Mother we'd obey her guidance, despite seeing the others around stuffing themselves with the enticing goodies.

The British army stumbled upon the Bergen-Belsen camp in April 1945 as it advanced across Germany. They had no previous knowledge of what they would encounter and were totally unprepared to deal with the situation. I heard it from them many times. They knew no one would believe them when they described what they'd found. They had to document it all on film.

They filmed the sights of the camp in the first days after the liberation: the burial of the bodies in the mass graves. The ceremonial incineration of the lice and typhus-infested barracks, watched by the troops and the former prisoners from a safe distance.

I saw the film on television in 1986. I remembered the smell of the thousands of corpses, which I had forgotten. I was probably so used to it at the time that it had ceased to bother me. And now the pictures of the dead, just as I had seen them, with those twisted limbs and sunken eye sockets. Then there are the German civilians, together with the mayor of a nearby town, having been ordered by the British to witness their own atrocities. They are holding handkerchiefs to their noses and averting their eyes. They stare openmouthed, shaking their heads, repeating over and over again, *"Wir haben nichts gewusst."* We didn't know anything.

It may sound wrong or politically incorrect, but I believe that many of the Germans really didn't know. The camp itself was quite distant from any settlement, the road leading to it off-limits. No obedient German would try to go to a place that was *VERBOTEN*.

The British ordered the male SS guards, wearing their now dirty and crumpled, formerly spick-and-span uniforms, to perform the disgusting task of burying the thousands of bodies. It gave me quite a bit of satisfaction to see those high and mighty *Übermenschen* humbled and degraded, dragging the corpses by their arms and legs, some of them already decomposing.

The film goes on: The camp-burning ceremony. The bulldozer, excavating earth for one of the huge mass graves. Open-air makeshift showers, where naked former prisoners bathe, not minding being filmed. And here are the SS women, lined up in front of the barracks, those fat, uniformed, large-bosomed brutes. Next there is the British military vehicle with the amplifier on the roof, driving along the central road of the camp. And then one sees the faces of the women prisoners behind the fence, and could it be . . . ? The girl in a dark dress with the bloated face, was that me? I think it was, and the shorter one just behind me looked like Margit; the face is not clear, but the hairline seems familiar. But the camera moves on too quickly.

A few days after the liberation, I started working with the British army. The familiar vehicle with the loudspeaker called for people who could translate from German to English and English to German. I volunteered to become an interpreter. Like everyone else, I was eager to have access to the soldiers' cigarettes and chocolate. I got a white armband with the letter *I*, which I wore on my sleeve. It was sheer chutzpah on my part to claim that I knew English. The English I had learned with Miss Pollak at the age of ten didn't prepare me for conversation in that language. German was no problem; it was my mother tongue.

I was attached to an officer, who sat in the former *Kommandatur* near the main entrance of the camp. In the beginning I did not understand a word of what he was saying, but then he started speaking slowly, and that improved the situation. Like every one of them, he was extremely kind to me. All the officers and soldiers were still in a state of shock after what they'd found in the camp, and each of them wanted personally to alleviate the suffering and tried to compensate for what had been done to us. They gave us presents, anything they could think of, even money, which of course we had no use for. My officer, for example, took off his wristwatch on the first day I came to work and wanted to give it to me. I didn't accept it; I was embarrassed. Instead I asked for cigarettes, at which he jumped up and opened a cupboard, which revealed a treasure of stacks and stacks of Woodbines, Craven A, and Navy Cut, the rations for the troops. He told me to help myself to as many as I liked, not only now, but whenever I wanted. I took two packets, which seemed to me a great lot, but I didn't want to appear greedy. The knowledge that I could replenish my treasure every day was more wonderful than the possession itself.

Of the three girls who had volunteered as interpreters, only I was placed in an office. Eva was attached to an officer, who was in charge of the burial of the corpses in the mass graves. He was driving around in a command car, and Eva had to interpret his orders to the Germans. I don't remember the third girl's name, only that she was a native of Brno.

A few days after the liberation, Eva's officer took both of us out of the camp in his car. We had to duck so that the guard at the gate wouldn't see us. The prisoners were forbidden to leave the camp; the typhus epidemic was already raging, people were dying, and the camp was under strict quarantine. But Eva's officer was young and reckless, and for the first time in years, we found ourselves beyond the fences, out in the open country.

It was May, or maybe still April, and along the road the cherry trees were in bloom. There were little villages, here and there a lonely farmstead, the fields were beginning to turn green, and all around was such heavenly, pastoral peace, without a sign of war or bomb damage, that we thought, *This cannot be true. Here we are, just a few miles from the worst hell human imagination can conceive, and for these people life has been going on as usual.* The war passed them by, the seasons came and went; true, perhaps their men were drafted to the army, and maybe they had to hand over their produce to the government. But what was that compared to what we had endured?

The officer stopped at one of the farms. A German *hausfrau* (housewife) came out, and he asked her for eggs. She didn't understand, shrugged her shoulders and gesticulated with her hands.

I spoke to her in German: *"Er will Eier."* He wants eggs.

She started wailing, "We don't have any eggs. We are hungry ourselves."

But then the officer barked a command, and she fell silent immediately. Then she walked into the henhouse and came out carrying several eggs in her apron. Excluding the one I was given in the family camp in Auschwitz, they were the first eggs I had seen in four years.

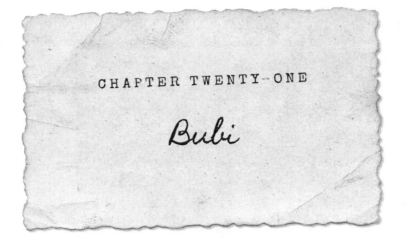

CHAPTER TWENTY-ONE

Bubi

I t was well known that most of the guards who had manned the camp vanished among the civilians to avoid capture, but a number of the personnel remained, and the British took them into custody.

It was not clear whether they belonged to the SS. They had no insignia—removed, of course, to look more innocent in the eyes of the British. Their appearance lost its military, commanding stance, and they behaved toward the British in a submissive, almost cringing manner.

They were put to work carrying the thousands of corpses, their disgust plainly showing on their faces, yet they dared not complain or refuse.

The female guards were locked in some rooms of the same hut where I worked. It was my officer who was in charge of them. One by one they were sent in for interrogation, and my job was to translate his questions into German and their answers into English. It was slow work, not only because of my poor English, but also because they tried to minimize their responsibility, saying they were only carrying out orders from above; none of them admitted to having given any commands or having tortured or beaten prisoners. In spite of that, they remained much more self-assured than the men.

My officer, whose name I have long forgotten, explained to me that what we were doing was only preliminary; we had to take down their personal data, their rank, and a short account of their career. Later they would be transferred to real prisons and charged at special war courts. And so every day, we processed a few, while I was undergoing a complicated process of change.

One of the SS women was a guard who had accompanied our group from Hamburg to Bergen-Belsen. She was called Bubi.

She was young, maybe twenty-five or twenty-six, tall and slim, with a rather pretty round face and very short dark hair, cut in men's fashion. Together with a number of other SS women, she had been assigned to the Neugraben camp in Hamburg before we were transported to Bergen-Belsen. Our guards were exchanged several times. The last were women, and they were the worst. They wore black capes that made them look like bats or angels of death. They beat us with sticks or whips, and their female commander was the most sadistic and inhuman of all.

Bubi was one of the earlier contingent. Her behavior was different. She would speak to us from time to time, even make jokes, but although she too carried a stick, she didn't use it on us. Soon she became friendly with one of our girls, and it became evident that what had been rumored about her was true. She was a lesbian.

In Neugraben I was in the same room as Lotta, the most beautiful of all our women. She was so beautiful that even in the same rags we all wore, standing among rows and rows of bedraggled women, her hair not cared for any more than that of all the others, she still attracted the eyes of everyone. Thanks to her beauty, she received better treatment in all the camps. In the family camp in Auschwitz, she was *Blockälteste* of Block 6. Her mother was also with us, all the while in the shadow of her striking daughter, quietly admiring her. Lotta was a few years older than me, but in Neugraben she befriended me and called me Didi, which I liked.

At first, Bubi managed to get assigned to the contingent where Lotta was working that day. During our march to and from work, she walked alongside Lotta, striking her black riding boots with her stick and having short exchanges of conversation with her. In time she grew bolder, staying longer and closer to Lotta, until she took to visiting her in our room.

We were about twenty-five women in the room. Two-tiered bunks with narrow gaps between them took up all the space. Lotta's bunk was the lower one in a dark corner, at right angles across from mine. When Bubi first came into the room in the evening, everyone thought it was a control visit. We froze, not knowing what to expect. But she casually told us to carry on, spoke for a short while with Lotta, and left. She repeated her visits more often and stayed longer. After some time she would spend whole evenings sitting on Lotta's bed, holding whispered conversations with her. Lotta would lie on her back, hidden in her dark corner, and we'd hear her burst into laughter from time to time.

Lotta was certainly not a lesbian, and I don't think that their relationship went beyond what we all could observe, but what prisoner would dare refuse anything to a powerful person, such as an SS guard? Besides, it was useful to have a friend higher up; maybe she would exempt you from the worst workplaces or even let you have some extra food. Most women were willing to do anything for a slice of bread, let alone something so trifling as pleasing someone like Bubi.

After bringing us from Hamburg to Bergen-Belsen, the job of our SS guards, including Bubi, was finished, and we didn't see them again.

But one day, after the SS staff abandoned the camp and left us locked up without food and water, a new prisoner appeared in our hut in Bergen-Belsen. It was Bubi. She sat down on the floor near Lotta with the rest of us, smiling, without any explanation. She wore street clothes, and if it wasn't for her round, healthy face with her short-cropped hair, she would have been indistinguishable from us.

Nobody took much notice of her. True, we might have wondered why she chose to suffer with us, risking hunger, infection, and lice when she didn't have to. I thought maybe she loved Lotta so much that she didn't want to be separated from her, even at such a price. Yet in those last days we had become so lethargic and indifferent that we didn't care what made Bubi join us.

But when the British arrived and liberated us, we knew that soon we would be fed and clothed and sent home, we started again to ponder what to do with Bubi. There were discussions, some saying that we must hand her over to the British and reveal her true identity. She was, after all, an SS woman, and we shouldn't shield her. Yet others thought that because she'd always treated us fairly, we should repay her by keeping silent and let things take their own course. She would probably be found out anyway, but let us not be the whistle blowers.

I never learned who was instrumental in Bubi's later fate, but, as I was working with the interrogating British officer, I saw her among the arrested SS women. I was undecided about my feelings toward her. I was pulled in two directions. On the one hand there was enormous satisfaction at the justice of our reversed roles. I—the former prisoner, who had been humiliated, starved, kicked and dehumanized—was now free and, in a sense, her superior. The former guard, who only a few days ago had power over my very life, was locked up and would probably be tried for her war crimes. It was elating but not altogether without conflict, because of all the perpetrators of our suffering, she had been the mildest and least harmful. The commanders, the sadists, and the murderers were hiding somewhere and might never be caught and punished. Should Bubi be the sacrificial lamb for the likes of a Mengele?

Then came the morning when it was her turn to be interrogated. She sat opposite the British officer, dressed again in her uniform, a narrow skirt and a tight-fitting jacket. I sat at the far end of the desk. When she recognized me, she seemed bewildered. Our eyes met, and for a moment her face expressed the gamut of feelings that passed between us. First it was surprise, which quickly changed to pleasure at recognition, then the realization of her new position toward my elevated status, and finally her eyes became pleading, as if she were appealing for help and understanding. The moment passed, and she lowered her eyes; neither of us had spoken.

I don't know if my eyes also reflected what I was feeling, but inside me I heard two voices, both equally imperative. The first screamed, *This is your enemy; have no mercy or pity on her, and treat her as cruelly as you were treated.* . . . *Avenge your suffering.* But the other voice said, *This person never harmed you;*

she is not to be blamed. And moreover, you are different from the Nazis: You are humane. You are incapable of being cruel.

The interrogation started. She stated her name, age, address, and the date she joined the SS. I have long forgotten it all except for the fact that her real name was not Bubi, of course. I translated everything accurately and matter-of-factly.

Then the officer left the room for some reason, leaving the two of us alone. In that instant, she turned to me eagerly and said, *"Hast du eine Zigarette?"* Suddenly there was no longer any dilemma. I knew what it meant for a smoker to be without cigarettes; my mother was a smoker herself. I had seen our women pick up the tiniest butts that had been trodden with a heel into the ground, which they later opened, rolling the scraps of tobacco into pieces of newspaper. They would burn with a flame and be consumed very quickly. The last bit, which could no longer be held between the fingers, would be stuck on a hairpin so as not to lose even the very last draw. And now I was in possession of any number of cigarettes, with permission to help myself to more as often as I wished.

Without a moment's hesitation, I took out the packet of cigarettes I had in my pocket and gave it to her. She had just hidden it in her clothes when the officer returned. A feeling of relief enveloped me, a feeling of satisfaction at my spontaneous reaction, without weighing if I had acted right. A nagging thought did disturb me, however: that if I told my friends, they would condemn my action. That is why I didn't speak about this incident for years.

For many years, I didn't know what happened to Bubi and also never tried to find out.[7] I had to take care of my own life and was not interested in the fate of our former guards.

---

7   In 1994, a German journalist, Rainer Hoffschildt, who was researching homosexuality in the concentration camps, approached me with the request to tell him anything I might remember about Bubi's behavior in Hamburg. From him I learned her real name, Anneliese Kohlmann, and that she had been sentenced to two years' imprisonment. More about her can be found on the Internet.

CHAPTER TWENTY-TWO

After the Liberation

My career as interpreter didn't last very long. Within a few days the British got things organized, the mountains of dead bodies were buried, the survivors got regular food and some clothes, and the ill were put into makeshift sickrooms. But the camp was so filthy and infested with lice and other vermin that it was necessary to move us out from there. I don't remember how we were moved; I must have been already sick by that time. I remember a clean room with four beds, a table, and chairs on the second floor of a red-brick building, which had formerly housed the Hungarian soldiers, the helpers of the SS, who manned the watchtowers. There was a whole campus of these buildings, with footpaths between them and a large central kitchen.

One of the buildings was turned into the British administration office, where my mother started working for the camp commander. Mother had been a secretary before she married; she knew stenography, English, and French besides German and Czech of course, and she could type in all these languages. She figured it would be beneficial to practice her skills, since she would have to be our breadwinner when we returned to Prague.

There was an interim period of which I have only a hazy recollection. I know

I was lying on the top of a three-tiered bunk in a large hall with many other women, while my mother balanced precariously on the ladder, trying to feed me or washing my arms and face. I must have been feverish most of the time; I felt a peculiar tingling in my fingers, which I get whenever I run a high temperature.

Like hundreds, perhaps thousands, of the prisoners, I had contracted typhus. Unlike most of the others, I survived. Mother told me afterward that I was taken to a makeshift hospital, where she saw that I didn't get much attention. She managed to get accommodation in a room shared by two other women and moved me there from the hospital.

The other two occupants were Mausi and her mother, Mrs. Hermannova. They had also passed the selection of Dr. Mengele and were with us in Hamburg and Bergen-Belsen. As we were living in one room, I was able to observe their relationship. Mausi's mother was a difficult woman, most of the time complaining about this and that, demanding attention and services from her daughter. We called her Mrs. Mausová, meaning Mrs. Mouse, behind her back. But Mausi treated her mother with loving care and kindness, never losing patience or showing irritation.

Next door lived a Dutch girl named Flora van Praag (such a name I couldn't forget!), who had a room all for herself. Her boyfriend, a British officer, somehow found her a piano, on which she played joyful tunes and dance music all day long, while in the evenings we heard her laughing with her boyfriend.

Mother was a smoker, and the camp commander allowed her to make free use of the officers' cigarette supply, which was stored in his office. She modestly took only one or two packs a day, and although she smoked a few, we still accumulated a hoard.

There was a man on the ground floor of the opposite building who sold fresh beef twice a week. He was an enterprising former prisoner who bought (or stole?) cattle from the surrounding countryside, slaughtered them, and traded the meat for cigarettes. In the morning Mother went with a few cigarettes to buy fresh meat. Since we had no kitchen utensils, Mother scraped the meat with a knife and made little patties, which she fried in a pan on an electric hotplate. We bought the knife, two plates, some salt, and butter from the cleaning woman, a German *hausfrau* whom the Brits sent to work for us. We paid her with the usual currency: cigarettes, of course. How I enjoyed these wonderful hamburgers! They helped me to recover quickly, and I gained weight and became stronger.

I don't know how long I was ill. I slept a lot, and when I awoke, the room was light and airy and my mother had nice things for me to eat, then I fell asleep again. But I felt better and better and then I could get up and walk a bit, to the toilet across the corridor and back. And all the time there were things to eat. We got meals from the central kitchen, as much as we wanted of everything; moreover, Mother traded cigarettes for all kinds of delicacies, such as eggs and milk. While I was recuperating, I often sat by the window, watching the people outside.

One morning I saw one of our young women dashing out from next door and embracing a British soldier in uniform. The soldier was her brother. Their family name was Pressburger. Her younger brother Harry had been sent as a youth from Prague to England, in the children's transport organized by Nicholas Winton. When the war broke out he joined the British army and was one of the liberators of Bergen-Belsen. There they stood, in the street, clinging to each other, crying, unable to let go.

We were thinking of the future, waiting to go home. (Home? There was none!) To be allowed to leave, we needed a medical certificate confirming that we were not carrying the typhus infection. Repatriation of the survivors was handled by several officers appointed by the camp commander. Mother and I went to register for repatriation, and it turned out that the officer was a Czech himself. I remember the lists pinned on his door, with names of missing people. Among them was Josef Čapek, the brother of the famous Czech writer Karel Čapek. I learned later that he had died at Bergen-Belsen.

The officer entered us on the waiting list but said that there was a shortage of buses and trains. Only small groups could be accommodated every few days.

While we were waiting, life seemed brighter every day. We enjoyed our freedom. The soldiers were eager for female company; they had strict orders not to fraternize with German women, but we, the former prisoners, were okay. The army organized film shows and dancing parties in the square; I could hear the music through the window. Each of us had by now acquired some dress or skirt, and whoever was fit enough was down there dancing.

I watched them from the window but didn't join them. I was shy and didn't know any dances. Also I had never danced with a man.

Meanwhile Mausi had become friendly with a Scottish army doctor named Sean, who often visited her, and sometimes they went out together. It even seemed that it might become a permanent match.

I also had a boyfriend, called Leslie. He wasn't an officer, just an army driver. I met him when he was sitting in his jeep and I asked him for a light. The next day he came to visit me in our room. He invited me to see a film. Mausi and Sean were also going to see it. When we left the building, Leslie kept back and let the two go in front. We walked a few paces behind them. He explained to me that in the British army, an officer must not be seen walking with a simple soldier like him.

I still remember the name of the film: *Lady Hamilton*. I didn't understand a word of what they were saying, but it was the first film I had seen since 1940, when the Jews in the occupied Protectorate of Bohemia and Moravia were forbidden to go to cinemas.

Another time, Leslie took me for an outing in his jeep. We drove through the lush countryside until we came to a forest. Leslie spread out a blanket in a clearing among the tall trees, and as we sat there, he started kissing me. His intentions were clear, but I was shy and frightened. Apart from a childish, innocent kiss from a schoolmate, I had never been embraced or kissed by a man before. Kissing Leslie was okay, but anything more was unimaginable. He was rather insistent, said that nothing would happen to me. He also told me quite earnestly that the British soldiers were strictly forbidden to consort with German women. Leslie took out something from his pocket to show me how he would protect himself from making me pregnant. I looked away, horrified and disgusted, and started crying. At that moment he must have realized that I was still an innocent child, pulled away, and began comforting me. He was very gentle, dried my tears, and behaved like a perfect gentleman. We met again several times before he moved on with his unit. I felt that, following the encounter in the forest, he liked and respected me more.

On the day of his departure, he came to say goodbye very early in the morning. We four women were still asleep when he quietly opened the door. I awoke as Leslie was discreetly tucking the blanket over my exposed behind, before he whispered his goodbye. He said he must hurry, because the truck full of his fellow soldiers was waiting for him below in the street with the motor running, but he just wanted to see me for the last time. I never heard from him again.

One afternoon there was an announcement from a loudspeaker, inviting women to come to a dance with the soldiers. This time it was not to be held in the square but in a hall in a nearby German town. I put on my black skirt and climbed on the truck with the other girls. We drove along tree-lined lanes until we came to a picturesque small town with colorful, old gabled houses.

When we arrived at the dance hall, it was empty, with chairs lined up along the walls. We were told to wait. After a while the soldiers arrived and the music began. There was a dance master, also in uniform, who called out directions, such as turn left or turn right or change partners. One of the dances was funny; the words went something like this:

> *You put your right hand in, your right hand out,*
> *your right hand in*
> *And you shake it all around*
> *You do the hokey cokey and you turn around*
> *That's what it's all about*
> *You put your left hand in, your left hand out,*
> *your left hand in . . .*

Then came the left foot and the right foot and so on. It was very amusing, and everybody laughed.

I sat on my chair next to the wall, and whenever a soldier came to ask me to dance, I replied that I didn't know how to dance. They bowed and went to ask another girl.

Then came the dance master himself. When I replied the same way, he just held out his hand and pulled me up. He said, "I am a dance instructor, and I will show you." Of course I looked down at my feet to see what I must do, but he lifted my chin and held me tight. "Don't look down," he said authoritatively. It was surprisingly easy: the feet just knew the right steps and at the end of the first round, I already felt confident. He danced with me several more times, and I enjoyed it.

It made me proud that he danced only with me, when he was not busy moderating.

Since then I have never had another dance lesson. I didn't need one.

My mother was very concerned about our future, all the time wondering how we would manage. We had nothing, no home, no possessions, no money, and also no husband or father who would provide for us. None of our close family could have survived; there was no one in Prague to whom Mother could turn for advice or help. Whatever we had owned had been confiscated by the Nazis: our modest bank account soon after the German invasion, and the rest of our household the day we were deported to the ghetto.

In the camp commander's office, Mother typed letters to my great-uncle Adolf in Palestine and to Aunt Manya in Prague, in which she described what we had endured. The letter to Palestine is now in my possession; my uncle gave it to me several years later, when I came to visit him in Tel Aviv. It had been opened by the British military censor. Mother had written in sober, unadorned sentences to say how we were deported to Terezín, then to Auschwitz, where Father had died, to Hamburg to work like slaves, and finally to Bergen-Belsen. She also wrote that all other relatives were most probably dead. Despite all her descriptions of the facts, the letter could not convey the pain, the suffering, and desolation we had to endure. Even as I am writing this, I feel that my words are not adequate. Human language doesn't contain terms to describe Auschwitz. The magnitude of those horrible experiences would require a new vocabulary. The language I know has no words to describe what I feel.

The weeks passed. It was already June, and we were still in the camp. Even now people kept dying; thousands of those who had been liberated succumbed to typhus and the consequences of malnutrition. Some had been already sent home; others like us were still waiting. Many could not return to their homelands and wished to emigrate to America.

We were informed that the Swedish government would accept a certain number of survivors to recuperate in Sweden, all expenses covered. The British doctors screened the candidates. Only the people who had a paper from the hospital, certifying that they were released from quarantine, were eligible. Mother and I decided to apply, and so did Mausi and her mother. We thought that in Prague no one was expecting us, so it would not matter if we returned a few weeks later. I had the necessary report from the hospital, but Mother didn't.

Help came from Mausi's Scottish boyfriend, Sean. He suggested that my mother enter the hospital on some pretended illness and have herself released after a few days. This way she would become eligible for the Swedish project. The doctor promised to take care of the necessary document.

And so Mother went to the hospital. It was located in one of the red-brick buildings, like the one where we had our room, but it was at the other end of the compound, quite a distance to walk. I accompanied Mother, carrying her bag with a few necessities; we already owned a toothbrush, soap, a few items of clothing, and, of course, cigarettes. I left her there in good humor; everything had gone smoothly, thanks to the letter from the English doctor. They gave her a real bed with sheets in a room with a few other women. The hospital was now much improved since the previous month, when I was there with typhus. It was, however, still critically understaffed; there were perhaps two or three doctors, but the few caregivers were volunteers rather than trained nurses.

I went to see Mother the next day. She was in bed, as she was supposed to be, but much less happy than yesterday. She complained of bellyache and, indeed, when she lifted the blanket to show me where it hurt, her belly was distended and protruded like a ball from the rest of her body.

We spoke of our intended journey to Sweden and worried together about how to keep our new possessions, since the Swedes did not allow anything to be brought in, not even our own clothes. They gave the people new clothes and other necessities. We understood that they wanted to prevent any infection or vermin from entering their country. Yet after the years in which our sole possessions were the clothes on our bodies and the bowl and spoon, we were attached to our newly acquired wealth. We each owned a coat; I had a pair of rubber boots stolen from the abandoned German store of the camp, a blouse, and a skirt, as well as a blanket and bedsheet allocated to us by the British army and a blue head scarf, one of two that we found in the lining of my coat when I and Eva Kraus participated in the looting of the camp stores.

Some time after our liberation, we received a few clothing items, used but clean. I suppose they were collected from the German population, to be distributed among the former prisoners. I got a pair of black bell-bottomed trousers and a few other items, but the trousers were the best. I was very proud of them. It would be a pity to lose such valuable items, which probably were also not available in postwar Prague. We planned to tie everything into a bundle and send it to Prague with the next coach that would take repatriates home. Someone may kindly keep it for us until our return. The Swedish sojourn would last only a few weeks.

Then Mother told me a few things that she wanted me to remember. I have forgotten what she said, but I knew they were important and wise words, such words as parents tell their children at momentous turns in their lives.

When I left, I promised to come again next day.

That evening Mausi and I were invited to a party. I was looking forward to it. It was a private occasion with music, not like the dances in the square, where anybody could come uninvited. It was held in the rooms of the higher rank officers, among them Mausi's Scottish doctor.

It was a very pleasant evening: there were cookies, chocolate, and drinks; the atmosphere was lively yet civilized. However, I didn't enjoy myself as thoroughly as I might have. At the back of my mind, I felt a nagging worry about my mother. She was probably suffering, and I also wondered why she had found it necessary to tell me those important guidelines for life. I wanted to go home, but I could not break up the party; we girls had been brought together in an army jeep, and I could return only with the others. Fortunately it wasn't very late when we got home.

Next day was the third day since Mother had entered the hospital, and according to the plan, she could now be released. I hoped she would feel well enough today. We had barely time to register for Sweden; if we delayed, we would miss our chance altogether.

I came to the room where I'd visited her the day before but realized I must have made a mistake because the bed was empty. I wanted to ask the women where my mother was, but then I saw her bag on the bed.

I turned to the women. "Where is my mother, where is my mother, where is my mother?" I demanded, my voice getting louder and louder until I was screaming.

Silence. No one answered. They all looked at me without a word. The silence became unbearable, but I knew already. Finally one of the women said in Slovakian, "*Tvoja mamička zomrela.*" Your mummy died. Then they were silent again.

"What shall I do?" I shouted. "What shall I do? What shall I do now?"

I grabbed the bag and started running back. All the way, dry sobs came out of my throat. It was a long way, some twenty minutes' walk. I wanted to cry, but I had no tears. I knew I should cry, but there were only those sobs like a cough, and I spoke aloud: "What shall I do? What shall I do . . . ?"

I was terribly worried what would become of me. If only I could remember what Mother told me yesterday. She knew she was dying—that was why she gave me this important advice for life. Yet I forgot what she said. I racked my brains to remember my mother's last words. Perhaps if I remembered, it would help me decide what I must do now. *What should I do? What will become of me?* I repeated and repeated the questions all the way, stumbling along with the cumbersome bag.

I burst into our room, where Mausi and her mother were sitting, each doing something trivial.

"Mother died," I yelled. "Mother died." They looked at me in disbelief. I could tell from their stares that they thought I had gone crazy.

"Sit down, come and tell us what happened. Calm yourself." Mausi spoke to me kindly, putting her arm around me, but she did not believe me.

"I'm telling you! Mother died. My mother is dead. What shall I do now? How will I live without Mother?"

I felt an enormous heaviness like a weight pressing on my chest from within, and all the time these sobs like hiccups continued. Yet I wasn't weeping. No tears came out of my eyes. I felt mainly worried, worried. *What will happen now? What shall I do?*

I felt so sorry for myself. I was alone. I had no one now. Mother was dead. Who would be with me? I belonged to nobody. I was only by myself. . . . No one would care. And I had forgotten what Mother told me yesterday. Was it yesterday? They were her last words. She was so wise; she had told me the most important things she knew, all the wisdom she learned in her life, and miserable creature that I was, I had forgotten her last words.

Suddenly it occurred to me that that wasn't all. Last night I was dancing. Maybe I was actually dancing the moment my mother died. I wasn't at her side. Mother died alone while I was laughing at a party. Who knows when she died? I hadn't even asked, I ran so fast.

Under the thick frozen layer that eclipsed all my emotions, there was the guilt. Already then I knew that I would never be able to forgive myself. The guilt for permitting my poor mother to die in that shabby way has stayed with me all my life. My mother's death has returned to me in my dreams in a hundred variations. If only I could return to that cursed night and undo the scenario.

CHAPTER TWENTY-THREE

Grave

haven't seen my mother's grave, nor was I present at her burial. The very same day I came with the news, Mausi took me to the repatriation officer and asked him to put me forward on the waiting list. She convinced me to return to Prague and not go to Sweden. Perhaps I would find some relatives or friends who would take me in. I waived my right to the Swedish recuperation; she told him that I was now an orphan and should be treated with special consideration. They spoke in Czech, and he was very kind and decent. He placed me on the next coach to Prague, which would be leaving the following morning.

There were no proper funerals at Bergen-Belsen. Yet I didn't want my mother to be buried in an anonymous mass grave. I wished her to have a separate grave with her name on it. This, however, I could not arrange in the short hours I had left until my departure.

Sean, Mausi, and another woman, Elly, who had been Mother's schoolmate back in Brno, promised to attend the funeral and see to it that Mother got a separate grave.

Some years after the end of the war, an organization was established in Hamburg, consisting of people who remembered the Jewish women who worked there during the war. Their aim is to commemorate our group of about five hundred women who worked in Freihafen, Neugraben, and Tiefstack. They have placed memorial plaques in the places where we were housed, and they write and speak about us to the younger generation.

In the late 1990s, the moving spirit behind the organization, Herr Heiner Schultz, invited a few of us former prisoners to visit Hamburg. I declined the invitation. I never wanted to see Germany again.

They kept sending more letters, politely trying to make me change my mind. I still refused. But then I received the itinerary they had planned for us and, among the various visits to *Gedenkstätten* (memorials), there was Bergen-Belsen.

That changed my attitude. It was a chance to see my mother's burial place.

There were six of us: four from Israel and two from the Czech Republic. Everything was arranged perfectly, accommodation in a hotel in the center of Hamburg, guided tours of important Jewish sites, meals in restaurants, transportation . . . Everything functioned without a hitch.

On the morning of our trip to Bergen-Belsen, I bought a bunch of flowers to put on my mother's grave. The camp is now an off-limits NATO base, but our hosts had arranged a special permit for us to enter. The cemetery is inside the fenced-in compound. The location of the memorial with the mass graves and the monument is some distance from there, on the grounds of the former concentration camp, which was burned down.

The cemetery looks like a well-kept park. There are no graves in the usual sense, but several rows of low green mounds, with sandy paths between them. Here and there are a few headstones with a name and a date.

How could I find my mother's grave? I walked among the rows and noticed that the dates on the stones rise chronologically. There were a few with the date May 1945, then June. I continued looking, and there was one with the date June 27. My mother died on June 29. A few paces ahead there was a tree. I decided that if one person was buried each day between the two dates, Mother must be under that tree. I placed the flowers on the elevated mound and stood there for a while. I was expecting something, perhaps a sign that this was the right place, that I was standing near my mother's remains. The others stayed apart, respecting my privacy.

But there was nothing. Everything around remained silent and green as before. However, I was sure now that I had done the right thing by returning to Germany.

CHAPTER TWENTY-FOUR

Return to Prague

The day after my mother's death, June 30, I was on the coach driven by its Czech owner, who was doing the shuttling as a volunteer. I carried two bundles, mine and Mausi's. She asked me to take it to Prague to be kept by her friend Ruth until she and her mother returned from Sweden. Of course, we had no suitcases; the things were just tied in an army blanket. What was in my bundle? A pair of black rubber boots looted from the German storerooms in Bergen-Belsen, a pair of blue British navy trousers with a "drawbridge" flap in front. There were also a blouse and a flower-patterned skirt, which the British had collected from the German population and distributed to the survivors. But above all there was my treasure: some eighty packets of British Woodbine cigarettes.

There were about forty people on the bus. I didn't know any of the other passengers. They were all liberated prisoners of various nationalities; for them Prague was only a transit station. I sat with a young Slovak girl named Marta. I felt very lonely. My travel companions were not aware that I had lost my mother just the day before. Even if they knew, they wouldn't have cared; everyone was absorbed with their own worries and fears of the future.

We traveled all day long across Germany, through cities demolished by bombs, while the bucolic countryside and villages were unharmed, peaceful and green. Our Czech driver kept driving until dark, because he didn't want to stay in German territory overnight. It was late evening when we crossed the border into Czechoslovakia. The bus stopped in the nearest town, Františkovy Lázně.

The place seemed lifeless. No one was in sight, and the windows of the old-fashioned hotels around the town square were dark. The area had been liberated just a short while ago, all the hotels were closed, and there were no guests. After several attempts, our driver found one hotel whose janitor, after hearing who the passengers were, was willing to let us stay overnight.

Such luxury! I was amazed. I had forgotten that such comfort existed. I walked along the carpeted corridors, through halls full of mirrors, polished furniture, and heavy velvet curtains. We got a luxurious room with a shiny bathroom and a huge double bed, meant for the rich, spoiled guests of a prewar era, who came to cure their ailments and show their jewels.

Two people had to share a room; my roommate was Marta. We looked strange in those surroundings. I wore my raincoat, my trousers, which had come from the British surplus stores, and my rubber boots. I had preferred to put them on rather than carry them. On my shoulders hung the two bundles. But most strange of all were those staring eyes reflected in the mirror. Could those be my eyes? And indeed, who was this tall girl whom I hadn't seen full-length in a mirror for the last three years?

I lay on the soft, springy bed on a white starched sheet covered by a fluffy light eiderdown and couldn't fall asleep. I turned and turned, and each time the bed heaved and bounced in response. The same was the case with my roommate.

Unlike the princess in Andersen's fairy tale, who couldn't fall asleep because of a pea placed under a pile of mattresses in order to find out if she was a genuine princess, the two of us were unable to fall asleep because the beds were too soft and springy. We had been sleeping on hard bunks for too many years. In the end, we just pulled off the fluffy eiderdown and spent the night sleeping on the carpet.

The following morning, our driver took us as far as Pilsen, his hometown. He took us to the railway station, arranged the tickets for us, and wished us a good journey.

We continued the rest of the way to Prague by train.

Part III
1945–21ˢᵀ CENTURY

CHAPTER TWENTY-FIVE

First Weeks in Prague

The train reached Prague by noontime on July 1. There I was then in my native town, alone, without Father and Mother, just two weeks short of my sixteenth birthday.

At the main railway station, our group was met by two people from the Repatriation Office. They handed each of us a pink identity card and took the people who had no place to stay to a nearby hostel. I left my two bundles there and set out to find Aunt Manya.

I remembered which tram went to the borough of Podolí, but I had no money for the fare. I showed the conductor my pink repatriation card, and he said I didn't have to pay. People looked at me strangely, and I realized that I must somehow seem odd to them. I didn't know why. I thought there was no visible mark on my person that could explain their stares. I guessed that it was the way I was dressed, with my rubber boots and a raincoat on a summer day. Only much later did I hear from others that something in the expression of the face, especially in the eyes, revealed the ravages of the years spent in Terezín, Auschwitz, and Bergen-Belsen.

I climbed the stairs to Manya's little flat and rang the doorbell. The door opened, and there stood my Aunt Manya. She did not recognize me. When she had seen me last, I was a child of thirteen, and now I was an adult of sixteen.

"Yes?" she said.

I couldn't answer.

"Dita?" she said doubtfully. I nodded.

She peered behind me down the stairs.

"But where is your mother?"

"Mother died two days ago."

"But that cannot be. . . . She wrote a letter. . . . She wrote that you both survived and that you were coming back soon. . . ."

And then she pulled me in and embraced me, and we cried together.

Incongruously, she said, "You are lucky to find me at home. I was just about to go out." As if I had come on a casual visit.

Suddenly she stopped and said, "You are not alone—your grandmother is alive! I wrote you at Bergen-Belsen, but I see you didn't get the letter. She survived in Terezín, and your Uncle Leo fetched her. She is staying with him, here in Prague."

Now I was stunned. Grandmother alive! Mother and I had mourned for her in Auschwitz when we learned from a woman who came in the May transport that Grandmother was on her deathbed. So she had recovered and was alive! She had survived three years in the ghetto.

Next day I went to retrieve the two bundles, mine and Mausi's, because Manya said I could stay with her. It seemed to her the most natural and obvious thing, and I was still too befuddled to think about the inconvenience I might be causing her.

Aunt Manya had been recently nominated principal of a special school for children with hearing problems. Thus this summer she wasn't on vacation like the teachers but worked through July and August. She lived in a one-room flat, but as the kitchen was quite large, she had turned it into a kind of living room with a spare bed.

Zdenka, Manya's sister, was delegated to visit Grandmother and prepare her for the news. "Slowly," Manya warned. "We mustn't overwhelm her. She is old and frail, and she is expecting Dita and her mother."

Zdenka told Grandmother only that Liesl was very ill. And so, in stages, the old woman was informed, and three days later, Manya, Zdenka, and I went to see her at last.

She was sitting in Uncle Leo and Aunt Verica's living room, her hands folded in her lap. Her gray hair was fastened with hairpins on her nape, her large, brown, somewhat protruding eyes filled with her great sorrow.

I told her how Father died, what Mother and I had suffered in Auschwitz and Hamburg and then in Bergen-Belsen. She wanted to know everything. She didn't cry; she just held my hand and stroked my head, and I felt her great, warming love. Her pain was enormous and unspeakable, yet I was numb. I spoke about people dying and going "into the gas" as a matter of fact. I knew that one was supposed to cry and mourn for the dead; I tried to feel sorrow but was unable to stir up any emotion at all. All I could feel was an icy wall around my heart. In later years I read articles by psychologists about the emotional damage the Holocaust caused the survivors and began to understand what had happened to me. I sensed this blunting of my emotions for many years, and I am not sure if I ever recovered completely.

For the time being I stayed with Aunt Manya, and Grandmother remained at Uncle Leo's. We would look for a flat and move in together, we hoped.

In the first days and weeks after our return from the concentration camps, survivors were searching for their families and friends. No one knew whether a dear one was dead, had not yet returned, or was perhaps hospitalized somewhere in Germany. If you met some acquaintance, you started asking, have you seen X, or have you met Y, or do you know anything about Z? People usually knew about their campmates, but there were so many different camps where we had been dispersed after Terezín and Auschwitz! On the walls of the Jewish Community Office there were lists with names of survivors and requests for information. Notices were stuck at railway stations and billboards with pleas for contact. Every day the radio broadcast more names, and one day I heard my mother's name. Searching for her was Mother's best friend, Edith, after whom I was named. I remembered her from a visit when I was about six. She took me to a toy shop and let me choose not one but three toys. She was sad to learn that Liesl was dead, but I never heard from her again.

Adjusting to normal life wasn't easy. I had no plans; it didn't even occur to me to think what I should do with myself. I owned nothing . . . had no income. Till then I'd never had to make any decisions; before the deportation I was a child and my parents took care of everything. In the camps we were sent here and there; the Germans were the masters of our lives, and we had to obey orders. I never thought that now I had to take responsibility for my life.

I was a guest in Manya's tiny flat, and I wanted to have a good time. I would eat all day long, but as much as I ate, I still remained hungry. The feeling of hunger went on for years after the war. It was not hunger in my mouth or my stomach, it was hunger in my head. It drove me to eat everything that was in the house; I never felt sated. I had already gained weight after the liberation and was now getting quite plump. In a photo from July 1945, my face looks really bloated. Much of my hair had fallen out after the typhus.

Food was still available only with ration cards, and there was a shortage of everything. Manya made sure to have at least enough bread in the house, because I was able to eat half a loaf at a time. I had nothing to wear. It was summer, and I wanted a swimsuit and a light dress.

Manya took me to several charity places, where I could choose a few items of used clothing and, most important, a pair of secondhand shoes. They were not my size, but I liked them. So what if they pinched my feet!

Before we were deported, my mother had given Manya some things for safekeeping. There were a few pillowcases with her monogram, which she had stitched for her dowry, one of her two coats, a tailored blue suit that she would not need in the ghetto, a few kitchen utensils, and, above all, the complete twelve-person set of china.

I remember the day when a salesman sat with Mother at the round table in the dining room and she leafed through a catalogue. She chose a white set with a silver stripe. I was still a small girl, but Mother said it was for my wedding. Manya arranged with some friends to keep our crate with the carefully packed china in their garden shed.

My mother's brother Hugo from Brno came to Prague before we were deported and took our photo albums. His wife was a gentile, which had protected him from the Nazi persecution. I am fortunate to have our family albums, a treasure that many of the survivors consider a most painful loss.

My parents had also lent a few pieces of furniture to a friend of Aunt Lori when we were evicted from our flat and had to squeeze into one room. That good lady kept them in her apartment throughout the war and returned them in good order. I never met her and didn't even know her name.

The matter of returning items to their owners was a painful and disappointing story. The experience of the Jews who returned was that the gentiles often claimed that the things were given to them as gifts, or that they had to sell them in order to pay for food parcels, which they sent to the ghetto, or even that they were lost in bombing attacks, although only a handful of buildings had been destroyed in Prague during the entire war. My experience was an exception; whatever my parents had hidden, although of little value, was returned to me without problems.

Manya would go out in the mornings, leaving me her ration card and some money to buy a few rolls and cheese. When she returned in the afternoon, she cooked a meal for us both. I didn't dare go to the grocery; I was ashamed because I didn't know how to shop. What did one say? "Give me" or "I want"? How much cheese should I buy? How much is one hundred grams, half a kilo? Too much, too little? Too shy to try, I stuck to the bread.

I spent many hours standing in queues at various offices. It was necessary to have documents. Without an identity card, one could not obtain a ration card. To get the identity card, one had to have a registration document from the police, who in turn wanted a document verifying my last address before the deportation. And so it went on and on. At the Jewish Community Office, I applied for support as an orphan. I had to get a document from the court to prove that my parents were dead. But there was no proof of their deaths, so they gave me a statement, which said only that they were allegedly dead. I needed copies of my school certificates to show the authorities that I was Czech and not German. It was an unending preoccupation.

But I also started to have a social life.

There were the two brothers Šabart, neighbors of my aunt Lori. They were a bit older than me, and both played the guitar. Lori invited Grandmother and me rather often for lunch, and then I would visit the two boys and sing with them the latest hits. I taught them the English words, which I had learned from the British soldiers at the dance events at Bergen-Belsen, and they eagerly wrote them down. I liked the younger brother; he was handsome, but he showed no interest in me as a girl.

Aunt Verica also tried to find company for me. The son of her friends who had just passed his matriculation exams at high school was going camping over the weekend with a group of his schoolmates, boys and girls. When Grandmother heard that I was going to be in a tent overnight with some complete strangers, she put her foot down. I mean literally. Poor Granny, she stamped her foot so hard on the floor that it must have hurt. I insisted stubbornly that I was going. She was so angry that she became quite exhausted. She could not educate me any longer; she had lost her authority over me. Her well-meant reasoning was of no avail. I'd had enough of being told what I could or couldn't do.

The youngsters were all paired; I was the only single. The boy who had invited me was very kind and attentive. But I was an outsider, and they had been schoolmates for years. We traveled by train for about half an hour, and they talked of things I knew nothing about, while what I could tell them about was from another planet.

We put up our camp near the river Sázava. The girls slept in one tent, the boys in another. During the night we had visitors: two Russian soldiers. The Russian "liberators" were still stationed in the country, and these two apparently had to patrol the nearby rail tracks.

The boys tried to make conversation with them, but they wanted women, and we girls huddled together in our tent, trembling with fright. It took quite a time to get rid of them; they kept trying to open the flap of our tent. We were in a panic until the boys convinced them with the help of a few cigarettes to go away.

"You see? Nothing bad happened to me," I told Grandmother the next morning, trying to appease her, but I felt her sadness at her realization that she was unable to guide me in place of my parents.

Another attempt by Aunt Verica happened when she arranged an outing with her next-door neighbor, a bachelor twice my age. He owned a car—an unusual luxury at that time—and invited Leo, Verica, and me to his native village, where he owned some property. Verica was immediately eager to accept, but I think she regretted it later.

We drove southward and after a while came to the outskirts of a small town, Budějovice. The man was the owner of a large country house and a mill but also, what is more, a large brewery. The beer is called *Budvar pivo*—in German, the name is Budweiser. The man seemed very keen on me, and it became so obvious that Verica insisted she and I share a room for the night.

Frustrated, the man shortened our stay and drove us back to Prague. And so I didn't become the girlfriend of the owner of the Budweiser beer brewery.

But Grandmother and also Aunt Manya talked to me about my future. I should learn, go to school again. In one sense, I was more mature than girls my age. I had seen torture and death; I'd learned to make myself inconspicuous so as not to draw the attention of the SS men. I had been surrounded by adult women who spoke freely about intimate matters, yet in some respects I was like a child, immature and naive.

Grandmother reminded me that I had almost no formal schooling, just the five elementary classes, and that my parents would have wanted me to study. I dreamed of becoming an artist but didn't think that one needed to study for that. Grandmother was helpless; I waved my hand at her suggestions. I painted my lips a bright vermilion, which I found gorgeous but which shocked everyone else. I went and enrolled at a course for tap dancing, because I wanted to be like Ginger Rogers. The first lesson was spent with a photographer, who took pictures of the girls in various positions, and I was delighted when I saw my photo displayed on the poster at the entrance of the dancing school.

CHAPTER TWENTY-SIX

Meeting Otto

One morning, when I was standing in a queue at the Ministry of the Interior, I recognized Otto Kraus, one of the educators on the *Kinderblock* in Auschwitz. It was he whom Sonia Shultz had pointed out to me in Terezín as the brother of Harry, the boy she fancied. And I had seen him daily in the *Kinderblock*. He was quite a good-looking man but a bit short, just my own height.

He recognized me, too, smiled, and said, "I remember you, the girl with the thin legs, sitting there with your books next to the chimney. I am glad you returned."

That was what we always said whenever we met someone who survived the camps. There were very few of us who came back, and none of them were children. I was among the youngest to survive Auschwitz, and only because at the "selection" I had lied about my age. With a few exceptions, none of the Prague Jews who returned were younger than fifteen or older than forty-two or -three.

We started talking, and Otto invited me to come with him to the theater on Tuesday; he had two tickets. It was six or seven weeks after my return to Prague.

During that time I had not seen a film or a play; it just hadn't occurred to me that I could again go wherever I wanted, that there were no longer any restrictions against Jews.

"Where are you going after you finish here?" Otto asked.

"To the *kille* to apply for an orphan's pension."

"I also have something to do there, let's walk together."

The Jewish Community Office was not far, and on the way we talked. We spoke about ourselves, and I was surprised and more and more astonished at how Otto described so well what I also felt: the hollowness of emotions, the lack of inner warmth, and the icy wall around the heart. His ability to put into words what I felt but could not express attracted and impressed me. I was glad that we would go to see a play together.

The play we saw was called *Nasredin's Escapades*; it was fun and not serious and stuffy as I had feared. During the play, Otto held my hand, and I felt flattered that this intelligent man thought me worthy of his attention. Much later he admitted that the second ticket was actually meant for another girl, whom he had been dating at the time.

It turned out that Otto was living in a flat that he shared with Honza, his friend and campmate, and Honza's wife, Ruth—the same Ruth to whom I had to deliver Mausi's bundle.

Otto was fortunate enough to be among the first to arrive back in Prague after the war. He knew that his father hadn't survived but was hopeful that his mother and brother would return from the camps. He therefore obtained the keys of a two-room flat in a quite presentable building. The flat had been abandoned by a German woman in such a hurry that she even left behind her clothes and food on the table. Flats were distributed by the housing committee according to the size of the family. But sad to say, none of Otto's family returned, and so he invited his campmate Honza Brammer and his wife to share the flat, in order not to lose the right to it.

Now I knew her address, I could bring her Mausi's bundle for safekeeping.

But things turned out differently. Otto suggested he would fetch it himself.

He came the next afternoon to my aunt's place, and from that day on, we started dating. We went for long walks, spoke about the camps and about our feelings of loss and loneliness. Another time he told me that at the beginning of the war, before the deportations of Jews, he was on a farm with a group of young men and women to learn about agriculture. They were Zionists and wanted to go to Palestine to become farmers and build the land.

He mentioned casually that both Ruth and Mausi were in the same group.

"Oh," I said, "you know Mausi?"

"I know Mausi more than well," he answered. "She was my girlfriend on the farm, and I almost married her."

I was taken aback and didn't know if I should feel jealous or be glad that he was now my boyfriend.

"Why didn't you marry her, then?"

"Because of my father. He said that only over his dead body would a son of his marry the daughter of a woman from Bielsko-Biala on the Polish border, practically an Eastern Jew."

CHAPTER TWENTY-SEVEN

Mausi

Mausi and her mother stayed in Sweden even after their recuperation period. Later they moved to Scotland. Perhaps Mausi still kept her ties with Sean, the Scottish doctor—I don't know. What happened was that she met a nice Jewish gentleman, a *mohel* (a man who does circumcisions) named Jack Grant, and married him. Otto jokingly called him Jack the Ripper. Only out of their earshot, of course.

They lived in Glasgow and had three children, a daughter and twins, boy and girl. Mausi was an exemplary mother and wife. Her mother lived with them until her death at a respectable age.

When Otto was on a summer course for English teachers in London in the 1960s, he was invited to Glasgow to visit the Grants. They welcomed him warmly, drove him around to see the sights, such as Robert Burns's cottage (Mausi knew that Otto also wrote poetry) and the lochs.

Once Otto asked casually whether Mausi was doing much painting. She was a bit flustered, became evasive, but Jack sat up, surprised.

"What painting?" he asked.

"Oh, nothing." Mausi waved her hand. "That was in the past."

Indeed, since their marriage she had not painted, and her husband never saw her pictures. He was a religious functionary, and she, being the "reverend's wife," felt that it was unbecoming for her to paint.

Yet, as the secret was now revealed, she went up to the loft and took down her collection of pictures. Not only were they very good and professional, but many of them were historical documents.

A few years later, the city of Glasgow honored her with an extensive exhibition and a catalogue with her biography. It was a great success, and Jack was extremely proud of his talented wife.

For many years they owned a flat in Israel, and we saw them quite frequently. Sometimes she came alone, and we spent many hours talking. I was very fond of Mausi; she was practical, straightforward, inquisitive, and loyal.

Our children knew about her past, and when they saw her, they would always repeat what I told them: "This is the woman who might have been your mother."

CHAPTER TWENTY-EIGHT

Teplice

n late July 1945, I found Margit again. She was back in Prague and lived with her father, Elmer Barnai, who had come back from the concentration camps. Her mother and sister, Helga, had perished. Mr. Barnai was offered a job as administrator of German properties in Teplice-Šanov. The position included a flat for his own use, a very important advantage. Flats were so scarce, it was almost impossible to find a vacancy. The flats that had been vacated by the fleeing German occupants were soon taken over by all kinds of people. The best homes were of course grabbed by the officials; the rest were allocated to returning prisoners or other citizens who flocked back from abroad to their liberated homeland. A Housing Ministry had been established, and people could obtain a flat only by applying for it. When Grandmother and I started looking for accommodation for ourselves, there was no longer anything available.

Margit's father invited me to live with him and Margit in Teplice, where we girls would go to school and have our own room. I jumped at the invitation. Grandmother was apprehensive; she didn't know who these people were. Mr. Barnai came for a visit and convinced Grandmother that I would be in good hands. He was eager for me to come, because Margit proclaimed that she would go back to school only if I came along. She felt too old to be a school-girl again. She was seventeen; I was sixteen. So my poor grandmother gave her consent. She knew she had no control over me anymore, and there was no prospect of a flat for her and me. What pleased her was that I would be at school again.

Otto wasn't so happy that I would not live in Prague. By now he was a student at the university studying comparative literature, philosophy, English, and Spanish. Every morning Otto and Ruth's husband, Honza, would leave together to go to university. Honza, who had almost finished his studies when the Germans closed the Czech universities, was now completing his PhD. Ruth prepared sandwiches for them, spread with mustard for lack of anything better. Otto got a modest scholarship, which he divided into three parts: a third went for food, a third for rent, and a third for culture. He bought books and went to the theater at least twice a week. And he started writing. But about that I learned only later.

In those months, soon after our return, he was still quite slim, and had he been a bit taller, he would have been quite good-looking. At first I found his round cheeks not so handsome, but he was so clever and it was so interesting and entertaining to be with him that I gave up my ideal of a tall, slim boyfriend.

When we began our relationship, schools were still on vacation, and apart from running around to the various offices applying for documents, we were both free. We met often, sometimes in town, more often at his place. It did not take long until we became lovers. I was totally inexperienced; besides some kissing, I didn't know anything about sex. But Otto was so gentle that I relaxed and relied on him. When I returned to Manya's place after our first lovemaking, I was sure everybody on the tram could read in my face that two hours ago I had stopped being a girl and become a woman.

In the middle of September, Mr. Barnai had the flat ready in Teplice, and Margit and I could move in. It was fully furnished with the equipment of the former tenant, a physician; even his medical instruments were still there. Like most of the Sudeten Germans, he must have fled to Germany immediately at the end of the war. Margit and I now had our own bedroom with a balcony, a white double bed, white wardrobes, a white dressing table with drawers, and a mirror. We felt like princesses.

Teplice, a well-known spa in the style of Karlovy Vary, was at that time full of refugees. They came mainly from the easternmost part of Czechoslovakia, which now belonged to the Soviet Union. The refugees flocked to the Sudeten towns that were emptied of the former German population and took over houses, farms, and businesses. They were nicknamed "gold diggers." There was also a large group of displaced people from other countries, who were waiting to go back home. Mr. Barnai employed one of them as our housekeeper. She made a wonderful milk soup with noodles but left soon to go back to her native Romania. We then started to buy our midday meals from a nearby hotel.

School had already started, but that was no problem. The whole state was still in turmoil, getting organized after the six-year-long occupation. We were put into the fifth grade of the Teplice High School, with students only one year younger, and the school director expected us to make up for the lost years. We had to take private lessons in Latin, provided by an old-worldly retired professor. Physics, mathematics, geometry, history, Czech language, and literature of the lower grades we should complete within the next two years.

Father Barnai, as I called him from then on, was appointed by the court as my guardian, and since I had two sources of income—a state pension as an orphan and a grant from the Jewish Community—I was no burden on him. Margit's father was very strict about morals; he felt responsible for our reputation, and we had to report where we were going. But we didn't always behave according to his instructions.

In spring there was a large student party, called Majales, for the whole school, with music and dancing. Father Barnai came along to chaperone us but left early and gave us a curfew. When Margit and I returned after midnight, Father Barnai met us at the door and smacked each of us on both cheeks with a pair of leather gloves. Why gloves, I don't know. Perhaps as a symbol for the thrown glove like in the challenge for a duel? Margit and I couldn't stop giggling and laughing into our pillows at the sight of Father Barnai in his long underpants wielding the gloves.

The flat was well equipped; there were carpets and bedsheets and curtains, pots and pans and all the kitchen utensils, and Father Barnai brought whatever we needed from the German houses he administered. He provided a gramophone and a lot of records. Margit, who had learned ballet before the war, taught me some steps, and we danced for hours around the table in the large dining room.

We both had nothing to wear, and that was a problem. The shops had hardly any wares, and the meager supplies were shoddy and unattractive. Moreover, one could buy them only with coupons, which might have sufficed for someone with a full wardrobe to replenish an item from time to time. But we needed everything, from underwear to stockings, not to speak of dresses, woollens, or coats. So Margit and I decided we would sew dresses for ourselves.

We bought a box of blue textile dye and dipped two bedsheets, of which there was a good supply in the flat, into the vat with the blue water. When they were dry, we began cutting them up. First we cut a round hole in the middle for the head. Then we stitched two seams at right angles to make sleeves—by hand of course; we didn't have a sewing machine—and then cut off the rest. When I tried to put the "dress" on, my head wouldn't go through, and the hole had to be enlarged. But the thing didn't look much like a dress—rather like a blue sack. So we added a strip around the waist to serve as a belt. On the shoulders we made several tucks and, in the end, stitched a hem around. In this attire we went to school. Strangely, no one in class commented or snickered at our models.

Margit and I were rather popular with the boys from the higher grades. Unlike the girls in our class, we were more mature, and we both smoked. During the breaks we would stand in the corridor behind the staircase with the older boys and have a cigarette. One day we were caught by the professor on duty and had to report to the headmaster. The punishment was harsh; we were expelled from school. Margit laughed it off; she wouldn't have minded quitting school, but I was extremely unhappy, especially because of Grandmother. What would she say? To lose my chance for an education for a stupid, petty breaking of the school rules?

Father Barnai tried to convince the principal to be more lenient. It turned out that the professor who caught us was an anti-Semite. We two were the only Jewish students in the school. We later learned that at the staff conference he was adamant and insisted on the punishment. Nevertheless, it was reduced to temporary expulsion. The next day I went to school after classes to speak to Mr. Weichet.

Mr. Weichet had been Otto's teacher in Prague before the war. Otto met him on the street a few days after his return from Terezín, and the teacher persuaded him to sit for his matriculation exam that very summer. Otto had already been in his matriculation class when the Germans banned Jews from schools. The advice was good, because Otto passed and could enroll at the university in the school year of 1945–46.

Otto knew that Mr. Weichet had been transferred to Teplice and told me to give him his best regards. It so happened that he became our homeroom teacher. Thus I believed that he might intervene on Margit's and my behalf.

I met the teacher in the empty corridor and told him about how I had started smoking in the camps because the women said that it made one feel the hunger less. The result was that my poor teacher started crying. I felt awful; I felt guilty for using this argument, even if it was the truth. But it was unfair on my part to cause his tears, and it embarrassed me deeply.

We were allowed back to school the next day; Father Barnai got a phone call from the school to tell him.

I wrote to Otto about the incident; we wrote each other almost daily.

His letters always began: *My sweet little girl.*

> *Prague 11.1.1945 (sic)*
>
> My sweet little girl, since I know how hard
> life is without cigarettes, chocolate,
> and love, I am sending the first two in
> natura. Unfortunately, the post office
> doesn't deliver love, therefore you must be
> satisfied with my loving you at a distance.
>
> Otto

On this occasion, though, he rebuked me, called me an irresponsible, immature child, and said he was disappointed in me. Afterward I took my studies more seriously to appease him and prove that I was not really stupid.

During the year in Teplice, I went to Prague twice for a few days. It was agreed that I would return for good at the end of the school year and continue school there. Otto said he could not love me at a distance and practically made me choose: either him or Margit. It was not difficult to decide, although I regretted having to leave the comfort of Teplice.

CHAPTER TWENTY-NINE

The Wedding

I finished the fifth grade of high school with Margit in Teplice and left with some regret, but I also looked forward to being with Otto again. The plan was that I should continue with high school.

Uncle Leo and Aunt Verica had exchanged their modern, three-room flat in the center of the city for a small one in Košíře, a shabbier section of Prague. They were about to emigrate to America and promised to leave the flat to Grandmother. The exchange was to be carried out after their departure. The deal was profitable for them, albeit done without the approval of the Housing Ministry.

I dutifully enrolled at the nearby girls' gymnasium but soon developed such a loathing toward the school that I just quit. Instead, I decided to attend a school for applied arts. As a child I used to spend many hours drawing dresses for my collection of paper dolls, and the adults of the family decided I had a future in fashion design. So I went about fulfilling their prediction.

I was now having a good time. Living with Grandmother was pleasant; she cooked and took care of me. For a while we were a small family. I got our furniture back from Lori's friend, and I loved the feeling of having a home again. I slept on the couch in the living room, and Grandmother used the leather sofa in the kitchen. It was a bit cramped, but as Grandmother was rather short, she managed.

Yet it soon emerged that the flat was infested with bedbugs. This was a nuisance, but we took it in our stride. These were nothing in comparison with the armies of such vermin in Terezín. We moved out for a few days while the flat was fumigated, but it helped only for a while, since the entire high-rise building was infested and the bedbugs soon found their way back into our beds. The bites itched, and I had to scratch myself, but otherwise I didn't mind. A minor inconvenience—bedbugs, ha!

I would leave for school in the morning, carrying my drawing board and paints. At noon I would buy a piece of pie or tart in a confectionery. Afternoons were spent with Otto, and in the evening I took the tram home. I felt free. Life was interesting, and Otto loved me. Only, when he took me to meet his friends, I became depressed because I felt so stupid and inadequate next to them. They discussed philosophy, politics, or new books and plays, while I was there among them like a decoration, pretty but dumb. I couldn't join their conversation and felt that even Otto thought me naive and childish. I remember how he tried to explain to me what philosophy was, and how I pretended to understand, although I wasn't sure I did.

The idyll lasted only a short time. Uncle Leo and Verica did not get the visa to America and needed their tiny flat back. For me there was no problem; I just took my few belongings and moved in with Otto. But poor Grandmother had nowhere to go. Uncle and Aunt moved in, and she stayed in the kitchen, making herself even smaller than she was, not to be in Aunt Verica's way.

I still attended the art school, but we were planning to get married.

It happened like this. We were returning from someplace in the center of town, and as we were waiting at the tram stop, Otto said in a quite casual tone, "I love you so much that maybe I will marry you."

He didn't ask, "Will you marry me?" or "Will you be my wife?" He knew it depended solely on his decision; there was absolutely no doubt in his mind that I might refuse.

I felt honored and elated.

There was, however, a major obstacle. One of the many documents that were required to get a permit for marriage was a certificate from the population census of 1930. The population of the Republic had three choices of nationalities: Czech, German, or Jewish. My parents, whose mother tongue and education had been German, registered as Germans. I was only six months old, so their nationality was mine, too, of course.

Now, after the war, I was a German, an enemy, and could not get the permit to marry. The Czech authorities had not yet managed to differentiate between the real Germans and the German-speaking Jewish survivors. I could even have been deported from Czechoslovakia to Germany.

It almost happened to Grandmother. Soon after her return from Terezín, she saw her name on the lists of the German citizens to be expelled, which were posted all over the city. She was alarmed and frightened, and when she told me about it, I just laughed. It was so absurd and obviously a mistake; I thought she should just ignore it. But I was wrong. Grandmother tried to get her name erased from the list, but all her efforts were in vain. In her agitation, she did something that for her was quite uncharacteristic.

She went to the prime minister's office and asked for an audience. They looked in disbelief at the little woman in her old-fashioned black hat, but she insisted: just tell him Katharina Polach wants to speak to him. The secretary smiled condescendingly but complied.

The prime minister came personally out of his office to greet her. Before the war he had been a member of Parliament and knew Grandfather well. It took only one phone call, and Grandmother's name was struck from the list.

I was not yet eighteen and, according to the law, still a minor. To be allowed to marry, I needed permission from the courts. Since Father Barnai was my legal custodian, I had to travel to the court in Teplice. On the appointed date we all—Mr. Barnai, Otto, and myself—appeared duly before the judge. First he just checked the data, but then he asked Otto, "What is your profession? What is your income? Where do you live?" The answers seemed to satisfy him, but then he sent the men out, and I was left alone with the judge. He looked me up and down carefully, probably to make sure that I was mature enough and normally developed. Then he leaned forward, smiled at me reassuringly, and said, "Is somebody coercing you into this marriage? Are you marrying of your free will? Are you sure you want to be the wife of this man?"

When I had answered, he explained, "In the meantime, until you are eighteen, you can either stay the ward of Mr. Barnai, or your husband can become custodian in his stead."

There was no question of my decision.

"My husband will be my husband, never my custodian."

I still did not have a permit to get married. I had the necessary domicile certificate and a document stating that I was single, an identity card, but I could not overcome the obstacle of the German census vote of my parents. Otto and I tried to have a Jewish ritual wedding. Rabbi Sicher, the chief rabbi of Czechoslovakia, had known Otto since he was born, having been Otto's mother's teacher at school back in Náchod, and he also conducted Otto's bar mitzvah. But even he couldn't help us. He was obliged to demand the same documents for a religious wedding as the civil marriage office.

Finally I decided on a ruse as a last resort. I put on my stiff wide coat, which a tailor had made for me from the military blanket I had brought from Bergen-Belsen. (I had no other coat, anyway.) It made me look larger, and again I stood in the queue at the Ministry of Interior. The clerk was a young man. I looked directly into his eyes and said, "I must have a permit to get married in a hurry. I am pregnant, and my boyfriend is willing to marry me. But if he has to wait, I know that he will surely escape."

His face shed the mien of officialdom, and lowering his voice, he asked, "Will it be all right if you get it next week?"

A few days later, I was finally in possession of the document I had spent so many months trying to obtain.

The wedding took place on May 21, 1947. By that time I was indeed pregnant. Much later, Otto admitted that it was crucial for him to know that I could bear children. He felt the loss of his entire family so acutely that the most important thing for him was to create a new one. I was naive but did have my doubts when he took no precautions. Yet he assured me that since it was only a short time after the camps, he had not yet regained his procreative powers. I was easily convinced and believed him; in my eyes he was the authority on everything.

When Metek Blum, Otto's best friend from Terezín, heard that I was pregnant, he became full of envy. He did not want to fall behind in achievements, and the result was that his daughter Sonia was born to him and his wife, Věra (née Joklová), six weeks after our first son, Peter Martin.

During the Nazi occupation, the Czech army had been dissolved. After the war all the men, even twenty-five-year-olds, were drafted for a shortened stint. As a high school graduate, Otto was placed in an officers' course. The huge military barracks was in Prague, near our Vršovice flat. Otto completed his six months of military service in May 1947.

While Otto was in the army, I lodged in his room in the Vršovice flat that he shared with Honza and Ruth. There were two rooms and a tiny cubicle behind the kitchen, where Ruth's sister Ditinka lived. Ruth and Honza were alternately absent for longer periods; still, for the five of us there was little privacy. We hoped that Otto would soon become manager of his father's factory, so we could at least live in a part of the Kraus villa. Soon after the Germans occupied Czechoslovakia in 1939, Otto's parents had been forced to sell their factory to a German for a ridiculous sum, but they never received their money, because Jewish accounts were blocked in the banks. The new German owner, by the name of Meyer, allowed the Kraus family to stay on in their villa until their deportation. When Otto returned after the war, he began the long process of claiming his father's property. It was a complicated procedure. The Czech authorities were in no hurry to restore properties to the Jewish owners; they dragged their feet and demanded endless documents.

Preparations for the wedding were not elaborate. I had my mother's blue suit, which Aunt Manya had stored during the war and which only needed a few alterations. I acquired a white blouse and a matching hat. One of Otto's few remaining distant cousins from Vlašim, who owned a shoe factory, provided blue shoes without the necessary coupons. I asked him to make me a pair with low heels; I didn't want to look taller than Otto.

Aunt Vala, a relative of Otto's, came two days early to cook and bake for the guests we invited for dinner. Otto managed to buy some beef on the black market, and Aunt Vala brought the provisions for several cakes. For two days before the wedding, I helped her, although I didn't know how to cook and bake. Before kneading the dough, as I was instructed by Vala, I took off the ring from my finger.

The ring was antique, a thick golden circle with a topaz set deep in the middle where the ring was wider. It had been Grandmother's gift on my twelfth birthday. She got it from her own grandmother. Before we were sent on the transport, I'd asked Zdenka to keep it for me. After the war, the first thing Zdenka did was pull the ring from her finger and hand it back to me.

When we finished baking the cakes and cleaning up the kitchen, I could not find the ring. Aunt Vala, Otto, and I looked everywhere; we even sorted the garbage. Nothing. We decided that it must have somehow got into one of the cakes.

Next morning, we took a taxi to the Clam-Gallas Palace, where civil marriages were conducted. A wide staircase led to the first floor, and, on the landing, several brides and grooms stood with their families. Each ceremony took fifteen or twenty minutes. It was like an assembly line.

On the stairs there was a great crowd of guests, many in uniform from Otto's officers' course. One of his old-time friends was Paťa. As we descended the stairs, new husband and wife, he pronounced philosophically, with suitably theatrical pathos: "From now on you will be even more alone than you were before."

Back at home, we had the festive meal with our guests. They were, of course, Metek and Vera, my aunts Lori and Manya, Grandmother, Otto's cousins Eva and Hanka Kraus, Aunt Vala, Margit, and Father Barnai. The cakes were cut, and everybody was warned to chew carefully, because my golden ring would be in one of the slices. But it wasn't. It just disappeared mysteriously and was never found again.

Otto consoled me: "The old ring was your maiden symbol. Now you have a new ring, the ring of a married woman."

In the afternoon we received a note advising us that we would receive a call from America. Uncle Otto Strass, the brother of Otto's mother, had decided to congratulate us on our wedding. Strangely, Uncle Otto's wife was also called Dita. There was no telephone in the Vršovice flat. The call would come to the office of the Kraus factory. In those times, overseas calls were a rarity and had to be mediated by the international telephone exchange.

After the last guest had gone, we washed the dishes, arranged the chairs and table, swept the carpet, and carried out the garbage. Then we dressed warmly, because in the office it would be cold, and went to wait for Uncle Otto's phone call. It was very exciting to think that we would actually be talking across these vast distances, as far as America.

It was announced for eight o'clock in the evening. But time passed; it was nine and then ten. The phone didn't ring. We sat on the uncomfortable office chairs and shivered. We couldn't just go home and let the uncle down. In the end, the call came at two o'clock in the morning. It went like this:

"Hello, is that you, Otto?"

"Hello, hello, Otto. Yes, it is Otto and Dita here."

"Congratulations on your wedding. We all wish you much happiness."

"Thank you. How are you, Uncle Otto? And how is Aunt Dita?"

"We are fine, all right. The girls also want to congratulate you."

A thin girl's voice said something incomprehensible in an American accent. After a while, another thin voice piped a few words, too. Uncle Otto continued:

"Why don't you come to America? Leave everything, take your toothbrush, and come to America."

"Thank you, Uncle Otto, but we would like to live here in Prague. This is our home."

"Okay. So bye-bye. And write. I will send you a parcel again soon."

And this is how we spent our wedding night.

CHAPTER THIRTY

The Kraus Factory

n the summer of 1947, Otto was at long last named proprietor of his parents' factory—not its owner however. This allowed us to move into the villa. The Treuhänder Meyer was expelled, together with all the Germans, from Czechoslovakia. The state appointed a manageress to run the factory. Most of the other employees remained from the time when it was still owned by the Kraus family. The villa was used as offices.

We turned two of the connecting rooms into our new home and moved in. There was a huge kitchen with an old-fashioned coal stove from the time before the war, when the family had employed a cook. This was no longer practical; we had it dismantled and bought an electric oven. The little cubicle behind the kitchen, where the cook had slept, became Otto's study. He had a desk, a chair, and a lamp there and could write undisturbed. His first book was *Země bez Boha—Land Without God*. When it was published to great acclaim, Otto was considered a promising young author.

As a published author, Otto was accepted in the circle of young Czech literary people. Thanks to the poet Kamil Bednář, who worked for Václav Petr, the publisher of Otto's first novel, Otto met Zdeněk Urbánek, Karel Nový, Bohuslav

Březovský (his wife, Dr. Březovská, was our pediatrician at the baby clinic), Ivan Diviš, Jiří Kolář, and others. They would meet in a wine cellar on Malostranské náměstí, discuss or read from their latest works, and drink wine. Otto wasn't a wine drinker—he would rather have had a cup of coffee—but those discussions were somehow inspiring. I once went with Otto, sat there like a decoration, listened to them, and felt privileged to be in the company of geniuses.

Ivan Diviš became a close friend. He often came to visit Otto in our cramped dwelling, and the two held long philosophical conversations. Once when we came to fetch him from his parents' flat, where he lived, Ivan's mother said to Otto, "I am glad he is going with you. With you he doesn't drink."

When Otto returned from the camps, he had no close family. His father had been murdered in the gas chambers of Auschwitz. His brother, Harry, was allegedly shot when he tried to escape during the evacuation of his camp. And Marie, Otto's mother, had died after the liberation, in a German hospital, like my mother, Liesl. Marie's sister, Ella, lived in London, and her brother, Otto Strass, in America.

But there was his mother's cousin, Aunt Vala, in the small town of Náchod, and she, her husband, Uncle Véna, and the children, Věra and Pavel, nicknamed Papen, were now Otto's closest, loving relatives. Before we were married, Otto took me to Náchod to introduce me and also to get their approval of his choice. Apparently, I passed muster.

We visited them frequently, and on one of our visits, we purchased two dozen tins of horsemeat. Food was still scarce, and most was available only with ration cards. Horsemeat was generally scorned, considered suitable only for the poorest of the poor, but the tinned horse goulash of Náchod could be bought without ration cards.

Papen studied pharmacology in Prague. Uncle Véna had a pharmacy near the main square in Náchod and wanted his son to take it over one day. Papen studied without much enthusiasm and became a pharmacist, but he never worked in a pharmacy. He played the trumpet, had a jazz band, and became quite famous.

He and his girlfriend, Milena, often came to visit us. Papen loved food; his handsome face was always flushed and shiny, as if the fat were oozing from his plump body. Then Otto would say, "Go to the pantry and kill a horse." And we would have a marvelous meal of horse goulash with potatoes.

Papen died on the stage as befitted his profession. He lifted his arms with the baton, fell over, and was dead. What a pity! He was still young, just fifty-two.

In the villa, I felt like a queen. I had a famous husband, two comfortable rooms, a small back garden, a large kitchen, and a car—an old, prewar box-shaped model Praga. In 1939, just before Hitler occupied Czechoslovakia, Otto's parents had made preparations to emigrate to England. They sent ahead a large ship trunk with clothes for the whole family, including their fur coats and even bed linen. The trunk stayed all the war years at one of London's train depots, undamaged by the heavy bombings. Now Aunt Ella sent it back to Prague. Oh, how wonderful that was! Suddenly we had blankets, sheets, towels, bathrobes; in short, everything we needed.

Our problem was Grandmother. She had no place to live. She was still staying with Uncle Leo and Verica. Their departure to America was delayed, and they were crowded in the Košíře flat. The shortage of housing had become even worse than in the first days after the war. One had to be on a waiting list at the Ministry of Housing, and people waited for years and years before they were offered a vacancy, which often turned out to be unfit for human habitation.

After much searching, Otto discovered a room for rent in the attic of an old house not far from us. Mrs. Adamová, the owner, was willing to let it to Grandmother. It was not a comfortable place; the entrance was from the backyard, the stairs were steep, and the heating inadequate. But there was no better solution. Mrs. Adamová was a kind woman, and she and Grandmother, who was so modest and adaptable, got along very well.

The baby was due in December, on Christmas day. But the twenty-fourth passed, and the next day, too. The first birth pangs started on the twenty-seventh. It was freezing, and Otto went out several times during the night to run the motor of the car, fearing it would not start when we had to rush to the hospital. The sturdy but ugly vehicle had remained standing without wheels on cinder blocks in the factory garage throughout the war. No fuel was available for private cars, not to mention tires or spare parts, so the German Treuhänder Meyer could not use it. When Otto was appointed manager of the factory, he found the car all dusty but in working condition. He purchased four second-hand tires on the black market. Such luxuries as new tires were nonexistent. He could, however, not find a fifth as a spare. Still, there were so few cars at the time that I felt proud and privileged to be seen in the stately six-seater.

In the small hours of the twenty-eighth, it was time to go to the hospital. Otto's best friend, Metek, who was a bit of a snob, opined that Otto could not allow his wife to give birth in a public hospital; it had to be a private sanatorium.

There were many hours of great pain, but everything went normally for a first child, and I didn't even need any stiches. The baby weighed 3.15 kilograms. Otto and Grandmother arrived shortly, and it was a great joy. The only shadow was when Otto told me that, as he was backing out from the yard into the street, he had run over our German shepherd puppy, Lump.

In those days, a mother used to stay in the hospital for three or four days after giving birth. But the next day I ran a fever, and it turned out that I had a furuncle in my right breast. Nursing became extremely painful. I was treated with the great new discovery, penicillin. It was administered by injection every three hours, day and night.

A week later I was pronounced cured and could go home with the baby. We had thought of a name a long time before its birth, not knowing, of course, whether it would be a boy or a girl. A girl would be named Michaela; that was certain. But for the boy we chose Peter Martin, the names of Viktor Fischl's two charming sons. Viktor was the brother of Otto's close friend Pata.

Yet the furuncle returned and was extremely painful. Otto rushed me to a general practitioner on our street, an old acquaintance of the Kraus family. He did surgery immediately. The right breast was damaged and didn't produce any more milk. The doctor told me that I would not be able to nurse my future children for more than a few short weeks.

After Peter Martin's birth, I don't know who was happier, me or my grandmother. She came every day, coddled the baby, and sang to him and would have held him in her arms all the time had we not forbidden it. It was the time of strict rules; everyone followed the advice of Dr. Spock's popular books. A baby got fed every three hours on the clock, and not when he was crying. Grandmother was old-fashioned, Otto said, and we had to obey the pediatrician. The doctor maintained that babies had to cry; it was good for their developing lungs.

By the way, our actual doctor was Dr. Epstein, professor of pediatrics, and before the war one of his students had been Dr. Mengele.

Otto decided that our son would not be circumcised. He did not want him to be marked as a Jew for his whole life. In Auschwitz, he had witnessed a frightful scene, when one of his fellow prisoners had his foreskin cut off by the camp barber "to make him a Jew." Otto himself had also not been circumcised because he'd been born prematurely. His parents delayed the procedure to wait until he gained weight and then just left it undone. For a Jew in Prague, it was an unimportant detail. But in Auschwitz he could have been the next victim of the barber with his blunt razor.

Peter was a very pretty baby, and I was a very proud mother. It also pleased me that I had him so young, and I planned how, when he grew up, I would dance with him. I was young but also silly and inexperienced.

One day I went to visit Ruth, our former flatmate, to show off my son. It was not far to go. I dressed the baby warmly, covered him in the pram with his downy quilt, and walked along the cold winter streets. When I returned an hour later, Otto and Grandmother were standing in the street with worried faces, turning this way and that, on the lookout for me. I probably hadn't told them where I was going, suspecting they wouldn't let me. What a dressing-down I got! How could you do such a thing, taking the baby out in the freezing cold, endangering him, he might get pneumonia, how irresponsible you are! And yes, I felt guilty, although I protested loudly, saying that I was mature enough to know what I was doing, and why didn't they trust me?

We now lived quite an orderly life. Otto worked hard running the factory, making efforts to obtain orders for ladies' lingerie and nighties. He would quote his father, who described his product as "work clothes for certain females." Raw material was in short supply, and the bosses of the textile factories had to be bribed. Our friend Metek accepted Otto's offer to become procurer at the Kraus factory. He was a wizard at the job. He himself had restored his father's distillery and thus had access to any number of bottles of brandy or whisky. No official at the Ministry of Commerce ever refused such a gift. And the rolls of chiffon, silk, and lace appeared regularly.

I tried to run the household with Grandmother's help. Every week I took Peter to the well-baby clinic, where Dr. Březovská examined him and noted down his progress. In the afternoon, we often visited Metek, his wife, Vera, and baby Sonia, or they would come to us. There were other friends, and of course cousin Papen with his Milena. One of Otto's former campmates, Zdeněk Eliáš (formerly Eckstein), would sit next to Peter and amuse him for hours. It was quite touching to see the two—the young man of twenty-four and the baby— giggling together.

Another friend, the poet Josef Hiršál, came to see us, too. But what he wanted was to have a look at the lingerie. In the evening after the seamstresses had gone home, Otto took him into the factory. When Hiršál saw the pile of ladies' panties on the packing table, he pressed an armful of them to his chest and then threw them high up in the air. As they floated down on his head, he jubilated, "So many women, so many women . . ."

Sometimes Otto would give Metek a few items of ladies' underwear. Some bureaucrats preferred them to Metek's whisky That made me terribly envious. Why should the wives of the officials get new nighties, while I got nothing? I still had barely anything to wear, and there they were giving things to people who surely had much more than I, and nothing was left for me. Even Metek took my side in the argument. But Otto insisted that the business had priority. The reason was not stinginess. Every roll of raw material was allocated by the Ministry of Commerce, and from each the factory was obliged to produce a fixed number of items. It was only thanks to the talented cutter, Mrs. Šandová, that one or two extra pieces were extracted from each roll.

I remember how hurt I felt when Otto's cousin Eva Kraus was getting married, and I, already visibly pregnant, came to the wedding in the only maternity dress I owned. It was black with a white collar, and Eva remarked, "At least for my wedding you could have put on a better dress."

A certain Mrs. Maternová had been appointed by the state to manage the Kraus factory when the German *Arisator*[8] was imprisoned after the war. Of course her office was the best room of the villa, while the accountant and two secretaries occupied the others. Mrs. Maternová was a short, plump woman of middle age, with blond hair always well-coiffed (her husband had a hairdresser's salon off Wenceslas Square) and carefully made up, with several rings on her pudgy fingers.

When Otto became proprietor, he did not dismiss Mrs. Maternová. He felt that he was not experienced enough to run the business by himself and thought he could rely on her. What a mistake that was!

Maternová had run the factory for almost two years. She was an ambitious woman, sly and false, who was in cahoots with two of the workers, the cutter

---

8 The Nazis called all non-Jews Aryans. When they expropriated Jewish property, they called it *Arisierung,* or "Aryanization," and the non-Jews they installed to run Jewish businesses were called *Arisatoren.*

and the head of the operation. The extra pieces that Metek now used as bribes had formerly been sold by Mrs. Maternová, who shared the profit with her two accomplices.

Of course, Mrs. Maternová was not happy that Otto became her boss. On the face of it, she pretended to cooperate, showing him the books and letting him make the decisions. But behind his back she did everything she could to undermine his authority. In our naiveté, Otto and I became quite friendly with her, until the Communist coup in February 1948.

CHAPTER THIRTY-ONE

A New Political Reality

Three years after the end of the war, the Communists staged a coup in Prague and took over the government. They called a multitude of workers to the Staroměstské (Old Town Square) under the pretext of supporting the labor unions. And then they went to President Beneš, claiming that the people were calling for his resignation. The ruse worked; the Communists came to power.

Suddenly there was a complete change of attitudes. An atmosphere of fear pervaded the lives of all. Former small-time functionaries became all-powerful bosses.

People, especially "capitalists," were summoned for interrogation; in every building informers were appointed to report on what they overheard from the tenants. There were even cases of previously known public figures disappearing without a trace. Red banners with pro-Soviet slogans hung everywhere. If one wanted to keep a job or send children to study, one had to become a member of the party. New "National Committees" issued "Loyal Citizen's" documents, without which no one could be employed. All privately owned factories and large businesses were expropriated by the state. They called it "nationalization."

The Kraus factory was one of them.

A few days after the Communist takeover, Mrs. Maternová called Otto into her office and, in the presence of the rest of the staff, handed him an envelope with a triumphant smile on her face. It was a *dekret*, a document stating that from that day, Otto Kraus was no longer manager of the Kraus Ladies' Lingerie Factory and had no authority. The factory was now the property of the state. He was not allowed to have any contact with the employees, neither directly nor by phone. Also, he had to immediately vacate the premises and hand over the keys and was not allowed to take out anything from the factory or the office. (Mrs. Maternová didn't even allow me to take back my own private sewing machine, which had been temporarily placed in the factory. She insisted that whatever was in the factory belonged now to the state. I was pleased when I heard later that her husband had divorced her.)

Actually, the Kraus factory shouldn't have been nationalized, at least not initially. At first only factories with fifty or more employees were expropriated. The government later nationalized even small businesses. At the time, only forty-nine employees, including Mrs. Maternová and the office staff, were registered in the Kraus factory. But Maternová falsified the numbers and so achieved her goal to become manageress again.

Yet what Mrs. Maternová was unable to accomplish, although she tried hard and tenaciously, was to have us move out of the house. We had to wait until we were allocated an alternative flat, and there was nothing available. During the war there had been no construction whatsoever. Many newly married couples had to live in the cramped flats of their parents, postponing the birth of children. Adult grandchildren moved in with grandparents, so that when those died, the grandchild would have a right to the flat. Families that occupied more rooms than they were allowed either had to take in lodgers or move to a smaller flat. Everything was registered; nothing escaped the watchful eye of Big Brother. And there were willing informers everywhere, a long-time tradition of the Czechs.

Maternová used all her contacts in the Communist Party to have us evicted, but there just wasn't anything available. She became hateful and harassed us constantly. She made the employees spy on us and report to her our every move. They told her who came to visit us, how long they stayed, when we went out, and when we returned. She even turned off the main electric switch on weekends, when the offices were closed, leaving us and the baby, who was then just a few weeks old, without light, heat, and warm water.

One night in late February, burglars broke into the storeroom of the factory and stole a large number of fabric rolls. The factory building stood at the back of the villa, and the bedroom window faced in its direction.

We were accused of purposefully allowing the break-in, if not perhaps even arranging it. There had been another attempt at a break-in the previous summer, while Otto was still manager of the factory, but he had heard the noise from the open window, and when he gave a shout, the burglars fled. Maternová argued that we must have heard the burglars like the time before and that we didn't call the police because the factory no longer belonged to us. But it was winter then, the window was closed, and we heard nothing.

There was no use arguing. Otto was summoned before the court. No lawyer dared to represent him, the capitalist oppressor of the working classes. He appeared alone before the judge, and when he started speaking, the judge shut him up, saying, "I don't speak to capitalists like you." However, there was fortunately not enough evidence, and the case was dismissed.

Yet in order to get any employment, everyone now had to present a document called a Declaration of Loyalty to the state. These documents were issued by the local branch of the Communist Party. There was no chance for Otto, the "collaborator with thieves," to get such a document.

My cousin Jenka came to our rescue.

Jenka was my cousin twice removed. She was a few years older than me and was married to Ivan, a functionary of the party. She too was a member of the party and believed wholeheartedly in the doctrine of social justice. They lived not far away, and the two of us often walked together with our babies in a stroller.

Thanks to her husband's connections, Otto was about to get the crucial certificate of state loyalty. I was told by Ivan to fetch the document instead of Otto. It was like a scene from a film. He instructed me how to dress, no makeup, not to utter a word, just say my name and wait. I was scared to death. I stood silently at the door of the gloomy office with grim-faced men sitting at several desks. No one talked to me. After what seemed to me like eternity, one of the men motioned to me with his finger to approach. He handed me a small piece of paper, and I left hurriedly, hoping that no one would intercept me. The document said:

CERTIFICATE

The Commission for Internal and National Security

We hereby certify that Mr. Otto Kraus ([date of birth], [address], Czech citizen) is, according to the evidence of the tenants and of the Workers Council, loyal to the Nation and to the State.

Signed: Secretary for National Security

Since Otto was a published author and had many good friends in the literary world, he was accepted at the Ministry of Culture as clerk for English literature. Any book that was published in the Republic had to be approved by the party *aparatchiks*. Otto liked the job, which consisted of reading new English books and writing a recommendation for translation. What aggravated him, however, was that his recommendations were often rejected for being "not politically correct." Writers of world renown were branded as rightists, imperialists, anti-socialists, or counterrevolutionaries. Otto was proud to be the only person in the "reddest" of ministries who was not a member of the Communist Party.

Jenka was instrumental not only in arranging this important document for Otto, but also in finding a solution for our housing problem. In the high-rise building where she lived was a tiny garçonnière—a bachelor flat—on the ground floor, occupied by an unmarried lady physician. Since the physician also had accommodation at the hospital where she worked, she was actually not allowed to keep the apartment. Jenka managed to have her move out, and the place was allocated to us. To refuse it was not an option.

It consisted of one room and a small bathroom with a toilet, a sink, and a bathtub. When the double bed, wardrobe, table, two chairs, and the baby's cot were moved in, there was hardly space to move. In one corner of the room there was a shallow recess with a sink and a two-ring gas cooker, above which hung a cupboard for the cooking utensils and foodstuff.

One morning, Jana, Pata's wife, arrived at our little garçonnière, lugging two big bags. She had decided we should cook jam. Fruits and vegetables were still in short supply in 1948, three years after the end of the war, and she had acquired several kilos of apples from somewhere. Peeling and cutting them took us three hours, but we had a good time talking and laughing together. While the apples with a lot of sugar were boiling, we played with my six-month-old baby, Peter.

When the fruit was cooked, we poured it into two large ceramic pots, which I had inherited from someone. We carried them to the window to cool, but halfway there, the pots broke from the heat, and the bottoms dropped out. The boiling-hot mess fell on the carpet, creating two steaming mounds and a lake, which the little carpet began slowly absorbing. The top of the mound could be saved, but much of our jam stuck to the fibers of the carpet. On our knees, we began scrubbing to save it. It was our only carpet.

Toward evening, we gave up. The sugar had hardened, and the carpet was like a board, impossible to roll up. But there was one solace: when people came to us, they would sniff and then always exclaim, "Oh, what a wonderful apple fragrance."

At this time, some of our friends were preparing to go to the newly created State of Israel. Some had already left, such as Ruth Bondy; her husband, Honza, was about to follow. This was an opportunity to swap flats. We would move to the

Vršovice flat, and Honza to our garçonnière. As two adults with a baby, we were entitled to two rooms, and we also wanted to accommodate Grandmother. Only no one must know that Honza was planning to emigrate.

It was accomplished through a mutual friend, a former fellow prisoner of both Otto and Honza's, who was a member of the Communist Party and had connections.

At last we were able to take Grandmother to live with us, and she was pleased that she could be with little Peter all day long. She was very discreet and never interfered or criticized us, although she must have had plenty of reasons to do so. I was young, not yet twenty, harebrained and incompetent. Peter was already a year old. She would hold him on her lap, sing to him in her quivery voice, and let him put the three pairs of her glasses on her nose, one on top of the other.

The idyll didn't last long. Honza had left for Israel; our best friends, Metek and Věra Blum, too. The regime became increasingly oppressive; whoever could was leaving. There was an atmosphere of urgency. People sensed that emigration wouldn't be allowed for much longer.

Otto decided we had to go. He knew that as long as he worked at the "red" Ministry, he wouldn't get an exit permit, so he quit. The Jewish Community offered him a position, and he readily accepted. In later years, he described himself as being the dismantler of the Zionist Movement in Prague. He was coached by the head of the Aliyah Department, a man who had been sent from Israel to manage the emigration not only of the Czech Jews but also of others, mainly Polish Jews, who passed through Czechoslovakia on their way to Israel.

At the Jewish Community Office, Otto was given a room with a desk, and when he opened the drawer, he found a million Czechoslovak koruna in cash. Agitated, he rushed to his Israeli boss, who calmly took the money and explained that these were the funds for Aliyah. Otto's work from the first day consisted of burning the evidence of how this and other moneys, which financed the Aliyah (ascent) of thousands of Holocaust survivors to Israel, were acquired. He and a woman secretary fed the little stove day after day with the telltale documents. His other task was to sell the symbolic shekel that every potential emigrant had to buy for ten koruna in order to register for Aliyah.

Otto had been a Zionist since before the war. I already mentioned that he intended to move to Palestine, as the land was called before it became the independent State of Israel. For two years, 1940 till 1942, he went on *hachshara* (agricultural training) to learn farming and husbandry. He had a romantic relationship to the soil, took Hebrew lessons, and read books about Jewish history and Zionism. He loved the fields and the smells of the cowshed. He dreamed of living in a kibbutz. Otto was influenced by A. D. Gordon, who wrote that the Jews should become tillers of the soil in a socialist land of Israel.

He learned to grow vegetables, plow with oxen, milk cows, and shovel manure in the cowshed. There were a number of such *hachshara* groups all over Bohemia and Moravia, working on large landowner farms. The farm where Otto had worked with Ruth and Mausi belonged to a monastery order. The monks expected the villagers to go to church every Sunday. The young Jews were a strange phenomenon, and the villagers feared that their liberal ways of life might influence their own daughters and sons. For Otto, *hachshara* ended when he was deported, together with his parents and younger brother, Harry, to the Terezín ghetto.

Under the British Mandate, immigration to Palestine took place clandestinely: people had to jump off the ship and wade ashore at night; often they were caught and imprisoned.

But since Israel had become independent, Jews were not just permitted but encouraged to immigrate and settle in the land. The meaning of the Hebrew word *aliyah* is "to go up, to rise"—thus whoever moves to Israel actually rises higher. The young state welcomed newcomers; the journey was even paid for by the Jewish Fund, and ships and airplanes brought Jews from all over the world.

In Czechoslovakia the possibility swept up a wave of enthusiastic Zionists, most of them survivors of concentration camps, to leave the old country and build their new homeland. Those who remained were either tied to non-Jewish partners or were planning to leave later, when they finished their studies.

We had been married for more than two years. I was young and inexperienced and followed Otto's decisions blindly, because I trusted him. He knew so much, and he explained everything to me, told me about kibbutzim and Jewish history, spoke about Theodor Herzl, the visionary of the Jewish State, and even taught me a few Hebrew words.

Life in Czechoslovakia was growing increasingly unpleasant. The regime was restrictive; people from the middle and upper classes were being harassed, and one could be imprisoned for such crimes as telling a joke about the government. People were fleeing over the border to Germany or Austria, and for us Jews, Aliyah was a welcome solution. The Czech authorities permitted, if reluctantly, emigration to Israel.

Yet the procedure was complicated, and we had to overcome many hurdles the bureaucracy put in our way. The first step was to make suitable arrangements with our flat. Grandmother would not be allowed to stay in it after we left. She declined to emigrate with us, saying, "I am like an old tree. Old trees cannot be replanted."

Otto's friend, the poet and artist Jiří Kolář, was desperately searching for a larger apartment. He lived in a one-room apartment with his wife, mother-in-law, and baby. If we exchanged flats, Grandmother could live in his, and he would get our two rooms. Yet it had to be done cleverly, so that the authorities would not be aware of the subterfuge. The details are too complicated to describe here. In the end, unfortunately, the planned arrangement failed—although we didn't learn this until after our departure. Kolář didn't get our flat and had to remain in the one room. Grandmother was not allowed to stay in ours and actually became homeless. Her only solution was to move to Brno, her former hometown, where she was promised a room in the Jewish senior home. While she was waiting for a vacancy, she found temporary accommodation with the Formáneks, her former neighbors. Her sister-in-law Olga, also a Terezín survivor, lived in the senior home, and the two had a lifelong, close relationship. Their fate was also similar in that they both had lost their whole families, except for one grandchild. My grandmother had me, and Olga had Pavel Uri Bass, my second cousin.

The next step in preparing our emigration was dealing with the bureaucracy. To be allowed to leave the country, we had to fill in forms, attach expensive stamps, stand in a queue, and hand them to the clerk. He, of course, demanded a pile of personal documents, among them an affidavit from the tax authorities, confirming that we didn't owe any taxes. Here arose a new problem.

For tax purposes, Otto's father had divided the assets among the four members of the family and they were listed as co-owners. The German Treuhänder, of course, never paid taxes for the former Jewish owners, and now the revenue authorities demanded back payments for the entire war period. No matter that all the members of the family, except Otto, had perished, that during the German occupation the Kraus family had no longer owned the factory. The tax people demanded their pound of flesh. And so we had no choice: either pay or forget the Aliyah.

And where does one find such money? I don't remember exactly how we scraped together the ransom. We were granted a certain reduction, and there was some money Otto had saved. At last we got the affidavit, and the application for our permit was duly accepted.

After a few months, we received our exit visa. Of course, this was not yet the final step. Every emigrant had to submit a detailed list of the items he intended to take with him. We were allowed to send a so called "lift" to Israel by ship. This was a large wooden crate containing our belongings. The list had to include every item—the baby's toys, diapers, our underwear, towels, sheets, pots and pans, spoons, forks, each book by title, every piece of furniture in detailed description. I have kept the list as a souvenir.

Again a few weeks passed before we got the list approved. However, many things had been crossed out. Thus we were forbidden from taking our carpet; my golden necklace and cigarette lighter; Otto's typewriter; not twelve cups and saucers but only six; not twelve forks and knives, only six; not eight bedsheets, only four. With the help of the Writer's Union, which appointed Otto as correspondent of one of the Czech newspapers, to write articles about Israel, he was later granted a special permission to take his typewriter after all.

But the story did not end there. Every item on the list had to be assessed by an official estimator. But since this was a time of mass emigration to Israel, the few licensed estimators were booked for weeks in advance. There was again a long wait until the day when a grim young man appeared and started examining all the items on our list. The procedure took hours; he handled each book, each handkerchief, slipper, and baby rattle, turning it over, spreading it out, and then writing down the price. Not the price of a used object, but the price it would cost in a shop. The sum was staggering. I never knew we had such wealth in our tiny flat.

The ransom we had to pay the state for allowing us to take our possessions abroad was 10 percent of the total. We decided to sell everything we could, except the things we were taking with us. The sale was set for the coming Sunday, but Otto thought there would be no buyers. To our surprise, the owner of a nearby laundry showed up and bought everything. She would have taken even more if we had anything else to offer.

Now there was money to pay the estimator and the state. The wooden crate, looking like a small ship container, was ordered from a carpenter, and we enrolled at the Jewish Community Office for the next transport. The Ministry of Interior at the time issued only a collective group passport to the emigrants. This ensured that nobody traveled anywhere else but to Israel. The Jewish Community was obliged to send a person with the documents to accompany the group up to the border.

The date of our departure was set for the beginning of May 1949. That was a new problem. The crate had to be packed at the railway station in the presence of the customs officials, and the date we were assigned was after the date of our departure. Somebody had to be present at the customs control, not necessarily the owner. But who?

The problem was resolved in the form of Stella Fischl, our friend Paťa's sister-in-law. Paťa was leaving in the same transport as us, and since he didn't have much luggage, we agreed to let him stow it in our crate. Stella promised to watch over the packing, and we were glad. We couldn't have found a more dependable person.

To take any money out of the Republic was not allowed. That didn't bother us because we had no cash left anyway. Otto's uncle from America had promised to lend us a certain amount for the beginning, which he would send directly to Israel. At the time we didn't imagine how differently things would turn out.

After paying for our obligatory shekel, the day came when we said goodbye to Grandmother; took our little Peter, aged just eighteen months, the suitcases, and the stroller; and hailed a taxi to the railway station.

Grandmother must have known that she would never see us again, but I was too preoccupied with all the arrangements to give it a thought. Today, now that I am old myself, I realize what a unique person she was, to send us off unselfishly, without a hint of self-pity or complaint. From Israel I wrote her detailed letters, describing our life, and she always answered, worrying about our future. Poor Grandmother! She had not long left to live. In winter, she became ill with pneumonia, and the Formáneks took her to the hospital. She died there, only ten months after our departure. Aunt Olga sent me a letter describing the circumstances, with a photo of the cremation ceremony. It shows a hall with three rows of old people in black, all acquaintances, none of them family members except for Olga.

CHAPTER THIRTY-TWO

Journey to ~~Israel~~

At the railway station on the day of our departure, there was a great commotion. Our group consisted of about a hundred people, boarding with their luggage for the first leg of the journey to Italy. Among them were a number of our friends: Paťa Fischl; the couple Eva and Pavel Lukeš, with Eva's mother, Mrs. Králová; Annetta Able with her husband and baby; Eva Weissová; Eva Schlachetová; and other acquaintances. Many were accompanied by family members or friends, saying goodbye, hugging, and wiping away tears.

We settled in the six-seat compartment, three adults on each side, with our little Peter moving from Daddy's to Mummy's lap and back again. For the toddler we had prepared a sleeping arrangement. It was a hanging mat, which we fastened to the luggage rack above our heads and padded with a few folded blankets. In fact, Peter was the only one who could sleep during the entire journey. There was no way for any of us to sleep. We sat upright on the wooden benches during the two days and the night. No one was allowed to get off the train at the stations where the train stopped. Sometimes it stood for hours until it moved on.

Food was no problem. Everybody had brought enough provisions and bottles of water to last the entire journey. But the trickle of water from the faucet in the dirty toilet was not sufficient to rinse one's hands, let alone wash the baby's soiled diapers. Disposable diapers were unknown then.

We had an ingenious contraption that had been invented in the Terezín ghetto, for heating the toddler's food. Peter was the only child in our carriage, and of course, he quickly became everyone's pet.

Soon we arrived at the border of Austria, and the excitement and tension rose. Our escort was a pretty, pert young woman, who entertained the customs people with drink, salami, and other goodies unavailable in the Republic. The purpose was to make them so happy that they wouldn't be too thorough with the luggage control. Moreover, she had a few bottles hidden in her compartment. They contained quicksilver, which, as we learned, is more expensive than gold. It was in this way that the Jewish community abroad was able to smuggle financial contributions to the young State of Israel. The moment the train passed the border, the joy and relief from the tension made us all shout and sing and clap hands happily.

One of our fellow passengers was Mrs. S, who had worked with Otto at the Jewish Community Office and actually assisted him with the burning of documents. Just before we reached the border, she asked Otto to keep a packet of cigarettes for her, explaining that she had more than she was permitted to take out of the Republic.

When the control was over and the customs people had left, Otto said, "For the favor I did you, let me smoke one of your cigarettes."

"Oh no, no, you can't," she cried.

In each of the cigarettes were rolled-up dollar bills. Otto stared at her, speechless. Had he been caught, the penalty would have not only meant prison but also that he would have never again been allowed to emigrate.

Apart from being sorry that we could not see Vienna and the Italian cities we passed through, the journey was uneventful. Sleep was impossible in the crowded compartments, but some people went to stand at the windows in the corridor and then one of us could nap awhile on the wooden bench, with a coat for a pillow.

On the second day I had my first glimpse of the sea. I had never seen it before, and my impression was of the enormous weight of this vast amount of water pressing the earth. Our destination was the displaced persons camp at Trani, a small seaside town in Italy. The camp had been established at the end of the war, and now it housed huge numbers of survivors from all over Europe, who were waiting for visas to America or Australia. Some of them had been there for three and four years and were very adept at trading currencies. Our accommodation was a huge shack with mattresses for dozens of people, without any privacy.

Each of us Czech Jews, even our little Peter, owned two and a half English pounds, the only money we had been allowed to take out of the Republic. As we were eager to explore the town, Mr. Krull, one of the veterans in the camp, exchanged our English pounds for the Israeli currency, with a small profit for us in Italian lira. And so we walked in a group to the town, where we sat in an outdoor café in the square, drank a glass of the local wine, and felt very grand.

Our ship was delayed, and we had to wait a few more days. Although the crowded and unhygienic conditions reminded us of the concentration camps, we were not upset by it, because now we were free. At last the *Galila* arrived, and we were taken to Bari, our embarkation port.

Instead of the sea liner that I had expected, a vessel more like a fishing boat than a passenger ship was anchored at the long, stone-paved quay. A wooden plank led up to the deck, and next to it there was a table where two people checked off the passengers from a list. A huge crowd of about fifteen hundred people with children, bundles, and suitcases jostled, squeezed, and pushed, without any semblance of order, to get on the ship. They screamed and gesticulated wildly, and we just stared at this uncivilized behavior. I was reminded of the scramble of the starved prisoners to the food barrels in the concentration camps.

They were Jews from Morocco and Tunis and Algeria who, like us, were on their way to Israel. Our Czech group decided not to join the melee and to wait patiently for our turn on the quay. We knew we had no chance to embark before the crowd. Someone told us that women with children were assured of good accommodation, and we believed it.

It was an exhausting wait. All day long a strong wind blew sand and grit into our faces, mouths, and hair. I wrapped the boy's head in my scarf, and we tried to screen him from the wind. The hours passed, everybody grew irritated; there was nowhere to sit, and there were no toilets.

Suddenly someone called our name: "Kraus? Is there a family Kraus?" It was a sailor from the *Galila*, and when he found us, he asked for a piece of our luggage, saying he would reserve places for us on the ship. We gave him our rolled-up bedding, without knowing who he was, hoping it was not a scam and thinking that we would perhaps never see our blankets again.

It was almost dark when we finally boarded. They led us down a flight of stairs and then another, until we were in a large storage room below the water-line. There was pandemonium: shouting and shoving, men and women scrambling for free bunks. The air was stifling, and already there was the stench of too many people together. Our blankets were nowhere in sight, and I found only one empty bunk, and none for Peter.

It was too much for me, and I started to cry uncontrollably. Where were our blankets? Where was the better accommodation for mothers with children? The bunk was so narrow that a slim person could hardly sleep on it, let alone with a child. How would we manage in such conditions for several days?

Otto decided he would look for the sailor who had taken our bundle. He came back after a while, a big smile on his face.

"Wipe away your tears, put on some lipstick, and come with me."

With Peter in my arms, I followed him up one flight, a second flight, and we were on the deck. Then higher still, to the upper deck. Here there were cabins, and one of them, in the middle of the ship, was ours. Our blankets were spread on three comfortable beds; there was a sink with faucets for cold and hot water, as well as a table and, on it, a bowl of fruit. Not just any old fruit, but oranges and bananas, delicacies we hadn't seen since before the war. It was literally like coming out from the netherworld straight into heaven.

After a while, the chief steward of the ship knocked on the door. He introduced himself, and it turned out he was related to the wife of Otto's cousin

Pepík. Pepík Kraus was the son of one of Otto's father's numerous brothers. Pepík managed to emigrate in time, before Hitler occupied Czechoslovakia. He had told his relative, the steward, to look out for us, and we now became his personal wards. We were invited to eat in the dining room for paying passengers, together with the captain and the officers. He told us we could use his private bathroom and gave me a cake of Palmolive soap, an unbelievable luxury!

Our cabin became also the refuge of many of our friends. Annetta came several times a day to nurse her baby away from the crowds; others came to have a wash at the sink because the communal shower cubicles were permanently overcrowded. There were twelve hundred people on the ship, which had a maximum capacity of six hundred. Those in the lower hold just spent the days on the deck, and most of them also slept there. Passengers got food tickets and were called to meals in three shifts.

But for me it was like a holiday. No cooking, no chores, just playing with my boy and getting a suntan. When we arrived at Haifa after three days, I actually didn't want to leave the ship.

Yet the three days on sea were the only good time of our entire Aliyah.

Dawn was just beginning when the ship arrived at Haifa and we saw the morning sun illuminating the wonderful town climbing up the slope of Mount Carmel. The sight was breathtaking. We were in the Land of Israel!

Otto's cousin Pepík was waiting for us at the port. When he spotted us on the deck, he waved enthusiastically. Yet it was late afternoon when we disembarked, mainly because I was in no hurry and the food in the dining room was so delicious. There was another queue to register the newcomers and the customs, and not even Pepík, who had acquaintances among the port personnel, could help. Besides, he was a taxi driver and had to get back to work. And yes, we were also dusted with the insecticide DDT, to kill any typhus-carrying lice on our persons. (The newcomers from the North African lands were deeply offended. They claimed that only they were disinfected with DDT, while new *olim*—immigrants on Aliyah to Israel—from Europe or America didn't have to undergo such demeaning treatment.

Once we were processed, a truck drove us to the tent city called Shaar Aliyah, just at the foot of Mount Carmel. It was May 16, my grandfather's birthday. What would my grandfather, the ardent social democrat, have thought of his granddaughter going to live in the Zionist Jewish State?

Our tent contained ten beds, and we shared it with Pavel, Eva, her mother, Pata, Manka, and two other friends. Apart from the hundreds of tents, there were a few wooden shacks in the camp, a kitchen, an office, a makeshift clinic, a few toilets, and a washroom. In addition, there was a long trough with faucets in the open, but the water was tepid. The compound was enclosed by a wire fence, and people were not allowed to leave. Free food was distributed three times a day, but many of the items were strange to us. We got pita bread and tahini, olives, and something called halva, which we guessed was made of crystallized honey and tasted a bit like caramel. If you had several containers, you had to keep the sweet halva away from the olives and sardines; if not, it would all run together in one bowl. The problem was not the lack of dishes but of hands to carry the vessels.

The first night it was very hot; it was the *hamsin*, the Israeli version of the sirocco. In the middle of the night, a sudden gust of wind blew off the top of the tent, and rain started pouring in. We moved our beds as far away from the hole as possible, but nobody could sleep anyway.

Every day following our arrival, Otto stood at the gate, expecting my uncle Ernst-Benjamin. He was my father's younger brother, who had managed to immigrate to Palestine at the last moment before the Nazi occupation. He knew we were due to arrive; we had sent him a telegram before our departure and another immediately upon our arrival. What we did not know was that he had become a policeman and could not get leave. There was no way to communicate with us, no phone, no mail address. In the meantime, all our friends had been fetched by their Israeli relatives. Our only daily relief was when cousin Pepík visited us in the late afternoons and gave us some coins from his earnings of the day and a bottle or two of fruit juice. After ten days of waiting, Otto decided to take things into his own hands and start acting.

We had expected, perhaps naively, that either Pepík or my uncle would advise us where to settle and where to look for work. Pepík was very enthusiastic and sympathetic, happy to have a relative nearby, after being for many years the only member of the Kraus family in Israel. He called Otto "blood of my blood," which became his sobriquet to our friends, when they spoke about him. But Blood of My Blood had no answers to our questions.

Then Otto got information about a better camp near Netanya. Next morning we climbed on the open truck with little Peter, our luggage, and a few other new *olim* and traveled to Pardessia.

Pardessia was similar to the tent camp we had left. There was also a fence and the same trough with faucets; however, there was a hole in the fence, and people left and entered through it without difficulty. There was a nearby bus stop, and Otto squeezed onto the bus, along with the shouting and shoving mob, and traveled to Tel Aviv, or rather Jaffa, to see my uncle at long last.

Uncle Ernst-Benjamin and Aunt Hadassa were glad to meet him, but no practical help could be expected from them. They had recently left Kibbutz Ashdot Yaakov, where they had met and started their family, and they were still in the process of settling down. Despite Uncle being a lawyer, trained to become a judge back in Prague, here he'd had to accept a post at the police and could barely make ends meet. Their dwelling was half of a flat in an unfinished Arab house in Jaffa; the other half was occupied by a large Bulgarian family of *olim*. There was only one shower room. Since the kitchen was taken over by the Bulgarians, the shower room became Aunt's kitchen, where she cooked on two petroleum cookers, which stood on wooden stools. Every Friday she removed everything from her "kitchen" to allow both families to take a shower. It was clear now that we could not expect solutions from either of our relatives.

Practical advice came from our friends Eva and Pavel Lukeš. They had settled in a village near Netanya, where they had relatives. Otto learned that Pavel worked as a farmhand and that there was work for him, too. He bought a kind of large, short-handled hoe called a *turyiah*, and he and Pavel became agricultural laborers. Every morning they would stand with a few others near the village silo, where the local farmers came to hire a hand for the day. Work consisted mainly of hoeing around the trees in the *pardessim*, the citrus orchards. These farmers were originally not farmers at all. They had been merchants, lawyers, or industrialists in Germany and Czechoslovakia. They emigrated just in time, before the war, paying large sums for entry visas to Palestine, then still ruled by the British. They established several villages where they grew vegetables and oranges and raised chickens.

Now the farmers would stand and watch their hired farmhand to make sure he was not straightening his back and being idle. At the end of the day, they paid him some measly wages, not before haggling with him about the lunch break.

In the meantime I stayed with little Peter in the huge camp, sharing the tent with strangers. The conditions were unspeakably unhygienic. There was no floor; the iron beds stood on the dusty ground. The food I fetched from the distribution point became covered with flies before I reached the tent. Soon the child got sick, first with diarrhea, but then he got an ear infection. He was feverish, did not eat, could not sleep, and cried incessantly. I became desperate. There was no choice; I had to get help from my family in Jaffa.

My aunt Hadassa was absolutely wonderful. She realized immediately what I had not been aware of: the baby's life was in danger. She took us to the Kupat Cholim health clinic, where we waited, together with dozens of other sick children, for our turn to see the pediatrician. It was the year of the huge wave of newcomers, mainly from North Africa, and the health system, not prepared for such multitudes, was collapsing from the pressure. There were not enough doctors, nurses, and hospital beds. In order to get a number to the doctor, Aunt Hadassa got up before daybreak and stood in the queue at the clinic. She returned around seven with number nine or twelve and prepared her own children for school. My little cousin Doron was in second grade, and Edna, not yet three, in nursery school. Then Aunt Hadassa accompanied me with the sick child back to the doctor; he spoke only Hebrew, and I could not communicate with him.

On the first visit, he pierced Peter's eardrum, and that eased the worst pain. But it turned out that in addition to everything else, he had now also contracted measles. Doctors' home visits did not exist, so the child had to be brought daily to the clinic, and the whole procedure, with the queue for the number, taking my young cousins to school and then returning to wait again at the clinic, was repeated day after day. Each time it took the whole morning. Of course little Edna also fell ill with the measles, but hers was only a mild case. At last Peter recovered, and we could think of settling somewhere to begin our new life.

While I was staying in Jaffa, Otto remained in the village, where he worked. He rented a room in the house of an elderly widow in return for doing her chores in the yard and garden. Thus he not only labored all day in the sun with his *turyiah*, but had to do more hard work for the widow every evening till dark. At weekends he came to Jaffa with a bag of tomatoes or cucumbers, which his farmer employers let him have for a discount. We both felt pangs of conscience for inconveniencing my poor aunt and her family. The four adults and three children slept in the two tiny rooms, one of which did not even have a window.

CHAPTER THIRTY-THREE

In the Village

After several weeks, in the middle of July, Otto came with the good news that there would be accommodation for us. The village committee had erected six wooden prefab units for rent to the *olim*. And so we took our little Peter, who by then was healthy again, and traveled to Shaar Chefer near Netanya.

The six new wooden huts stood on a hill. Each contained four one-room units, and two families shared a tiny shower room and toilet. There was no electricity and no road. The nearest grocery was two kilometers away, which made shopping a very strenuous enterprise. I had to drag the pram with little Peter through the deep sand, and the way back, weighted down with the groceries, was even harder.

Our neighbors were Pavel; Eva, who was five months pregnant; and Eva's mother. We shared the shower with them as well as the huge tin pot and oil-burner on which we heated water for washing and laundry. There was no boiler. In summer we drank tepid water; in winter we took cold showers. Together we bought a secondhand icebox. The iceman came three times a week with blocks of ice wrapped in sacks. With a big screwdriver and hammer, he would chop off half a block for those who could afford a larger icebox or one third of the block for the likes of us. We wrapped it in two layers of sacking to make it last. One had to open the box as little as possible, so that the ice would not melt before the next purchase.

Our small unit contained one room and a cubicle with a little sink with a fake-marble work top on each side. The dishes and provisions were stored on two shelves underneath it, concealed by a curtain. I did my cooking on two oil cookers. The fuel was called *naft*, and it was sold from a barrel by a man who came once a week on a horse-drawn cart. The wick of the burners had to be changed frequently, because it smoked and blackened the pots.

But even here in Israel, like in postwar Prague, food was scarce. Not only did we have very little money, but it was the time of *tzena* (austerity). It was barely a year after Israel's perilous War of Independence, and the country was in the process of absorbing hundreds of thousands of newcomers. Thus its reserves were sorely depleted. There were even ration cards for certain items. Yet since the village's livelihood was mainly chicken farming, the birds that could not be marketed due to a broken wing or other damage were plentiful and cheap. Also there was no scarcity of eggs, either cracked or misshapen.

We lived hand to mouth. Every morning Otto went with his *turyiah* to the village depot to be hired as laborer for the day. In the late afternoon, Otto brought his wages, with which we paid the next day's expenses, the *naft*, the ice, and the cinema ticket for the weekend film that was screened outdoors on the wall of the local culture hall.

I also tried to earn some money. I offered my services as a seamstress to the farmers' wives, to shorten or lengthen their dresses or to patch the elbows or knees of their husbands' trousers and shirts. There wasn't much demand, but from time to time, I did get some work.

In the meantime we received notice that our crate had arrived in Haifa port and that we should fetch it soon; otherwise we would have to pay a storage fee. The cost of the freight itself was a few hundred pounds.

Fortunately there was Aunt Ella, Otto's mother's sister in London. Hers had been a wealthy family who lived in a luxurious villa in Liberec in the north of Czechoslovakia. She and her husband managed to flee just a few hours before the arrival of the occupying Nazis. They left everything behind and escaped to London, where their son was studying. The British did not give them a work permit, and during the whole war Aunt and Uncle made a meager living, he by threading beads, and she by sewing and crocheting dresses for Jewish ladies.

When Aunt learned that we had to pay the freight for our crate, she promptly sold her fur coat and sent the money. She was that kind of person: warmhearted, down-to-earth, practical. We heard the story of the fur coat many years later, not from her but from a mutual friend.

After a few months in the village, those of the *olim* who were considered suitable by the village committee were offered memberships in the Cooperative. They invited Otto for a discussion and told him that for one thousand pounds we would be given a two-room house, a small henhouse, and an adjacent plot of three dunams (a dunam is a ten-by-one-hundred-meter area of land) for growing vegetables.

Now was the time to turn to Otto's American uncle, who had promised financial help. Otto was a careful planner; he would never have taken the risk of emigrating with a wife and child with just with the paltry seven and a half pounds we were allowed, and without any sort of financial backing. Before our emigration he had contacted Otto Strass, who owed the Kraus family quite a large amount of money, borrowed before his emigration, and asked him for a loan. This had to be done secretly by word of mouth, not, God forbid, by mail, which the Communist censors might read. Only when Otto was assured of the forthcoming help did he start planning our Aliyah.

The American uncle promised the money, and Otto accepted on condition that it would not be a gift but a loan, which we would repay.

The loan never materialized.

The next letter from America brought the sad news that Uncle Strass had died. A tumor had been discovered on his brain, and he died on the operating table. He was only in his early forties. His wife, Dita, and two young daughters were now left without support, and we were without the hope of a loan.

Otto decided to use his farming skills to start growing vegetables himself. We rented three dunams and a mule to plow the field, which had lain barren for several years. Moishe the mule was owned by the Cooperative, and as the saying goes, he was stubborn. He declined to enter his stable. Taking him out was no problem, but he just refused to go back in.

In the end Otto found the solution; he made him walk in reverse, tail first. I had to lead Moishe, holding the reins near his head, and when we reached the end of the field, make him do a U-turn for the next furrow. One time, I must have somehow been on the wrong side of the animal, because suddenly his hoof landed on my foot. I cried out, which made him freeze. No matter how much I hit him, he remained standing on my foot. Only when Otto overcame his laughing fit did he come to my rescue. Fortunately, the soil was soft enough for my foot to sink in and there was only little damage.

As Otto considered himself a professional agriculturist, he decided not to grow what everybody else did, such as cucumbers, onions, and peppers. Celery was a rare plant then and fetched a good price, and so did cauliflower and lettuce.

Every day in the late afternoon, when Otto returned with his *turyiah* from hoeing the orchards, we would go to our field. It was hard work. While little Peter played with some toy at the edge of the field, we carried the heavy pipes with the sprinklers from place to place, each time uncoupling the sections and fixing them together again a few rows farther on. We also bought a few sacks of chicken manure and spread it out with shovels. The sprinklers had to be turned on after sundown to save water from evaporation in the heat of the day, and one of us had to return to the field later at night to turn them off. Automatic irrigation was as yet unknown.

The climate in Israel is favorable, and the yield was quite good. The price of the produce varied. Sometimes it went up; other times it sank below cost. At the end of the year the calculation showed that although we hadn't lost, the balance was merely the acquisition of the pipes. No debt but also no profit.

What now? Saving the one thousand pounds needed to settle in the village became unrealistic. Staying as farm laborers was not an option. After a whole year in Israel, we had made no progress.

Ever since our arrival at Haifa, various *shlichim* (emissaries) had come to the tent to attract new members for their kibbutzim. One of them, David, had urged us to come and see his kibbutz. It had been founded many years before by pioneers from Czechoslovakia, Romania, and Poland. He continued to visit us in the village, and every time, he repeated his invitation. This time we went with him.

The kibbutz was a pleasant place with lawns, much greenery, attractive kindergartens, and a communal dining hall. For supper there was bread, margarine, olives, tomatoes, cucumbers, sardines, jam, and tea. But to top it all, each person got a bowl of fresh sour cream.

That did it! I fell in love with the cream, and we moved to the kibbutz as prospective future members.

But that is already the next story.

CHAPTER THIRTY-FOUR

Givat Chaim

was looking forward to moving to the kibbutz. We had a number of friends there, some of whom had come on the same ship with us, some of whom had been members of the Zionist movement where Otto was active before the war. I was hoping that life in the kibbutz would be easier than in the village.

Kibbutz Givat Chaim is one of the oldest established kibbutzim in Israel (*kibbutz*—singular; *kibbutzim*—plural), founded by Zionist pioneers in 1933. Givat Chaim was named after Chaim Arlosoroff, one of the early leaders of the Zionist movement. It is located in the Hefer Valley in central Israel, near the town of Hadera. The kibbutz movement was divided into several left-oriented streams, from the extreme to the more moderate, but the basic social structures were similar. The main tenet of the movement was equality of all its members. Property was owned by the collective, and the motto was *everyone contributes according to his ability and receives according to his needs.* This ideal was, of course, never quite achieved, even with the best of intentions; some members were always more equal than others.

So, for example, when our small family joined the kibbutz, we were given the most unattractive work, which the old-timers hated to do. I was put to washing dishes in the kitchen—by hand, of course, as the kibbutz was not yet able to afford a dishwashing machine. My hands were immersed in the soapy water for hours until they were sickly white and furrowed like the underside of a mushroom. Moreover, the number of eaters exceeded the number of plates, spoons, forks, and knives, and I was constantly rushed to work faster, so the *chaverim*[9] needn't wait for a clean plate to start eating.

Otto became a kitchen boy, who hauled the large heavy pots and milk cans, although he'd asked for work in the fields, telling them of his two years' apprenticeship on the farms in Czechoslovakia. But the principle of the *sadran avoda* (the person whose task was to appoint the *chaverim* to the work areas) was to assign you to the places that were short of hands and not where you, the greenhorn, wished to work. The rationale behind this absurd and shortsighted policy was: *We did our stint of the disgusting kitchen and the sanitation chores; now it's your turn.* It drove away dozens of prospective new members.

David, our new friend, who was very pleased that at last he had managed to lure us to the kibbutz, took us around, showed us the cowshed with its dozens of cows—which, every year, received Israel's first prize in milk production—the ducks, geese, and chickens in their modern coops, the orange grove, the banana orchard, the vineyard. We visited the clinic and sickrooms, the children's houses with their well-equipped playgrounds, the laundry, the communal dining room, the culture hall with its library and music room, and the bakery, which baked fresh bread for the members every day. There was also a cobbler who repaired all the shoes, and a clothes store, where the laundered clothes were sorted, mended, and ironed, and where a seamstress even sewed new dresses for the *chaverot*.

Otto and I were duly impressed, but what I wanted to see most was the room where we would live. The old-timers, who had initially lived in tents and later in makeshift cabins, were now already established in solid semidetached rows of houses. Each family had a single room with a porch, but since the children slept

---

9   A kibbutz member was called a *chaver or chavera*, meaning "friend" or "member." Plural forms are *chaverim* and *chaverot*.

in dormitories, one room was sufficient for a couple. The kibbutz had recently erected several rows of wooden huts, with rooms of about fourteen square meters per unit and a lawn at the front. Our double bed, a small coffee table, and two chairs were all we could squeeze into the room. The rest of our furniture, sent in the container all the way from Prague, was gladly accepted by various neighbors. In this way, our friend Paťa got the green sofa, one of the three pieces saved from my childhood home. It was very useful to him and his lady friends— good-looking Paťa was now single again, having divorced Jana back in Prague. The green sofa would move to other locations but would eventually return to my possession.

For the first few days, we did not have to work. It was necessary to acquaint our little boy, Peter, with the new environment. Children in the kibbutz lived in separate homes, not with their parents. For security reasons, the children's houses stood in a cluster in the center of the settlement.

Peter was two and a half years old and spoke Czech. Now he had to live with children whose language he didn't know, with a nurse who didn't understand him. We took him to the toddlers' home to get acquainted with the nurse and the other children. Nurse Zipora welcomed us warmly but insisted that we give the boy a new name, because Peter was not Hebrew and the children would not be able to pronounce it. She urged us to decide fast, so that she could tell the children what to call the new boy. Otto and I pondered over it in the evening and decided to call him Shimon. There was certain logic in the choice. Shimon of the Bible was named Peter after his baptism. We just reversed the procedure; from Peter, the Christian, he became Shimon, the Jew. Besides, I liked the name.

I stayed with Shimon in the toddlers' home every morning, until he gradually agreed to remain there alone. In the evening after a shower, he was put in his cot, like the other five toddlers. I held his hand until he fell asleep, and then I left, as did all the other parents. Kibbutz children were used to it, and they said good night and fell asleep. However, we were inexperienced parents; we didn't realize what it means for a small child to lose his language and his name, or to sleep away from his parents, among strange children.

Shimon bit the other kids, and the parents complained, showing us the imprint of Shimon's teeth on the arms of their offspring. Of course he bit them, what could he do? They spoke to him in a language he did not understand, and when he spoke, they stared at him uncomprehendingly. And Mummy and Daddy were gone, too! I still fear that the damage we involuntarily caused our eldest child might have played a role in his later mental problems, despite the doctors' reassurances that it wouldn't have; the pangs of sorrow and pain for Shimon's unhappy life are ever-present.

It took a while until he started communicating in Hebrew and stopped biting. He was two and a half and had been quite verbal in his native Czech. He continued calling me Mámo, until one day when he was already about five, he asked me, "Why do I call you Mámo when all the children call their mothers Imma?" He had completely forgotten his Czech. From that day I was also Imma.

There was something in the structure of the kibbutz that remained an enigma for me. Everybody was equal, true, but there were still differences in status. Some members thrived on the reputation they had acquired long ago. Nachum, for example, was considered an outstanding worker—a quality most highly valued—but I saw him lingering over his breakfast longer than anybody and having long talks with the electrician or the boiler-room manager, instead of being at work. Some people enjoyed privileges or special considerations that I did not understand.

Also I wasn't sure if the kitchen manager was my boss. Did she have the right to order me about, or did I have the right to say no? For the first year all newcomers were not full members, only candidates. Would they accept me when our membership was discussed by the general assembly? Perhaps I'd do something wrong, and they might not vote us in?

I was confused and did not feel at home. Often I had attacks of migraine and upset stomach. On the one hand, there was freedom—no household to take care of, no shopping or laundry—but I also could not relax, because I sensed that I was constantly under observation. As a matter of fact, the feeling that this was only some provisional and impermanent episode remained with me throughout the seven years we lived on the kibbutz. I never unpacked all my suitcases, symbolically and literally.

Although the children were separated from their parents most of the day, they were still the most cherished and pampered treasure of the kibbutz. There were the babies' and the toddlers' homes and the kindergartens with the little chairs, beds, and plenty of toys, swings, slides, sand pits, and toy tractors. Each toddlers' home had two units for six children. There was a bedroom, a large play-cum-dining room, a shower room and cubicles with tiny toilets, a roofed porch, and an outdoor playground with a colorful wooden fence around. The lower school grades lived in dormitories with an attached classroom, while the older children went to the proper day school at the edge of the kibbutz. All the staff, including the teachers, were kibbutz members. When the kibbutz needed another nurse or teacher, it would choose one of its members to study the profession. Of course, a person who was not willing could refuse. On the other hand, if someone wanted to be sent to study something for which the kibbutz had no use, it would be vetoed by the general assembly.

There were, however, some exceptions. First of all, the kibbutz still upheld the principle of voluntary help for the good of the nation. They would send an experienced *chaver* to help establish a new kibbutz along the border or to coach street kids in the cities. If a member brought up some promising idea for a new source of income, it would often be supported by the general assembly.

Thus, for example, there was Honza Beck and his Bubatron. Honza was crazy about puppets. He was an adult with a child's soul. With his deft hands he carved and painted the heads and limbs of the puppets, invented an ingenious mechanism for their movements, and built a mobile folding stage. With a staff of helpers, he would tour the country with his shows of fairy tales.

The most beloved of his productions was a tale in which Buba Ziva (*buba* in Hebrew means "doll")—so named after the first baby born on Kibbutz Givat Chaim—played the main role. Buba Ziva also became the heroine of a children's hook, and Honza's Bubatron became extremely popular all over the country. He came from Czechoslovakia a long time before the war but could still speak Czech. Honza was a cheerful person, full of energy and crazy ideas. We became very good friends, and our friendship lasted until his early death.

The main income of Givat Chaim came from the canning factory Gat, later Pri-Gat. Initially it produced orange juice and jams, but it gradually branched out to pickling olives and canning all kinds of fruits and vegetables and salted peanuts. During the citrus season, huge trucks arrived daily and unloaded grapefruits and oranges. After the juice was extracted, the pulp was left outside, where it grew into veritable mountains and fermented, its scent permeating the entire kibbutz for the whole winter. It was the cattle's favorite food. By the way, the cows also loved music, and Franta, the cowshed manager, had the radio playing classical music all day long. It was the secret of their huge milk production.

Like most kibbutzim in Israel, Givat Chaim not only grew agricultural products on its lands; in winter it also tended vast state-owned fields of crops in the Negev.

Two or three *chaverim* would load a tractor and other agricultural equipment onto a truck and drive to the south, where they stayed for lengthy periods, sowing, cultivating, and harvesting. In those times the Israelis were still full of pioneering zeal, readily volunteering for tasks for the benefit of the nation and the new state. I liked this spirit, and when I was asked to donate my free Shabbat to pick grapes or other urgent chores, during what in Hebrew they so aptly call "the burning season," I never refused.

Another voluntary contribution of the kibbutzim to the welfare of the state was the absorption of the members of the so-called Youth Aliyah movement. The movement's aim was to take care of youths who had come to Israel without their parents, sometimes orphans, but also children of large families that had not yet settled down and were still in the tent camps.

The kibbutz offered them accommodation, an instructor, and a housemother to look after them. They were at school part-time, and they worked and learned Hebrew part-time. It was a good way to introduce the teenagers to life in their new country. The kibbutz, of course, did not do this without ulterior motives. It hoped that the youths would stay and become members. The state also contributed toward the cost for their upkeep.

Yet I really never could adapt to the notion that, in order to be a true female kibbutz member, one had to give up all cosmetics, high heels, and earrings. To look well-groomed was generally disapproved of. In the cities, kibbutz women would be recognizable by their unattractive clothes, with hair either short-cropped or gathered in a ponytail. When I went to visit my friend or uncle in Tel Aviv, I carried my high-heeled shoes in a bag, changed into them on the bus, put on lipstick and makeup, and hoped that I would not meet anybody from the kibbutz.

Kibbutzniks wouldn't use an umbrella in the pouring rain; it seemed to them an unnecessary luxury. They rejected the polite social behavior of their former homes; they were the new revolutionaries, who didn't dance the waltz or tango but rather the hora and at the table talked with their mouths full. Instead of wedding ceremonies, the *chaver* and *chavera* just declared before the general assembly that from now on they were a couple, and they moved into a room together. From that moment, they were considered married. This, however, changed after the state started establishing ministries with departments and officials demanding documents—in short, a bureaucracy. Then even kibbutzniks had to marry, with a rabbi, of course.

Our friend Arnošt once told us that, on his wedding day, he missed the bus when returning from work in town. The rabbi, however, was in a hurry and couldn't wait. Another kibbutznik replaced Arnošt and married the bride in his stead. The rabbi wasn't informed.

Otto and I were still *olim chadashim*, which means "new immigrants," and therefore entitled to a grant from the state, as well as Hebrew instruction for half a year. We knew nothing about the grant—the kibbutz received it on our behalf—but we did get Hebrew lessons. This was, however, a complicated issue.

The entire group of newcomers was supposed to receive instruction twice a week for two hours. First of all, there was no permanent classroom; each time we had to find a room with chairs and tables, but usually there was no blackboard. Our instructor was Ruben, also a former Czech. But as our group consisted of Polish, Hungarian, and Czech newcomers, there was no common language in which to explain the Hebrew words. Ruben tried Yiddish, which we Czechs didn't know, but could work out with our knowledge of German. The problem, however, was increased by the fact that Ruben didn't know Yiddish, either, only German. He nonchalantly overcame that obstacle by improvising and changing the gender of German nouns. For example *das Haus* (the house) became *der hois*, or *die Arbeit* (the work) became *dus orbeit*, and, as a last recourse, *der Bart* (the beard) was *dih bohrt*. Instead of the German personal pronoun *ich* (I), he would say *yach*. Another obstacle was that often Ruben was otherwise occupied and didn't appear for the lesson. Or some of the students would be drafted for urgent tasks that couldn't be delayed, and the lesson wouldn't take place for lack of participants. I doubt that in the end we got more than a dozen Hebrew lessons.

I picked up my Hebrew at work, in the kitchen, the dining room, the laundry, and the kindergarten. Many kibbutz members didn't know German, Czech, or English, so I just had to learn Hebrew. I remember once, when I used the exclamation *Ježíš Maria* (Jesus Mary), which was a common expletive for all Czech-speaking persons, no matter whether Jews or Christians, I was rebuked by a *chavera*: "We Jews do not say this in Israel."

A great help was our new friend Matti Megged. Matti was a salaried teacher, not a member of the kibbutz, and he and his wife, Hanna, lived in the hut next to ours. Matti was especially interested in our Czech group, because he had recently been in Prague—something to do with arms for Israel. We had to communicate in English and the little Hebrew we knew, with the rest in gestures. I remember Matti telling us something that happened to him in Prague. When he and an Israeli friend were traveling by tram one day, they commented on the big tits of a girl who was sitting in front of them. She kept her eyes lowered, but after a while, when she rose to get off, she remarked casually from the corner of her mouth, "Not only does she have big tits, but she also speaks Hebrew." Today this wouldn't surprise anyone, with the hundreds of thousands of Israeli tourists, but in 1948 no one knew Hebrew in Prague.

Matti spent many hours with Otto and me, asking lots of questions, wanting to know everything about our pasts.

He was an exception; most Israelis didn't want to listen to tales of the Holocaust. Much later I heard that Prime Minister David Ben-Gurion himself had said that any man who survived the camps must have been a *Kapo* or collaborator with the Nazis and any woman survivor a prostitute. No wonder, then, that the kibbutzniks dismissed the whole matter with a wave of their hands, saying, "Yes, yes, all right, but you don't know what we had to undergo here, with the war, the Arab armies, the Palmach."

An important feature of kibbutz life was culture. Every week two films were screened in the gym hall: one for adults, another for children. Several times a year every member got a ticket for a theater performance in Tel Aviv, Hadera, or Netanya. Transportation was provided. We sat on benches on the open back of a truck, wrapped in a warm coat or blanket over our Shabbat clothes. I remember the first Hebrew play I saw. It was called *He Walked in the Fields*, and I understood neither the plot nor the dialogue.

Once a year, a kind of book fair was set up in front of the culture hall and each of us could choose one book. Of course they were all in Hebrew. I always donated mine to one of the senior members. Often there were lectures about various subjects, and, above all, there were concerts. In those years, even top musicians and actors were willing to perform in the kibbutzim, usually for a small fee but also for free.

So, for instance, Frank Pelleg, the noted harpsichord player, gave a series of lectures about baroque music, playing samples on the piano. He would arrive in the afternoon, but, as the performance was in the evening, the *chaver* of the "culture department" would search for someone to host the artist. Pelleg was originally from Czechoslovakia, where his name was Pollak, so Otto and I readily volunteered, and we hit it off with him perfectly. We became real friends and later visited him and his wife, Inge, several times at his home on Vitkin Street in Haifa. I remember him telling us how he'd smuggled the musical score of the opera *Brundibár* to Israel.

During the forty years of the Communist regime in Czechoslovakia, Israel was considered a western imperialist enemy, and travel between the two countries was severely restricted. But Pelleg was invited to perform in Prague. There he met Eliška Klein, the sister of the well-known composer Gideon Klein, who perished in the Holocaust. She had in her possession the score of Hans Krása's children's opera *Brundibár*, which had been staged at Terezín, where it was a huge success, and everyone who was in the ghetto remembered and loved it. Eliška entrusted the manuscript to Pelleg, and he carried it to Israel in his suitcase. It was a risky undertaking, since the authorities forbade such "national treasures" to be taken out of the country. The customs people searched the foreigners' luggage very thoroughly, especially for propaganda material. Had he been caught, it would have certainly caused a serious diplomatic incident. But apparently the customs officials didn't have instructions to confiscate musical scores, so it stayed safely in Pelleg's suitcase.

In 1955 Pelleg entrusted the score to Otto, who, together with the music teacher Adi Nir, staged the opera with the kibbutz children. It was the first production of *Brundibár* in Israel. The performance took place in Givat Chaim when we commemorated ten years since the liberation of Terezín. It was attended by dozens of survivors from all over the country.

Not only did we have artists from "outside"[10] providing our entertainment, but we also had our own choir, conducted by the kibbutz music teacher, and even an amateur actors' group, led by Chanan, a theater aficionado. The choir rehearsed in the evenings after work, and the songs had to be ready for festivals such as Pesach and Chanuka.

---

10 People or places not part of the kibbutz were referred to as being from outside. Some *chaverim* had parents outside. The barber who came twice a month to trim our hair was from outside. Matti, the teacher, was from outside. Children from outside often came to vacation with their kibbutz relatives.

The principal festival to which the *chaverim* paid the most serious attention was, however, neither Pesach, Rosh Hashanah, nor Yom Kippur, but Purim. Purim is a lesser feast commemorating an event in ancient Persia. Queen Esther, who was Jewish, and her uncle Mordecai saved the Jews from being killed by the evil Haman. Purim is celebrated with masks and costumes, much like carnivals in other countries.

Preparations started many weeks in advance. Fancy costumes were sewn or constructed and decorated, and elaborate charades were prepared for the big event. Every year a theme was chosen in addition to the traditional Megilat Esther story. Once it was *the Twenties*; other times, *On the Beach* or *At the Zoo*. One memorable charade was *Pre–World War I Fashions*.

Our friend Paťa was the producer, and we, the Czech group with a few of our Hungarian and Polish colleagues, acted as figures in the charade. We rehearsed in the communal shower room late in the evening, having first put our children to bed. Everyone came up with new funny characters, and we laughed nonstop.

The scene was a public park with a nanny pushing a cardboard pram, behind which crouched chaver Efraim with a baby cap and a pacifier. There was an elderly couple, he with a top hat leaning on a walking stick, she wearing a huge hat decorated with a whole garden of flowers. Eva and Peter wore children's shorts and played ball. A policeman swung a baton, and a young couple petted on a bench. It looked like a photo of bygone days.

There were prizes for the best costumes. One year the winner was our plumber. He had constructed a whole mock flushing toilet, with the water tank, including the pulling chain, on his back, and the toilet seat like an apron in front.

None of the kibbutz members were religious; no one wore a kippa. The food cooked in both kitchens—the children's and the adults'—was not kosher. In the first years, when there was still a shortage of food, our kibbutz even raised pigs for meat. The pigsty was hidden behind the cowshed and the pigs prospered from the leftovers from both kitchens. The pigs were a beloved attraction of the kindergarten children. Some of the cooks were *chaverot* from Czechoslovakia and Hungary and knew how to make a proper goulash. Yet a few members, who came from Jewish traditional families in Poland or Romania, were unable to overcome their distaste for pork and asked for vegetarian dishes.

All the Jewish feasts were celebrated. At Pesach there was a Seder meal in the huge gym hall, all decorated with garlands and flowers. Our ideologue, Chaver Segal, rewrote and modernized the Haggadah, which he turned into a celebration of spring and freedom, even though Israel's exodus from Egypt was mentioned in passing. But we drank the proscribed four glasses of wine, and our choir, of which I was an enthusiastic member, sang the traditional songs. There were always many guests, mostly close relatives of the kibbutz members, and we all felt uplifted by the truly wonderful evening.

There was another festival called Chag Ha'mayim, meaning "in praise of water." I think it might have been an ancient tradition of prayers for rain, which the kibbutz revived. It took place outdoors in the fields in late summer. The audience sat on bales of straw. The young girls, in colorful wide-skirted dresses, and the boys, in flowing shirts, danced merrily on the stubble, and the highlight of the feast was a sudden stream of water shooting up high into the air. It was a marvelous, happy celebration. I wonder if there are still such feasts in the kibbutzim today.

CHAPTER THIRTY-FIVE

My Career as a Cobbler

My dishwashing stint did not last very long. In the kibbutz it was understood that members would work wherever they were placed; the only exceptions were women in advanced stages of pregnancy, or convalescents.

When I was pregnant with our daughter, Michaela, I was allowed to work in the sewing workshop as a helper to the seamstress, which was considered "light" work. Sara, the dressmaker, was a thin, pale woman with a sulky expression, who on principle was opposed to saying a good word about anybody and would never praise my work. I could sew the straightest seam from beginning to end, yet the maximal sign of satisfaction was a wordless nod while she handed me the next garment.

If Sara was thin, her husband was even thinner. His chest looked like the inside of a soup plate, and the knees that protruded under his floppy khaki shorts were the thickest part of his legs. In time the two of them produced a baby boy with limbs like toothpicks.

The husband used to come to the sewing workshop to discuss some important topic with his wife In his quiet monotonous voice, such as who would fetch the milk and bread for their afternoon tea from the dining room and how many slices they would need. Sometimes he would return to say that perhaps he should bring only four slices instead of five.

Still, I loved working in the sewing workshop, because I was fond of clothes, and being close to the source enabled me to have the first pick of the material when the rolls of fabric were delivered. Women in the kibbutz were allocated one work outfit per year and a Shabbat dress every other year. I still remember the sky-blue dress that was meant for work but was so pretty that I wore it on Shabbat, although it was made of the cheapest material. At least two *chaverot* imitated it after me.

After my daughter was born, I was allowed to continue in the sewing room for several weeks longer. All the babies were kept in the infants' home, and the mothers came from their workplaces to nurse them every few hours. It was therefore convenient to work in the kibbutz and not in the fields or orchards. But after my baby was weaned, I was again considered an able-bodied laborer who didn't need to be coddled by light work.

After supper I was called before the "labor officer." Every year a kibbutz member was obliged to become the "labor officer," whose job it was to appoint workers to the various sectors: a hated but necessary task. As the year progressed, the "officer" usually became more unpleasant and aggressive. He was constantly short of people, as demand always exceeded supply. Here, someone fell ill and had to be replaced; there, another worked on Shabbat and had to be given a free day during the week; a third one had to go to Haifa to visit a sick relative.

For some disagreeable jobs there were just no takers, so they had to be foisted on the newcomers. The new aspirant members were more easily persuaded to wash dishes or mop the dining-room floor after they had been told that all the old-timers had done these jobs when they first came to the kibbutz. Of course everyone had to contribute, even if it was not in his or her line. A green new-comer just couldn't counter such a morally charged demand.

As I was already a full member who had passed her dishwashing phase, Ezra, the labor officer, offered me more appealing jobs. I could become a helper to one of the kindergarten teachers or an assistant to the cook, while another person was needed in the vineyard to pack the grapes into crates. I shook my head.

"I would like to do something with my hands, some kind of handicraft. I am good with my hands, I can sew quite well—"

"No, no, those jobs are only for the disabled. You are young and strong."

We parted without a solution.

For the next few days I was sent all over the place to substitute for various absent workers. I didn't like any of those jobs. Soon it was my turn to do night-time guard duty. Every female member was taken off her regular work once or twice a year for two weeks. The males did night-time guard stints with a weapon on the kibbutz periphery. The children slept in the children's homes, and it was necessary to listen for children crying. In winter we had to make sure the children were warmly covered and hadn't kicked off their blankets. When children cried, we'd give them drinks and comfort them until they fell asleep again. If a child cried for a long time, we would wake up the mother. We knew every child, and of course also where their parents lived.

I liked night duty, because when I finished folding all the diapers from the huge baskets in each of the nurseries I would sit on one of the porches, where I could hear the sounds from the other buildings and knit or read. During my stint the year before, I had produced birthday presents for our little son, a picture lotto game made from cardboard, and some stuffed animals. The best part of the night watch was at dawn. From every room emerged the sleepy-eyed *chaverim* in their overalls and khaki hats[11] on their way to work, while

---

11 The most popular head covering in Israel used to be a khaki cloth hat, which was practical not only as protection against the hot sun but also to wipe the perspiration from one's face or as a receptacle for the oranges or nuts one gathered under the trees. It was called a *kova tembel. Kova* in Hebrew is a hat and *tembel* is a fool. And, indeed, the person with the hat pulled low over the forehead looked somewhat foolish. The iconic drawing of "little Srulik" in khaki shorts and the *kova tembel* became a kind of symbol of Israeliness . . . of pioneering, volunteering . . . salt of the earth.

lucky me was looking forward to a sweet sleep in my bed. At noon I got up, showered, went to the dining room for lunch, and then had free time until it was time to fetch little Shimon. I loved it.

But two weeks later it was over, and I had to decide on a permanent workplace.

Ezra seemed to have relented. He now offered me a job at the barrel-making plant. Wasn't it a craft requiring skill, which I had demanded? Here was work with timber, fresh-smelling wood—certainly I would enjoy that?

It sounded good. I knew the workshop where the finished barrels were stacked along its outer wall, the virgin chestnut planks lying in neat rows inside. Wood is one of my favorite materials, and I looked forward to handling it and producing such useful objects as barrels. The principal customer for them was our canning factory, which needed them for pickling olives.

Ezra accompanied me personally and told Lova, the barrel boss, "Here's the new worker you asked for."

Lova looked me over doubtfully but seemed not disinclined to give me a try. The work I was supposed to do did not require much physical strength or prior knowledge. He led me to a machine, a kind of tall metal frame with a slot and something like a press. He pushed a lever and two buttons, and the thing started rumbling. Now he demonstrated what I must do: pick up a narrow board from a pile of cut-to-size pieces and shove it into the slot. In went a straight plank and out came a bent one, much like a banana or a cradle. It was really not complicated or difficult to learn. They watched me put two or three planks through the press, Lova nodded, and the two men walked away.

And so I worked at it for hour after hour. At the far end of the workshop were other machines attended by a handful of *chaverim*, but the noise was so great that conversation was impossible. I bent down, picked up a plank, pushed it into the slot, went around to the other side to remove it, placed it on the pile—one layer facing right, the next one left—went back again to the front, bent, picked up another piece, shoved it into the machine, on and on and on without pause. The day seemed interminable; time did not pass. I was getting dumber and number by the hour. At long last it was over; the machines were turned off, and I could go home.

But I had made up my mind. Despite the friendly material, despite Lova's satisfaction with the output of my first day, I was determined not to remain a barrel maker.

I have to pause here and provide some explanation about the status of women in the kibbutz. The basic philosophy of the whole kibbutz movement was the absolute equality of its members. Property was owned by all: each member had equal rights and responsibilities. Managing positions such as treasurer or kibbutz secretary were filled by rotation. No person was worthier than any other, be they field laborers or teachers, plumbers or accountants.

Yet beneath this enlightened liberal ideology remained the age-old conviction of the male of the species: that he was master of the universe, and despite his benign indulgence toward the female, he was still her superior.

For example, no woman was a truck driver, a job that enabled the men to save some money for their private use. Truck drivers got an allowance for food on their long hauling trips but took sandwiches from the dining hall and spent the money on sweets for their children. Naturally they never admitted the real reason for their monopoly, claiming that it would be above a woman's endurance to drive a truck.

None of the *chaverot* could travel abroad like Lova, who went to Italy every year to personally select the timber for the barrels. In the kitchen, however, all the staff were women, except, of course, for the "kitchen boy," who lugged the milk cans and heaved bucketfuls of peeled potatoes into the huge vats.

I resented this macho attitude. I felt that the labor officer was only waiting for me to give up and admit that these male tasks were too much for me. I returned to him saying that the deadening labor at the wood-bending machine was not to my taste, and, as I considered myself a reasonably intelligent person, such robot-like work would turn me into a cretin. He nodded condescendingly. "I knew it," he said, "but you were so eager to do a man's job."

"I can do some of the men's jobs," I reminded him.

I was referring to my stint in our canning factory, where I'd sat at a long table along with other *chaverot*, filling tins with grapefruit segments. Once, on a night shift, the man who'd been operating the tin-capping machine had uttered a scream and jumped backward. His finger had been caught in the machine. He had to be taken to hospital. What now? The whole shift would be lost. There was no one to fill his place on such short notice. I offered myself as a substitute. I had watched David at work, and it looked rather simple. The cans would come sliding along a winding chute. He picked the nearest one with his left hand, and, with his right hand, he reached for a lid from the stack and put it on top of the can, then pressed a pedal. The machine clamped the lid on, and the closed can rolled on to a moving belt, where it was packed by the women into cardboard boxes.

The foreman was doubtful: Should he allow a woman to operate such a sophisticated contraption? He dragged the labor officer from his bed, not daring to decide on his own. They conferred together, glancing in my direction. At last the foreman approached me and said, "Would you really try? It is dangerous; you saw yourself what happened to David."

They stood with bated breath, one on each side of me, and watched me perform the perilous feat, which no woman had ever been allowed to do. It was child's play; one only had to be on guard to protect the fingers. Soon I developed a rhythm, and the shift could go on. In the end, the usual quota was filled, and I felt elated to have pierced the balloon of their male self-righteousness.

"There just isn't a vacancy in any of the workshops at present," Ezra told me, having consulted his list. "The only job is in the cobbler's workshop. But as you are not a skilled cobbler"—he looked up at me and grinned—"you couldn't possibly fit in."

"I might become an apprentice and learn cobbling on the job," I ventured.

Ezra shook his head. "You probably don't know Yaacov the cobbler. Nobody would want to work under him."

I did know Yaacov; his youngest boy and ours were the same age and lived together in the same kindergarten. I saw him every evening when we were showering our children and putting them to bed. He didn't look frightening to me. "If Yaacov doesn't object," I said, "I'm ready to try."

The next day I started my career in the shoe-repair shop.

The cobbler's workshop was located in a spacious low building, well ventilated by large windows on all four sides. It was shaded by eucalyptus trees, which had been planted when the kibbutz was still young. Around the inside walls ran shelves on which lay in disarray shoes of all sizes, colors, and ages, together with the shoemaker's lasts (wooden foot-shaped models used to produce shoes). There was also a small locked room where Yaacov kept the leather hides, the uppers, stocks of needles, twine, and knives. The greater part of the storeroom was filled with discarded old shoes, all those that in the course of years had been declared unmendable. There were also boxes with pairs of shoes made to measure by Yaacov's own hand, which had been rejected by the people for whom they had been created. He didn't throw them away, in the hope that one day they might fit somebody else. They were Yaacov's skeletons in the cupboard, and he tried to forget their existence.

As with the women's dresses, every member was entitled to one pair of sandals a year and one pair of Shabbat shoes every third year. Work shoes were more readily available, and if you brought your worn-out ones, you could obtain a new pair. Of course the discarded shoes were never thrown out, but added to the pile in the storeroom, and when that became filled to capacity, a new mound was created in a corner of the main room.

Traditionally, Yaacov and his helper, Mimon—of whom more later—produced all the shoes themselves. When I joined the workshop, the growing number of kibbutz members had already made it impossible to catch up with the demand for shoes. So a decision was reached by the general assembly, which convened every Shabbat evening, to buy the children's footwear and the work shoes at the central kibbutz supply store in Tel Aviv.

Of course, this obliged Yaacov to travel to Tel Aviv at least once a week. He received the usual allowance to cover the fare and a meal in town. Poor Yaacov; he must have stayed very hungry, because as we were putting our children to bed in the evening, I enviously eyed the sweets he brought his little son after a day in Tel Aviv.

For the *chaverim* and especially for the *chaverot*, Yaacov sewed quality shoes. The client would sit on the only normal-height chair in the workshop, place his foot on a sheet of paper, and Yaacov would trace its outline with a pencil, bunions and crooked toes included. Then he would measure the instep and arch with a tailor's tape, write them on the paper in thick characters of his very own hieroglyphs, adding the name—first name only—and also the customer's wishes as to color and type of leather.

With the men the thing was easy; they could have the moccasin style or the classic shoe with shoelaces, colors either black or brown. The women were choosier.

"I want the same model as you made for Miriam, only with a higher heel and not in white, but in green. You know, not dark green, but a light shade to go with my new Shabbat dress."

Yaacov, tight-lipped, would nod and add a scrawl on the paper.

A week later the *chavera* would appear to fetch her new shoes, but Yaacov would send her away: "Perhaps next week—ask me on Thursday."

Thursday came and went, another week passed, and another. Five or six weeks later, the shoes were ready, with high heels, all shiny and new in their box. Only instead of green, they were white.

"But I asked you to make me green ones," wailed the woman.

"What are you saying? I wrote it down here. See? Exactly what you wanted. White like Miriam's."

The *chavera* had one of two options. Either she took the white pair or she left it in the cobbler's shop and waited for her next turn two or three years later.

A third possibility was out of the question. It was well-known on the kibbutz that Yaacov suffered from a heart condition, and no one dared to make him lose his temper, which might lead to hypertension and, God forbid, a heart attack or worse.

Sometimes it wasn't the color but the size that was wrong. Yaacov might have written Chaim on the footprint paper, but there were three Chaims on our kibbutz, and the foot of the tallest one was, of course, two or three sizes larger than that of the short Chaim. The small one could perhaps take the large shoes and stuff newspaper into the toes, but tall Chaim could never wear the small shoes of short Chaim.

And so the orphaned, unclaimed shoes added to Yaacov's skeletons in the cupboard, gathering dust in the locked storeroom. From time to time he managed to palm off a pair on some indifferent member who was oblivious to changing fashions. None of us dared to mention the rejects in front of Yaacov.

I started my first day in the shoe-repair shop full of goodwill and eagerness to learn the trade and to make myself useful. I got an enormous blue apron, took my place on the low stool at the worktable, and put a thick wooden slab on my lap. A heavy cast-iron tripod was placed on the slab. All the hammering was done on the tripod, and in the first few weeks my thighs were blue, violet, and yellow. After some time I got used to the ache and didn't mind it any longer.

I was given the special cobbler's hammer with a wide blunt end and a forked front, which could be inserted under bent nails to pull them out. Yaacov gave me an old sandal and told me to replace the heel.

"The heel is built of layers; you insert the screwdriver between them and peel away layer after layer until you reach the one that isn't worn down. You make a paper pattern of its size, copy it onto a piece of leather, and cut out the new heel. You nail it on with these medium nails, taking care not to leave their sharp end sticking out on the inside."

How I loved it! Mending old things and making them useful again is one of my life passions. Sandal after sandal, heel after heel, I repaired away and didn't even feel the passing of time. The foot odor that emanated from the sandals didn't put me off. Only one thing kept bothering me: What if I did something wrong, made some blunder, or asked a silly question that might make Yaacov angry and raise his blood pressure? I tried to behave with restraint, meek as a lamb, which is not in my nature, but I always said yes and watched his face for any sign of displeasure.

I had good reason to be wary. I had seen with my own eyes the frightening scene when Baruch, one of the most respected old-timers on the kibbutz, demanded new Shabbat shoes a year ahead of his turn. Baruch was a heavy, large man with an awkward lopsided gait, and his shoes simply did not last the required term. He held them in his large hands, and there was no question that they had ended their life.

"This year you are not entitled to new shoes" was Yaacov's verdict.

"But I cannot wear these any longer," implored Baruch.

"I said you are not going to get another pair this year. Come back next year. And that's final."

Any other *chaver* would have given up and perhaps worn his sandals during the cold winter months or his work boots on Shabbat. But Baruch was a stubborn person. He didn't relent but continued to explain in his slow, even voice that, in spite of the rules, he must get a new pair of shoes, though it was against the principle of equal rights. . . .

Yaacov didn't answer. We fell silent, stopped hammering, and stared at him. He puffed up his chest, his face became red, his veins stood out on his forehead, and it looked as if at any moment he would succumb to an apoplectic seizure.

When Baruch saw what he had caused, he stopped midsentence and started retreating backward to the door like a crab. He was soon gone altogether, with the ruins of his old shoes still in his hands. Yaacov's face gradually regained its normal color, and after a while he was able to resume his work.

I had a terrible feeling that Yaacov wouldn't survive many more incidents like this.

Despite this, I had devised a plan to reorganize the shoe-repair shop and make it function according to the highly valued principle of equal rights. Yaacov's system was not a system but rather chaos: When a *chaver* or *chavera* brought their shoes to be mended, they would be deposited next to his stool, where they formed a smelly mound. He then took the top pair, which might have arrived the same day, mended it, and perhaps the next one, too. Meanwhile, another pair had arrived, so that the top ones were always done first, while those on the bottom stayed forever unmended. When the owner came to fetch his boots, they were still deep under the pile, sometimes for weeks.

Yaacov would shrug his shoulders.

"You can see yourself how much work we have; your turn hasn't come up yet."

Most people accepted the answer, afraid to rouse Yaacov's ill humor. Some, however, grew desperate because they had no spare boots to wear to work. For them Yaacov had the perfect solution: he would reach behind him and hand over another repaired pair from the shelf. Those, of course, belonged to somebody else. When the owner came to claim them, Yaacov would declare the missing boots unmendable—they just had to be thrown away—or he might explain that they were under the pile somewhere, waiting to be repaired.

I realized that I would have to proceed very cautiously, perhaps even secretly, to introduce order into the shoe-repair shop.

On a day when Yaacov was in Tel Aviv, I removed a few pairs from the top of the heap next to his stool and placed them in a row on the shelf in the order of their arrival.

I awaited Yaacov's reaction with trepidation the next morning. Nothing happened; there was no comment. Perhaps Yaacov was even glad that the heap had miraculously decreased. And so each week when he was away, I would arrange the incoming shoes, one behind the other, and slowly the system became established. Yaacov seemed relieved that he was rid of the complaints of his fellow kibbutzniks. With time they ceased to turn to him, and gradually I became the go-between. Yaacov could work away in his corner, cutting out the soles and heels from the large leather hides, and didn't have to listen to the talk around the worktable. He even let me sweep the floor but only around the clutter, of course, so as not to disturb the accumulated junk. After a few weeks the place looked friendlier, somehow brighter, and the people who arrived with worried expressions on their faces left with smiles.

Working in the shoe-repair shop had one great advantage for me. I am a late riser, and getting up at dawn at five thirty, especially in winter in the dark, is sheer torment for me. People who work in the kitchen, in the children's homes or with the farm animals, could not be late to work. But the shoes were neither hungry nor did they cry for me, and so it didn't matter if I started work at half past seven or at eight. I often remained alone at the end of the workday to complete my eight and a half hours. I could tell that Yaacov didn't approve, but he tolerated it in silence. The weeks passed, and I felt more and more settled. Yaacov taught me to repair other things besides heels. He was a master shoemaker, having learned the craft when he was a young man back in his native Hungary.

Not so his assistant, my colleague Mimon, whom Yaacov insisted on addressing as Maimon. Mimon was an outsider—that is, he was not a member of the kibbutz but a paid employee. This was an exception, because originally the kibbutz was entirely self-sufficient. Everything was produced by the members themselves. We grew our own vegetables and fruit, raised chickens and ducks and cattle, baked our bread, built the houses, produced the furniture, ran a school for the kibbutz children, and even had a drama circle and choir to provide our entertainment.

Mimon was not a cobbler by profession. He was one of those people with golden hands who can do anything. He only had to look at a tool or machine to know immediately how it worked; he could take it apart and put together again without a problem. He was tall and lean, with tough muscles, and his neck seemed as if someone had pulled it upward; he had a huge Adam's apple sliding up and down its whole length. He was from Morocco and was unable to pronounce *sh*.

"Salom, Sosana," he greeted the kindergarten teacher, "your soes are finised, they're on the self."

Mimon had a wife and child, but he rarely mentioned them in conversation. In the three years the two of us sat at the worktable on the low stools at right angles from each other, six days a week, eight and a half hours daily, he talked about many things: about his numerous brothers, his old home, or his army service. In passing he mentioned, "We have a new baby."

"I know," I said, "you already told me some time ago."

"That was the one before," he corrected me, "the boy. Now there is a girl again."

"*Mazel tov!* So now you have three."

"Thanks. No, now we have four."

In the beginning Mimon used to come to the kibbutz by bus. But as soon as he earned a few lira, he bought an old motorcycle. The trouble was that the motorcycle used to break down in the middle of his journey, and Mimon would arrive at work pushing his heavy vehicle, panting and sweating. He left it parked in front of the shop, and the moment Yaacov left on some errand, Mimon would squat next to the machine and start fixing it. Often he stayed for hours after work, tinkering with the engine and cursing under his breath. Sometimes he got a ride to the nearest town to buy a spare part. He was, however, a happy-go-lucky, optimistic type of person. Each time the motor started and didn't die on him, he became full of childlike joy and believed that from then on it would run smoothly forever. Yet the machine would let him down again and again. He must have invested his entire meager wages in the contraption, until he finally gave up and sold it at a loss.

But Mimon was not a man to travel by bus like other mortals. He needed the motorcycle to boost his male ego, to feel like the king of the road. Soon he bought another motorbike: "But a much better one, a real bargain." Poor

Mimon; his bargain turned out to be no more reliable than its predecessor. Only now Mimon was ashamed to admit another failure. He kept the broken-down vehicle hidden behind an abandoned building and attempted to repair it after work when no one was around.

Our best days were when Yaacov was absent and we were free to talk. Mimon was a born storyteller, but in front of Yaacov he would never hold forth, so as not to appear to be neglecting his work. He knew lots of fairy tales, long convoluted narratives of magic birds, prophetic dreams, and pursuits of revenge. Most times I couldn't make head or tail of the stories; they meandered so that there remained no connection between the beginning, the middle, and the end. It was all very absorbing and fascinating, but I suspect that he was inventing the tales as he went along. In later years I found a similarity between Mimon's stories and the way of certain people who mix reality with imagination, so alien to our modern, rational way of thinking.

As the months passed, I learned more and more about mending shoes. I knew how to sew torn straps onto sandals on the sewing machine, and I could polish finished heels with wax by the rotating brushes. I was able to sharpen my long cobbler's knife by myself, no longer having to ask Yaacov or Mimon to do it for me. It was necessary to sharpen the knife several times a day, so that it could cut through the tough leather as if it were butter.

Once a month, an elderly man used to come to buy old shoes. He was an *oleh chadash*, a newcomer from Romania, who spoke Yiddish but no Hebrew. With Yaacov he could communicate, but with Mimon, who knew Arabic, French, and Hebrew, conversation was rather difficult. Over his shoulder he carried an empty jute sack, which he dropped on the floor in happy anticipation of a friendly talk. I, being a woman, was not considered a partner. Yaacov was not the type to encourage chumminess. Only Mimon remained.

"Where did you learn shoemaking?" the man began.

"Yach nisst ferstayn" (I don't understand) was all Mimon had learned to say.

The man disregarded Mimon's declaration and embarked on a long account of his woes and misfortunes, how he was cheated here and robbed there, how the government promised all kinds of assistance and in the end he got nothing.

Mimon nodded in sympathy. He grasped that the man was complaining, though he understood not a word.

"You good, good. You are understand," the poor man managed in Hebrew. Afterward he started sorting out the discarded shoes from the mountain in the corner, first making two heaps and then checking each shoe, boot, or sandal against the more acceptable specimens. In the end he stuffed them into his sack and the haggling over the price began. Yaacov was no businessman; he knew that the old shoes were worth nothing, but he couldn't disappoint the peddler, for whom the bargaining was the heart of the transaction. After the negotiation ritual, Yaacov agreed to the man's initial offer, and they shook hands.

The Romanian then stood his full sack near the door, went around the worktable to pat Mimon on the back, and shook his hand vigorously.

"You good, good," he enthused. Then he heaved the sack over his shoulder and left.

They were pleasant days in the shoe-repair shop. In the nearly three years I worked there, I was promoted to mend Shabbat shoes, and I replaced worn-out soles the professional way, with the invisible stitch. With a sharp knife one makes a diagonal groove in the new leather; with an awl one pricks a small hole and then inserts two needles from opposite sides with a waxed twine, to attach the new sole. When it's done, one must smear shoemaker's glue into the groove and then close the flap so that the seam becomes invisible. Sometimes I even assisted in the construction of new shoes. My hands became callused and rough; neither soaping and scrubbing nor rubbing them with lemon could remove the brown and black color from the cracks in my hands. Worst of all were the dark rims that accumulated around my nails and stayed there long after we had left the kibbutz.

There lived on our kibbutz an important *chaver*, a politician who often went abroad on official state missions. He considered it a great achievement that the kibbutz had enabled a woman to become a cobbler, thus providing living proof of the equality between men and women. Before one of his trips overseas, he decided to use me as a propaganda gimmick.

One morning he persuaded old Mr. Heller, the aged father of one of the *chaverot*, to take a photo of me at work. The old man owned one of the two cameras on the kibbutz. He circled the worktable trying to find the best angle and the proper light, told us to look this way and that way, to say cheese, and finally snapped a few shots.

Armed with these historical photos, our prominent *chaver* traveled abroad, convinced that my pictures would prove the most enticing bait for the Jewish diaspora to make Aliyah and join the pioneers in the new State of Israel. He believed that a picture of a female cobbler would make all the Jewish women come flocking to our kibbutz.

He did not recruit one single newcomer. I suspect that my photos had an adverse effect. I think that when the rich Jewish ladies of Argentina saw me sitting with the tripod, mending old shoes, they got scared, thinking that if they came to live on the kibbutz, they would all have to become cobblers.

CHAPTER THIRTY-SIX

Dining Room

The dining room of a kibbutz fulfilled several purposes. Primarily, of course, it served the three meals of the day: breakfast, lunch, and supper. In the one-room living quarters of the *chaverim*, there were neither kitchens nor any cooking utensils; at most they had a hotplate and a kettle. They could make tea or coffee, and perhaps boil an egg, if they had good relations with the chicken-farm man or with Chava, the manager of the food storeroom. The only meal one had at home regularly was in the afternoon with the children. We would take home a few slices of bread from the dining room and spread them with jam, of which there was no shortage due to the Pri-Gat factory. It was also possible to have afternoon tea in the dining room. On the tables were jugs with tea, bread, and tins whose label proclaimed SARDINES AND OTHER FISH. People sneered: *Yes, one sardine and one shark.*

But the dining room was also the place where we held our weekly general assemblies. The kibbutz secretary—a job also filled by rotation—would announce the agenda, and the members voted for or against each item. These could be the purchase of a new tractor, or approving someone's demand to be allowed to take driving lessons, or the announcement that Eva and Arieh are from now on a couple and want to move into a room together. While the discussion went on, many of the *chaverot* knitted, and there were whispered conversations. When it came to the vote, everyone participated: some raised their hand for yea, and some for nay, and I'm not sure they always knew exactly what they had just agreed to or rejected.

One had to read the various important notices at the entrance to the dining room. There was, for example, the list of the three people whose turn had come to do night watch this week, or the announcement about two free places in a car that would be traveling to Tel Aviv the next morning, or a notice to the public that Efra and Gerti Schalinger had hebraized their name and were from then on called Shalev, or the warning that from eight o'clock that night till the next morning the water main would be shut off, due to the cleaning of the water tower reservoir, where accumulated sand had blocked the flow.

After supper the tables were occupied by the various committees. Here, the *chavera* responsible for matters of health distributed money to people who had to go by bus to the various HMO specialists in town. She knew the exact price of a ticket to Tel Aviv or to nearby Hadera. When I had to see the gynecologist or have an X-ray, I used to go by the auto stop and, with the money I saved, buy sweets for the children. In those days most drivers in Israel would give you a lift, especially if you were a pretty young woman.

There, at another table, sat Ayko, the man who distributed razors and condoms. The weekly allocation was two of each. He was stingy with his wares; if someone asked for a third condom, Ayko would accuse him of wastefulness. "Can't you recycle them?" he would grumble. He himself was a bachelor, who had his gray hair cut once a year and walked around without a shirt or jacket in all seasons, exposing his leathery brown chest with a tangle of white hairs. He also was a sports buff, a champion on the parallel bars.

The busiest of all was the *sadran avodah*. This was a most unpleasant job—coordinating work assignments. He or she had to find workers to fill in for someone who had fallen ill or who, for some other weighty reason, could not work next day. If it was the electrician, the cobbler, or the accountant who was missing, it did not matter so much. But what if the cows, the chickens, or the children had to be fed? The only people who were free were those who were having their Shabbat—that is, who had worked on Shabbat and got a free day on a weekday in exchange. But who would be willing to give up a free day? For all their Zionist zeal, the kibbutzniks wanted their Shabbat. After all his persuasive efforts, the poor *sadran avodah* often had to man the post him or herself.

At other tables sat groups discussing various plans. For instance, there was the topic of vacations, to which every member was entitled for ten days once a year. Going to a hotel was out of the question; the vacation allocation would not buy even a single night at a third-rate hotel. Many people had family in Haifa, in Tel Aviv, or in villages, but most wouldn't want to impose on them. The best option was to take a tent and go camping. A discussion was held about the location. Often someone was sent out to scout for a suitable place.

I remember with nostalgia the week in the abandoned Arab village of Ein Hod on Mount Carmel. It was completely empty except for a Jewish couple with a child, who had started a primitive kiosk in one of the abandoned houses, selling cigarettes and drinks to people who passed through on their way to settlements higher up.

The houses were bare; instead of windows and doors, there were just holes. We picked one where the wind blew through and moved in. The vacationers, as well as the equipment, were brought up by the kibbutz truck. We carried iron bedsteads with their mattresses; pots, pans, oil cookers, plates, and cutlery; food for a week; anti-mosquito spray; toilet paper; first-aid kit; rucksacks; straw hats; and swimsuits into the house and started planning our itinerary. Despite the breeze that cooled the building, we preferred to sleep on the flat roof. My fondest memories are of the warm nights, when I watched the stars and the moon above me and listened to the sounds, the plaintive hoot of the owls and the music of the cicadas.

There were ten of us—men and women in equal numbers. All of us were one half of a couple; the other half had to stay behind in the kibbutz to take care of the children. They got their turn with the next group.

The organizer of our group, Efra, had already checked the surrounding area and located the spots that were of interest. So on the next day, we walked to the ancient crusader fort at Atlit, and the day after, we went along the track on Mount Carmel, and then to Haifa with its Bahai Temple, then one day at the beach at Tantura—in short, a whole day's outing for each day of the week. On our return to base in the late afternoon, we all participated in the preparation of supper, usually soup, salad, an egg, bread, cheese, yogurt, olives, and sometimes boiled potatoes or spaghetti.

I went on two such camping vacations. The second was in western Galilee next to Kibbutz Gesher HaZiv, where we stayed in an empty citrus packing plant in the middle of the orange groves. This time I was with different people than in the former group, but there was one thing in common to both: several halves of couples had arranged it so they could have a little fun on the side with the opposite-sex half of another couple.

Among the many jobs I did during our seven years in the kibbutz was a stint in the dining room. It was shift work, either from six to half past two, or from half past eleven to eight in the evening. When we first came to the kibbutz, there were long tables with benches seating four at each side. The two people at the end had it easy, but the two in the middle had to climb over the bench holding on to the shoulder of the neighbor, who was often just lifting his spoon with soup, which he spilled, of course. Or if three people finished and got up and you were the one sitting at the end of the bench, your weight would tilt it up and you slid to the floor. Later the kibbutz bought square tables with two chairs at each side. Since there were never enough knives, because they got nicked for home use, each table was allocated two knives to be used in rotation. It didn't help when the "economist" of supplies bought new knives. Within a few weeks they were gone again.

The food was brought from the kitchen on trolleys with shelves, on which the main course, meat or fish, was already on the plates—soup plates. One ate the soup after the main dish, to save washing another set of plates. The side dishes, potatoes, noodles, or rice, stood in unlimited amounts on the table. For the vegetarians among us, there was a portion of quiche or fried breaded cauliflower. The vegetarian would call out "*Bimkom*," which in Hebrew means "instead," and receive the meatless dish.

After the meal I had to clean the tables, lift the chair legs up, and wash the floor. And there were also always some latecomers who had to be served. Then the tables had to be prepared for the next meal.

Friday evenings the dining room was transformed into a festive hall. White tablecloths covered the tables, with flowers everywhere. Everyone entered freshly showered, the *chaverim* wearing their well-ironed white shirts, and the *chaverot* in their best dresses, saying "*Shabbat shalom*" to one another. The food was also prepared with special care and served in the finer dishes. There was often a cultural program after the meal.

I was not the only waitress, of course; there were several of us on duty each shift. One time the kibbutz committee decided to employ a labor-saving specialist to teach us how to be more efficient and to reduce the staff. He followed our work in the dining room for more than a week, taking notes. He then proposed a new schedule.

It didn't work. The trouble was that he had modeled his arrangement on my performance. It turned out that my colleagues were not as quick as I and could not fit some tasks into the labor-saving specialist's calculations. The outcome was that two people were employed to do what I had been doing alone. Nobody said it aloud, but I knew they were all annoyed with me.

CHAPTER THIRTY-SEVEN

A New Job for Otto

fter Otto's stint as kitchen boy, he became *sanitar*, together with our next-door neighbor Chanan. Their job was keeping the communal bathrooms and toilets clean; emptying the trash cans; exterminating rats, cockroaches, and other vermin; and unblocking clogged-up water pipes. It flattered them to be so indispensable. The *chaverim* always needed their services urgently, begged them not to delay and come immediately, the sink was overflowing, the ants had invaded the food storage, a cockroach was seen in the toddlers' home. And the two *sanitars*, sitting on their wagon with the equipment, drawn by the kibbutz mule, would answer with serious faces that first they must finish the more important tasks, cleaning the bathrooms or emptying the trash cans. They would often get bribes in the form of eggs—from the chicken coop boss—or a cup of genuine Brazil coffee from Anita, the newcomer from Latin America, who was hysterical because she had seen a mouse under her bed.

The job, however unsavory, had one big advantage: namely that they were their own bosses—nobody interfered with their schedule, and the *sadran avoda* could not call them up to fill in for some missing worker. Otto was very happy with his work and became quite knowledgeable in matters of plumbing and sewage. He was not a handy person by nature, but his motto was *if a stupid plumber can do it, I can certainly do it as well.*

Sometimes his job necessitated delicate discretion. One day a certain *chaver* took him aside, so that no one could overhear them, and asked Otto if he had anything to get rid of lice. "Not in my hair, but body lice." A few days later, another *chaver* came with the same complaint. And when the numbers rose, Otto started to make discreet inquiries and managed to find the source of the spreading epidemic. She was a pretty, young, single newcomer who had recently joined our kibbutz. With some lotion secretly supplied to her, the problem was solved.

Yet he didn't remain a *sanitar* for long, and it was my fault.

One afternoon, the current *sadran avoda* came to our room looking for Otto. He was out somewhere, so he turned to me, asking if it was true that Otto had studied English at the university back in Prague. "That's right," I answered proudly.

"Do you think he could teach the kids English at school?"

"Of course he could," I replied, without a moment's hesitation.

"Tell him to see me tomorrow morning."

I could read the relief in the face of the *sadran avoda*.

So from one day to the next, Otto rose from the lowly job as *sanitar* to the elevated position of an English teacher. He received two respectable shirts from the clothes store to replace his blue worker's outfit and began his new career.

In fact, it was not an English teacher that our kibbutz needed but a Hebrew literature teacher. The neighboring Kibbutz Ein HaHoresh had a wonderful literature teacher: the writer Hanoch Bartov. Their school principal was ready to lend him to us, but his condition was that we provide an English teacher for the school in Ein HaHoresh. Both sides agreed and the switch was approved. Thus the two teachers would walk several times a week over the fields and through the orchards that separated the two settlements, to teach in each other's kibbutz. In the morning and again in the afternoon, they met in the middle of the way, circling the large puddle in the footpath in winter from opposite sides. Yet the matter was more complicated.

The Ministry of Education in Jerusalem was duly informed of who was to be the next English teacher for grades five to eight at Givat Chaim's elementary school. He was, however, not Otto Kraus but Chaver Yaacov. Chaver Yaacov was a licensed teacher with years of seniority who hated teaching and worked in the boiler room. And no wonder: English was the most unpopular subject in Israeli schools, because of the British occupation. Refusing to learn English had been a way to demonstrate Jewish defiance. Many a teacher fled from the rebellious classes, and there was a permanent shortage of English teachers. For instance, the one before Otto quit after being locked in the broom closet by his students.

This attitude lasted long after the British were gone and changed only gradually when the Israelis realized that there is a world out there with people who don't understand Hebrew. The kibbutz, of course, preferred receiving the salary of senior teacher Yaacov to that of Otto the beginner, who even had no proper teacher's license. Yet the arrangement lasted just one year. When the headmaster of the Givat Chaim School heard how popular Otto had become at Ein HaHoresh, he decided not to waste this boon and kept Otto in the school in Givat Chaim.

Since Otto wasn't a graduate of some teachers' college and hadn't been indoctrinated with theories about teaching recalcitrant children a foreign language, he invented his own curriculum. He used songs and jokes, and in a short time the kids started looking forward to the English lessons. The parents were surprised at Otto's popularity, recalling the many teachers who fled after their first week in class. The highlight of his success was the end-of-school-year-play called *How the Elephant Got Its Trunk*, based on the story by Rudyard Kipling, which the children performed in English. It was about a curious little elephant who wanted to know what the crocodile ate for dinner. "Come nearer, little elephant, and I will tell you," said the crocodile, and the elephant came nearer and nearer, until the crocodile got hold of his nose and pulled and pulled, and as the elephant pulled back, his nose became longer and longer, and that is how the elephant got its trunk.

Even now, after sixty years, you may ask the grandmothers and grandfathers of the kibbutz, and they will tell you how the elephant got its trunk. In English.

CHAPTER THIRTY-EIGHT

Locusts

I n those days there was no way in the kibbutz to make a public announcement. No one had a telephone, and there was no intercom; television was as yet unknown in Israel. In lieu of a public loudspeaker system, there was a piece of iron pipe that hung by a chain on a pole in front of the dining room. In case of fire or another emergency, the nearest person banged on the pipe with a hammer or anything that came to hand; the sound was heard in the farthest corner of the kibbutz, and everybody came running.

One day the alarm was sounded, and the cry was "Locusts!"

Indeed, we heard the approaching hum like a thousand beehives, and soon the sky became dark with a huge cloud of locusts. It was imperative that they not land on our fields and in our orchards. A few members had experienced locust invasions before and ordered, "Take pots and pans and lids from the kitchen and make as much noise as you can."

We dispersed all over the area, shouting and yelling, banging the metal lids with ladles. Everybody was there, school kids, little ones, men and women; all left what they had been doing in order to save our crops and gardens. The plan was to let the locusts settle late in the evening, because when it is cold they do not feed and they can be sprayed and destroyed. It took the whole afternoon, but we succeeded. There was a smaller cloud of them the next day, which was chased away without doing much damage.

Among the newcomers in our kibbutz there were a few Moroccans who were happy when they saw the locusts. They picked up the insects, thrust them into pots, and quickly slammed the lid over them. They claimed that they were a delicacy.

One of them, Shoshana, the mother of a boy who was in the toddlers' home with our Shimon, invited us to come over to her place and share in the feast. I shuddered at the thought, but Otto did go. He said the roasted locusts were among the most delicious foods he had ever tasted.

I have already mentioned some of the places that provided the necessary services for the kibbutzniks, such as the bakery and the seamstress's workshop. We also had our own laundry, with huge washing machines, which washed all our clothes. There were separate bins for white towels and bed linen, for dirty overalls, for socks and stockings and for more delicate blouses and shirts. At the beginning of the week, we sorted our dirty clothes into the bins, each item marked with a personal number, and on Friday we fetched the clean, folded pile from the shelves in the clothes store.

There was an electrician, Hans, who not only maintained everything that was connected with electricity but also repaired broken sockets or short circuits in our rooms and fixed our hotplates. We had a carpentry workshop, where three or four *chaverim* produced little chairs for our kindergartens, built wooden fences, and attached legs to broken chairs. A skillful person could go there, pick some discarded piece of wood, and fashion a toy for his children or a shelf for his room. Otto made a beautiful crayon box for Shimon's birthday and a board with letter tiles made of plywood for Scrabble, the newest popular game.

There was also the shoe-repair workshop, which I've already described, and the tractor mechanic's garage. In later years, when I came to visit old friends in the kibbutz, I heard that they had a resident dentist and even a cosmetician and hairdresser.

We were more fortunate than many other kibbutzim in that we had our own doctor, Dr. Ebl, who lived in Givat Chaim with his family. He was a colorful character, whose many pronouncements made the rounds of the kibbutz. I suspect they were being embellished as they progressed.

He was from Vienna, a veteran of World War I, of which he repeatedly reminded his patients. If you complained of a pain in your shoulder, he would immediately tell you that when he served in the field under Kaiser Franz Josef, he had such severe pain in his shoulder that what you described was nothing compared to what he suffered then. Any disease of a patient, he'd had it, too. The only exception was Fruma, who complained that she could not get pregnant. But he consoled her, saying, "You are lucky that you are not a cow."

"Why?" she asked, perplexed.

"A cow that cannot get pregnant is slaughtered for meat."

It was his kind of humor. Another *chavera* reported the following conversation:

"Doctor, I have such pain in my back that I cannot lie down."

"You must sit on a chair with a straight back."

"But the pain continues even when I sit."

"Then I recommend that you walk or stand."

"When I walk or stand, the pain is even more unbearable."

"If you cannot lie, sit, walk, or stand, the only thing that remains is to hang yourself."

I am not sure that was exactly what Dr. Ebl said, but I wouldn't put it past him. Yet he was a dedicated practical physician with a lot of common sense.

Dr. Ebl liked Otto, and they often chatted, the doctor happy that he could talk with him in German. On one occasion, Otto spoke about my recurring migraines and stomach problems.

"Herr Otto," Dr. Ebl said, "take your wife and children and leave the kibbutz. When you live outside, she will be well."

It made sense. After seven years I still didn't feel settled down. For me life in the kibbutz was something impermanent, a kind of transition period. It would be unreasonable to wait longer in the hope that I would start feeling at home in Givat Chaim. It had to be admitted: I was not a kibbutz type.

However, this was not the only reason that Otto decided to look for another place for us to live. He too had a dilemma with the kibbutz movement, and that concerned his writing.

About a year after we came to the kibbutz, he started writing a novel called *Mountain Wind*. It was about a fictional kibbutz somewhere in the Galilee region, populated by characters, each with his or her problems. Among them was a child: an asocial loner, who did not fit in with his group. The cause for his almost autistic behavior, hinted at by the author, was that children spent just a few hours a day with their parents and slept in separate children's houses. It was an issue about which there were different opinions within the kibbutz, with some claiming that it was unnatural for children to grow up in a collective, away from their parents from the day they were born. However, the ideologues of the kibbutz movement and their adherents believed that not only was it not harmful, but it actually created healthy, unspoiled, and socially integrated individuals.

When Otto submitted the book to the publishing house Hakibbutz Hameuchad, the editors were not happy with what they perceived as criticism of the educational precepts of the movement. They met with Otto and tried to persuade him to make changes in the book. They wanted to publish it but were apprehensive of what it might do to the reputation of the kibbutzim in Israel. They sent one of their editors, the writer Alexander Sened, to talk to Otto.

Alexander was tall and lean with reddish hair and thick glasses. When he arrived in Givat Chaim, I thought that his face looked familiar. Suddenly I remembered where I had seen him. I took out our photo album and showed him a snapshot of Otto and his friend Metek taken by a street photographer in Prague a short time before our Aliyah. The man walking behind them was Alexander. It was true; he had been in Prague on a mission at the time. What an amazing coincidence!

The two had a long discussion about the novel, but Otto would not be moved.

Alexander offered him an attractive proposal as incentive. The publishing house would enable Otto to study for a year at any university of his choice. This sounded very appealing, and they decided to talk it over again. For that meeting, we would go to Revivim, the kibbutz in the Negev desert where Alexander lived with his wife, Yonat. Alexander and Yonat were not only a couple; they were a team, writing books together.

I will never forget the place. A green settlement with plantations irrigated by saline water, but around it in all directions, nothing but the dry brown desert as far as the eye could see. The members themselves also drank the same water, so their coffee tasted salty. They depended on their well, because the National Water Grid that was being built had not yet reached the southern regions. "But we are used to it," they'd say, smiling.

But, memorable as the visit was, it did not achieve the hoped-for result. Hakibbutz Hameuchad decided not to publish Otto's novel.

He offered it to a private publisher, Hadar, and a contract was signed. Now Otto had to make up his mind about which of his two life dreams to give up: the Zionist dream to be a pioneer in the Land of Israel, or his dream of being a writer and publishing books. Publishing the novel against the wishes of the kibbutz meant that he could not stay in Givat Chaim any longer.

It was not difficult to find work as an English teacher. There were several offers, but in the end we decided to move to Hadassim, a children's village with a high school.

In most cases, when people decided to leave the kibbutz, it was considered a kind of betrayal. The old-timers would accuse them of using the kibbutz like a springboard, just to learn Hebrew, get acquainted with life in Israel or acquire a skill, and finally to selfishly abandon the community.

We were surprised at the expressions of friendliness and regret at losing us when the members heard of our decision to leave. What flattered Otto most was the praise of one of the oldest and most valued female members, who told him, "I respect you, not only because you were a good teacher, but mainly because you were a good laborer."

CHAPTER THIRTY-NINE

Hadassim

We had found our new home when Avi Fischer, our friend from Prague and from the *Kinderblock* in Auschwitz, heard that we wanted to leave the kibbutz and came to Givat Chaim to tell Otto that his school was looking for an English teacher. Avi himself was now a teacher in Hadassim Youth Village, where he also resided with his wife, Hanna, and their three children.

Hadassim was an unusual institution. It had been established a short time after the end of World War II in order to absorb children survivors from Europe. Located among citrus orchards, not far from Netanya, the campus consisted of dormitories, school buildings, sports facilities, a large dining hall and kitchen, parklike lawns and trees, a swimming pool, and several semidetached bungalows for the teachers and staff. It was supported by the Canadian Hadassah-WIZO organization.

In order to integrate the survivor orphans, the institution accepted an approximately equal number of Israeli students. They lived together, learned the new language, and formed friendships. In later years, when the first students graduated and left, Hadassim accepted many children of diplomats who didn't want to drag their children from country to country. But there were also always a certain number of kids from broken homes or social cases.

The directors, Yirmiyahu and Rachel Shapira, accepted Otto gladly. English teachers were a rare commodity, due to the fact that Israeli students still hated the language. When our two children, Shimon and Michaela, heard that their schedule would not be very different from that in the kibbutz, and that moreover they would live with us parents and have their own private room, they were thrilled. We were assigned a three-room bungalow, with a little garden around. As it happened, it was next door to Avi.

But what would I do? I wasn't a teacher. Not working wasn't an option; a teacher's salary is too small to keep a family, even if we didn't have to pay rent. I accepted a job in the school dining room. My boss was Malvina, a Polish Holocaust survivor, who was gruff, unsmiling, and never pleased with me. But from my stint with Yaacov the cobbler, I was experienced in dealing with difficult bosses, so I avoided conflicts.

After some time, however, I rose in status and became a tutor of students who needed help in English. In the middle of the school year, the headmaster asked me to substitute for a teacher who went on maternity leave. I was scared. I had never had enough self-confidence to stand in front of an audience, but Otto urged me to take it up. He promised to prepare me for each lesson. With trepidation, I started, but I found that it wasn't so difficult, and by the end of the year I felt quite confident. During the next few years, I attended evening courses and intensive seminars during the school vacations and at the end passed the teachers' college examinations and got my license.

I was a conscientious but uninspiring teacher. In Otto's classes one could hear bursts of laughter; he was amusing, and the students loved his lessons. Even now, when they are grandfathers and grandmothers and scattered over the continents, they remember him with nostalgia. He had the talent to make witty, humorous comments; he told jokes or acted out scenes from Shakespeare's *Julius Caesar*, which was part of the curriculum. He took hold of a broom, quoted Caesar—*Et tu, Brute?*—and let the broom clatter to the floor.

In one of the classes, he had a Persian student who would constantly interrupt the lesson, asking the meaning of this or that word. Once, when Otto had a cold and often sneezed, Farshit asked, "What in English does one wish someone who sneezes?" With a straight face Otto told him, "One says, 'Drop dead.'" The class smiled but kept mum. Otto sneezed a few more times and each time Farshit wished him, "Drop dead, teacher." Suddenly he stopped and cried, "But *dead* means 'dead'!" Only then did the class burst into loud laughter. In private Otto later commented, "Better Farshit than near shit."

I envied Otto's ability to be so interesting and popular in his classes. I was a teacher for twenty-eight years. In the later ones, I prepared the upper two grades for their matriculation exams. My students would pass their exams quite well, but in the commemorative brochure, with photos of all the graduate students and their teachers, they forgot to include my picture.

Not long after we came to live in Hadassim, there was an exhibition of the pictures painted by the children in Terezín, at the Yad Vashem Holocaust memorial in Jerusalem. I was invited to attend the opening ceremony. The organizers had located me, thanks to my signature on one of the pictures. I took the bus to Jerusalem. There were speeches by the Yad Vashem director, Dr. Arieh Kubovy, and other officials. As I walked along the walls of the exhibition hall, I recognized names of children I had known. They had painted what they saw around them, the three-tiered bunks, the funeral hearses drawn by men, transporting bread loaves to the barracks, gallows with hanged men. But there were also locomotives, airplanes, children playing, and butterflies on flowers. Under each picture was the name of the child, his or her age, and the words *did not survive* or *perished*. I knew many of them; some had been my friends. I felt like I was at a funeral.

Suddenly I saw a drawing in black and white. It depicted a church and a row of roofs and was signed: *Dita Polachová*. I had forgotten it, but now I remembered what made me draw it. I was trying to depict the moment after sunset, when all the colors faded and the black roofs were sharply outlined against the luminous sky. In my picture, however, the contours are not sharp, since I drew it with black chalk, which easily smudges.

It was a bad moment. I realized with distress that my picture was the only one in the exhibition without the word *perished* under it.

My admiration of Otto's intellect—his ability to analyze difficult topics and express them clearly, his encyclopedic knowledge of so many subjects—began on the day we first met in Prague after the war. I was so inexperienced, so inadequate next to him! I still felt like a child, while he was an adult.

Otto was blessed with a marvelous sense of humor. With his jokes and witty observations, he was always the center of the company. He once admitted to me that as a youth he was ashamed for being overweight and that his talent to amuse was a way to compensate for this flaw. When Otto and Paťa were together, their conversation was a firework display of brilliant witticisms and creative ideas; they inspired each other. Another of his talented, bright friends was Rejšík in Kibbutz Naot Mordechai. When the three were together, we wives only listened and laughed. I admired not only Otto's sense of humor but his talent to observe global trends. He sensed developing political crises and economic changes. For example, when his graduating students asked him what he thought they should study, he advised them to learn Chinese. He'd already predicted in the seventies the rise of China as a world power.

For many years the relationship between me and Otto was unequal: he was the dominant male, and I the docile wife. Until one day in Hadassim, when I was about forty.

We were on the way somewhere, and I was driving. I had been driving already for a number of years. I often did our shopping in Netanya, since in Hadassim there was just a small grocery store that wasn't well stocked and was more expensive. As I shifted gears going uphill, there was a screeching sound, and Otto exclaimed, "Oy!" and closed his eyes like he was in pain. Up till then, I would have apologized or tried to justify my mistake. But this time I just blew up. "Stop criticizing me and teaching me all the time. When you drive uphill, it happens to you, too, and I don't comment or correct you. I have been driving enough years and don't need your advice any longer."

Otto was in shock; he couldn't understand what was happening. This was the beginning of my growing up and becoming an adult. My outburst was childish, but the fact that I demanded to be treated as an equal . . . that was new. In the weeks that followed, our marriage was in crisis. Suddenly I had my own opinions and no longer uncritically accepted everything he said. Otto even thought we should part. But our bond was strong and survived the crisis.

I think that in later years, he was quite glad that I had changed. Not long after his heart attack, he got cancer of the stomach. He was very ill, and for the last years of his life, he was grateful that I took over responsibilities and he could depend on me. It bothered him that I stayed with him all the time, never left him alone. He would tell me, "Go out, have a good time, and forget me." He resented being a burden, certain that I would begin hating him if his dependence limited my freedom. I embraced him, but he insisted, "Go, go. I will be all right."

<hr />

The boarding students in Hadassim had a free weekend twice a month. They went home on Friday after school and came back Saturday night or early Sunday morning. Teachers who lived on the campus were expected to provide a substitute home for students who had nowhere to go. For a time we had Annie, a pretty girl of fifteen, whose mother was in a mental hospital and whose father was unable to care for his three children.

For one school term, there was Shulamit from South Africa, who had just lost her mother; her father had sent her to our boarding school after he'd remarried. And we also had the Czech boy called Honza Rohan, who did have both parents, but they lived in Germany. All remained lifelong friends, although now they are scattered across different parts of the world.

Parents would also come to Hadassim to visit their children or meet the teachers. New ones asked their way to the dormitories or classrooms. Often when a parent saw Otto walking, they would ask, "Do you also have a child here?" He would politely explain that he was a teacher. But one day it happened that a person asked him, "Do you have a grandchild here?"

When Otto came home, he said to me, "As long as they thought I was one of the parents, that was all right. But to be considered a grandfather shows that the time has come for me to stop teaching. I will study graphology."

He enrolled at the Tel Aviv University, and within two years he became a graphologist. The university didn't give diplomas to the graduates, just a certificate, acknowledging that the student had attended the graphology course. Otto could now join the Association of Graphologists, and after a short time he became a respected member.

He stopped teaching, and soon the clients began arriving. Otto enjoyed his new profession enormously. He joked, saying, "If no one wants to read my writing, at least I can read theirs." Who were the clients that wanted to have handwriting analyzed? For one, companies, before they accepted new employees; also kibbutzim, to screen potential new members; youngsters who couldn't decide what to study or who wanted to know more about their new boyfriend or girlfriend; and also parents, who wanted to find out if the man their daughter was marrying was not a crook.

Graphology was a lucky choice, not only because Otto loved it but also because he could continue working when he became ill with cancer of the stomach. Sometimes he would sit with his microscope over the piece of paper for hours and then exclaim, "Eureka, I have cracked the puzzle!" He explained that his work was much like that of a detective.

CHAPTER FORTY

Rosh Pina

Otto loved Galilee, because he could fish there in the river Jordan or in Lake Kinneret. Almost every time we had a longer holiday or in the summer vacations, we took our car and traveled north. At first we had a jeep. We bought it when we received money from the German government, compensation for the forced labor we'd had to do during the war. It was a battered vehicle, which had served in North Africa in World War II and didn't want to start unless rolled down a hill.

A few years later, we bought a better car. It was produced in Israel and was called a Susita, after a mountain on the Golan Heights. It was an ugly van without windows, but roomy and dependable. We used to drive it to the youth hostel in Rosh Pina.

Rosh Pina is a picturesque village in the north of Israel, with a view of Mount Hermon, whose top half is covered in snow in winter. Above the village is a spring whose clear water cascades down, along the first houses, and then suddenly vanishes underground. Rosh Pina lies on the eastern slope of Mount Canaan; on the western side is the famous kabbalist town Safed.

In Hebrew, *rosh* is "head" and *pina* is "corner." But together they mean "foundation stone." The village was established by Baron Edmond de Rothschild near the end of the nineteenth and the beginning of the twentieth centuries, for the new Jewish settlers from Romania. The idea was that they would make a living producing silk. They planted mulberry trees and raised silkworms. The project, however, did not take off. The trees remained, but the settlers gradually left, and many of the quaint stone houses stayed empty.

With the establishment of the State of Israel in 1948, a new wave of settlers arrived. The houses were soon filled again, and new ones had to be built in a hurry. Those were not as pretty as the first ones, which had thick stone walls and red roofs. The new ones were semidetached, and each unit consisted of a single room, a tiny kitchen, and a shower.

Once, when we came to the youth hostel in Rosh Pina, the manager asked, "How many youths are you bringing?"

Otto said, "Just the two of us."

The man looked at Otto's gray hair and remarked politely that we didn't seem like youths.

It was necessary to look for different accommodation. Tsippi, our Hadassim colleague, owned one of the new houses in Rosh Pina and generously let us stay there. At the same time she suggested that we could purchase one for ourselves; there were a few for sale.

We drove to Safed, to the district office that managed the ownerless houses. They were very surprised to learn that someone wanted to buy such a poor hovel when, in the neighboring town of Hatzor, one could purchase a proper house with two rooms for almost the same price. They pointed at some rusty keys on the wall and said, "Help yourself."

We returned to Rosh Pina and tried to find the houses by the numbers on the keys. The streets had no names. The local people would tell us, "Oh, that would be the one below the school," or "Probably opposite the Shlomoviches." Then I spied an abandoned house—it had holes instead of a window and door, but it was nestled prettily under tall eucalyptus trees. I fell in love with it at first sight and only hoped that it belonged to one of the keys.

On the porch of the second half of the house, we saw an old woman. "Yes," she confirmed, "this is number sixteen B. I am Mrs. Ungar, and who are you?" She smiled happily when she heard that we might buy the other half.

"Oh, then I will have pleasant neighbors," she said. "The old cobbler died five years ago, and since then, I am here alone."

We peered inside. The room showed evidence not only of the late owner's profession but also of his vice. The entire floor was covered with old shoes and empty bottles.

When Tsippi heard that we were buying the house next to Mrs. Ungar and how much it cost, she said resolutely, "That's not the way to do it. You must bargain. You must tell them that there is no window and no door, the doorstep is missing, the roof has a hole, in the shower is nothing but a pipe sticking out of the wall, and there is no sink in the kitchen."

In Safed, they nodded their heads and promised to send an estimator. A few weeks later, the verdict arrived, and the price was reduced by 25 percent.

Each trip to Safed had to be carefully calculated, because we were only free on school holidays, but as everyone knows, offices also don't work on holidays. From home to Safed, the distance is 150 kilometers, and with the narrow pot-holed roads of those times, it took three hours each way.

Of course the ruin needed extensive repairs to make it habitable. We found a young, eager architect in Safed who had just finished his studies. We arranged to meet him halfway between Safed and Hadassim and discussed the plan over a table at a filling station. My dream was of a house with an enclosed yard, like they have in Greece, where grapes would hang overhead from a pergola. He sketched a plan on a piece of paper and offered to personally supervise the workers. We employed a builder, Shimon Azrad, who came from Safed in a suit and tie, with a briefcase under his arm to impress us. He knew very little about building, because he was actually a housepainter's assistant. But we discovered that only a few weeks later. The architect couldn't have supervised the work very diligently. There was a new entrance door, but it didn't fit and couldn't be locked; the additional room, designed by the architect, had a crooked wall, so the roof couldn't be attached; and so on. In the end everything was somehow patched up, and we traveled to Rosh Pina to take over our new house. By then the school year had ended and we were on vacation.

The architect smiled, but we could see that something was bothering him. After a while, he admitted sheepishly that he'd forgotten to design the drainage for the toilet. The result was that we had to hire the local plumber, who came with a helper, pickaxes, and shovels. They dug a deep hole in the rocky ground and a ditch for the pipe. The eucalyptus trees loved it. They sent thin tentacle roots boring into the pipe and didn't even mind that the water came from the toilet.

The final bill for the improvements exceeded the price of the house. But we didn't regret it. We spent all our vacations and holidays there with our sons (sadly, Michaela was no longer alive) and later with our grandsons.

People would ask us, "What is it that draws you to Rosh Pina? Do you have roots there?"

And Otto would answer, "Yes, we do, and they clog up our sewer pipe."

CHAPTER FORTY-ONE

About Friends

Some of the people with whom we had traveled to Israel were already friends or acquaintances; we also met a few new ones on the train. Paťa was the former: he was already friends with Otto from Terezín. At first he too lived in Kibbutz Givat Chaim, but he soon left to join a theater company, because he was an actor. In midlife, he decided to become a psychologist. He and his wife, Betty, went to America. When he finished his studies, they returned with their American-born son, Mike, and Paťa worked at the psychology clinic of the kibbutz movement in Tel Aviv. We visited each other frequently. Otto and Paťa died a few years apart, but Betty and I are still in contact.

Annetta and her sister Stěpa are twins, and in Auschwitz they were among Mengele's "experiment" subjects. Annetta and her husband, Jirka, also lived in Givat Chaim for a number of years but later moved to Australia. Annetta is now a very fit widow of ninetysomething, has three children and a lot of grandchildren and great-grandchildren. Stěpa lives near her.

Eva Weissová didn't stay in Israel. She married Karel Gross, who was one of the children sent to England from Czechoslovakia at the beginning of the war. He loved England and didn't want to live in Israel. She moved to London with him. They had two daughters and a son, and we visited them many times. Eva and I had been friends since Auschwitz. She died two years ago, and I miss and long for her very much.

Eva and Pavel Lukeš remained in Shaar Chefer. They were our closest friends throughout the years. When Otto and I retired, we played bridge with them twice a week. In 2017 we lost Eva, and sadly Pavel died in 2019. They had a son, three grandchildren, and two great-grandchildren.

The only one who stayed on in Givat Chaim was Eva Schlachetová, who changed her name to the Hebrew Michal Efrat. She and I were roommates in Hamburg and Bergen-Belsen, where both our mothers died. In Prague she studied graphics, and in Israel she became a well-known illustrator of children's books. She had a son, three grandsons, and two great-grandchildren. We would meet quite often and always had a lot to talk about. Sadly, when I was writing this story in 2018, the news came that Michal died in her sleep.

The friends described here are just those with whom we came to Israel on the same train and ship. There were many others with whom we kept in contact, but most of them are friends from before the war or from Terezín and Auschwitz.

CHAPTER FORTY-TWO

Later Years

When Israel became an independent state, it was befriended by Czecho-slovakia. Our pilots were trained there, and the Czechs sold us weap-ons. But this changed drastically when the Czechs realized that Israel hadn't come under the influence of the Soviet Union, as they had expected, but had instead allied itself with the United States. Israel was viewed as an enemy of the socialist Czechoslovak Republic. *Zionism* became a curse word. The Czech ambassador was recalled from Tel Aviv, and Israelis couldn't get visas to visit Czechoslovakia.

Only a few courageous friends kept writing to us in Israel. It was known that anyone corresponding with the "West" was suspected of spying, and their let-ters were vigilantly read by censors. Aunt Manya didn't write; we received news about her only a few times from her sister Zdenka. Margit, of course, wrote often and sent photos of her daughters and later her grandchildren. Vala and Véna from Náchod stayed in contact with us all the time, and, when they died, Věra continued writing without fear. But many friends vanished from our lives.

We were actually banned from our former homeland, much like our fore-fathers who, with Moses, were destined to wander in the desert for forty years. Figuratively, of course, because Israel in modern times is far from being a desert.

When we came to Israel in 1949, just a year after the establishment of the independent state, the country was, if not really a desert, still very underdeveloped and backward. Along the narrow, potholed road that we traveled from the tent camp to Tel Aviv, we saw untilled land full of weeds and thorns. I remember my disappointment when Uncle Ernst-Benjamin proudly took us for a walk to show us Tel Aviv. The seashore was littered with junk; shabby kiosks sold lemonade. On Allenby Street, the shopwindows were dirty, the displays heaps of unattractive wares.

Someone who saw it then and came today would think it was another country. Instead of the bleak houses, there are modern buildings and tree-lined streets. Tel Aviv's promenade is a jewel of sandy beaches, with high-rise hotels and restaurants that can compete with the choicest of the world. Every former swamp is turned into arable land; there are four- and six-lane highways full of traffic. . . . Truly a vibrant, strong country.

In March 1989, exactly forty years after our departure, Otto and I traveled to Prague. Czechoslovakia was still under Communist rule. Otto and Ruth Bondy had been invited as delegates to participate in a symposium held in Terezín, commemorating the Auschwitz family camp. I was permitted to come along as the delegation's photographer.

It was a weird experience. At the airport we were met by a Communist functionary, who took us into his office. The official welcomed us with flowery party phrases and, with a wink, offered to give us entry visas on a separate sheet, so that they wouldn't be seen in our passports. The poor man thought we would be in trouble on our return if the Israeli passport controller discovered that we had been in Czechoslovakia!

Next day was free, and we walked the streets of our native Prague, visiting the places where we grew up, our schools and favorite parks. We passed the National Theater, stood on the Legií bridge, and Otto said, "Look, the Vltava is still flowing. . . ."

We had completely erased our old country from memory. It was as if Czechoslovakia had ceased to exist for forty years.

But just a few months after that memorable visit, the Communist regime ended with the famous Velvet Revolution, and the country became a democracy again. Now we could visit whenever we wanted. We reconnected with old friends: Otto with his literary people—Joska Hiršál, Zdeněk Urbánek—and with former campmates Pavel Stránský, Jirka Franěk, and others. I also found my childhood friends Raja and Gerta, and some of the girls from the Terezín *Heim* L 410 and the *Kinderblock*. I heard that they routinely met once a year in the Krkonoše Mountains. I had a great wish to see them, and the following September, there was a happy reunion.

Gerta Altschul, 1945

It was a memorable event, and since 2006 I have joined them every year for a few days. From Israel came other Terezín survivors, some with their husbands or adult children. Among the regular participants were Ella Weissberger from America, from Prague came Helga Hošková, and from Brno Anna Flachová (Flaška). Even two of our former educators from the *Heim* once participated: Eva Weissová from England and another, whose name I have forgotten, from Sweden.

We usually lodged in Hotel Horal in Špindlerův Mlýn. Every day we would either take the cable car to the top of the mountain, go on walking tours, or swim in the pool. We sang tunes from the opera *Brundibár* or songs by Voskovec and Werich. But what we did most of the time was talk, remembering the past and the many lost friends. Sadly, each year there were fewer participants, and the last time only three of us came.

By a lucky chance, I also discovered another person from my prewar years. It happened on one of my Prague sojourns. My friend Flaška from Brno invited me to a concert that her talented son, Tomáš Hanus, was going to conduct in one of Prague's quaint, ancient churches. The program included the premiere of a work by a contemporary composer, Jan Klusák. After the concert Flaška took me to the dressing room to introduce me to her son. There were several other men waiting for the conductor to change into street clothes and go to celebrate with the composer.

All through the concert I had been thinking about the name Klusák. Before the war, my parents were friends with a couple named Porges. I remembered that the wife's maiden name had been Klusáková. We often went on day trips with them and their little son, Honzík. It was with Mrs. Porgesová and Honzík that my mother and I shared a summer vacation home in a villa in Senohraby in 1937. We went swimming together in the river Sázava or walking in the woods. But I didn't play with Honzík, because he was five years younger than me.

At first I didn't dare approach the famous composer. But as we stood there waiting, I worked up the courage and asked him, "Excuse me, but were you by any chance in Senohraby as a child?"

"Yes, I was," he replied, nodding.

I wasn't yet sure, so I asked, "And was your father's first name Otto?"

"Yes," he said, surprised, and looked at me curiously.

"I was there with you," I blurted out.

The other people became interested, stopped talking, and watched us. With amazement in his voice, he said, "You are Edith Polachová?"

I could only nod and whisper, "And you are little Honzíček."

The room was silent; Flaška wiped her tears, and I was overcome by emotion.

Then Honzík said, "Mother and I thought you didn't return. We looked for you. My father died in the war. I still have the special ruler you gave me when we came to say goodbye before they deported you. I use it for the lines when I'm composing."

Flaška wanted me to join them for the celebration, but I was too overcome by emotion and needed to be alone.

But the next morning Honzík came to visit me, holding a large briefcase. He took out the ruler, which showed the wear from years of use. Then he opened his family album. There were photos of trips with both our parents and also from Senohraby. I have the same photos in my album.

Since our reunion, we meet once a year. Some time ago Honzík invited me to the premiere of his opera *Filoktétés*, which was staged at the National Theater. We are good friends now; the age difference doesn't matter any longer.

CHAPTER FORTY-THREE

Otto's Writings

When Otto was asked what his profession was, he would answer: "My true calling in life is to write, but I make my living as a teacher." Indeed, he never stopped writing. After he corrected the students' papers and prepared the lessons for the next day, he would sit at his desk or under the tree in the front garden and write. Sometimes he sat for a long stretch just staring into the distance. He would explain, "Don't think that I'm idle. In fact I'm working hard—I'm thinking." Yet publishing remained a painful disappointment. After the Hebrew translation of his first novel, *Land Without God*,[12] and the next novel, which resulted in us leaving the kibbutz, no publisher was interested. The main problem was language. There was no translator from Czech to Hebrew in Israel, except Ruth Bondy, but she was busy with her own writing.

Otto then started to write in English. He felt that his Czech was getting rusty, and, anyway, all day long he was immersed in English, so he felt at home in it. Computers didn't exist yet; Otto wrote in a large notebook with a

12 This was the translation of *Země bez Boha*, his first novel, published in Prague in 1947.

Parker pen donated by a rich uncle. I would then type it on our Olivetti type-writer, making three copies with blue carbon sheets between. But no one wanted to publish English books in Israel. He would send his manuscripts abroad, to England, America. But each time, he got refusals: "Sorry, but the topic doesn't suit us." Sometimes no reason was even given. It frustrated him, and he started doubting his talent. "Maybe I'm not a good writer." But after some time, he would recover his confidence and go on creating. He just couldn't give it up.

And finally recognition arrived. When the Communist regime in Czechoslovakia fell and democracy was reestablished, a number of his English manuscripts were translated to Czech and published in rapid succession. Even after his death, some of his previously unpublished works appeared.

CHAPTER FORTY-FOUR

At the Imperial Museum

I n the first years after my return from the concentration camps, I remembered my experiences in great detail. When I met people who were survivors like me, we spoke about Auschwitz and Terezín and Bergen-Belsen. But we didn't open up easily before the others, the uninitiated, whom we felt were unable to comprehend.

In later years, when we had children, Otto and I spoke freely about our years in the Holocaust. We didn't mind that the children listened, too. And so, among other things, my younger son, Ronny, remembered that I once told him that after the liberation of Bergen-Belsen by the British army, I happened to be filmed by the army photographers who were documenting the camp.

In 2002 Ronny searched the Internet and learned that the documentary films are stored at the British Imperial War Museum. He contacted the museum and was informed that anyone who wishes to view them can do so by appointment. Ronny urged me to travel to London, and after some hesitation, I decided to go and also use the occasion to visit my good friend Eva Gross, who had moved from London and lived in the south of England.

At the end of May 2002, I sat for two days at the Imperial British War

Museum In a small studio, surrounded by stacks of round tin boxes containing reels of film, and watched on a small screen the horrors of Bergen-Belsen. The boxes had tags with dates, descriptions of the scenes, and the names of the film crew. This enabled me to choose the parts in which I might be seen and eliminate others where it was less probable.

The experience was very harrowing. I watched the bulldozers scooping out the earth for the mass graves, the burial of the thousands of bodies, most of them naked, some already in a state of decomposition, the skeletal surviving prisoners wrapped in blankets, facing the camera with their sunken eyes, reel after reel, hour after hour.

Toward noon on the second day, I suddenly recognized Eva Kraus, Otto's cousin. She was filmed in conversation with some officer, smiling and wearing a head scarf that was familiar. We had found two identical scarves in the pocket of a coat when we, together with other prisoners, looted the German storehouses in the camp a few days after the liberation. The scarves were blue with white polka dots, and we each took one.

The film rolled on, and suddenly I saw myself.

I am wearing a jacket and the polka-dotted head scarf tied under my chin, standing next to a soldier who sits in a jeep. He offers me a cigarette and lights it for me. On my left arm is the white armband with the letter *i*, denoting "interpreter."

I stopped the reel as instructed. I was so excited I couldn't speak and sat motionless for a while, trying to calm down. When I'd started my search, I really did not expect to find anything. It was so long ago, so improbable, a crazy idea! And now there was proof that it happened, that I had really been there. Suddenly it was no longer a vague memory, something perhaps not even true. It rose from the distant past and became a hard fact.

Even the staff of the museum were excited at my discovery. They had experienced only rare cases when survivors recognized themselves positively in those documentaries. The museum people made a copy of the video and mailed it to me. It arrived within a few days at Eva's place, and we watched it together.

It is a very short scene, lasting just half a minute. But for me it is an immensely important document. Events I remember from the concentration camps might be distorted or might even not be true, they happened so many years ago. But here was tangible evidence, historical truth. This was filmed in Bergen-Belsen, and that was me in the jacket and head scarf. And I also remember the soldier; he was a redhead. That was Leslie.

CHAPTER FORTY-FIVE

Trips and Returns: Journey to Japan

One day in the spring of 1996, I got a phone call from Aliza Schiller, the administrator of Beit Terezín. Beit Terezín is a memorial site established in Kibbutz Givat Chaim, which serves also as a library, museum, and archive. Aliza told me that a female journalist from Japan would like to talk with me. A meeting was arranged at my place in Netanya, and that is how I met Mrs. Michiko Nomura.

She was interested to learn about the life of the girls in *Heim* L 410, about our drawing lessons with Friedl Brandeis, and also about me. Before we parted, Michiko asked casually, "Would you come to Japan if you were invited?"

Without a moment's hesitation, I replied, "Of course."

I did not take it seriously; it sounded so unreal. But I did not know Mrs. Nomura's determination.

In May I got an invitation to Japan, signed by Michiko Nomura, to attend the Terezín Children's Picture Exhibition. Now I was really thrilled.

A plane ticket was waiting for me in Paris, and my flight on All Nippon Airways started there on a Sunday morning. I was obliged to leave a day sooner, because in Israel there are no flights on Shabbat. This was a marvelous bonus. I had never been to Paris, and now I got the chance to see the Champs-Élysées, the *Arc de Triomphe*, and Notre-Dame Cathedral, as well as a lot of Czech-speaking, gaping, weekend tourists.

I wasn't sure if I would be reimbursed for the Israel-to-Paris flight and the hotel; therefore I booked a cheap room for the night to and from Japan, which I later regretted. When I slept there on my return, I fell from the overhanging mattress of the narrow bed and knocked my chin so badly that half my face turned blue. Otto nearly didn't recognize me when I got home.

I used the one and a half days to see as much of Paris as possible. On Sunday I went to the airport, where I met Mrs. Andela Bartošova, the curator of the pictures in the Jewish Museum in Prague, who was also invited. We flew close to the North Pole, and I was amazed by the sights below. At times I thought I was looking at a map in an atlas, with splotches of green, brown, and blue and no sign of human habitation. Most of the passengers were Japanese, and they were very quiet and disciplined, so unlike our noisy, chattering, circulating Israelis.

The flight landed the next day around midday, and at the exit from the plane, we were stopped by some people who had a wheelchair and were calling out, "Mistel Klaus, Mistel Klaus." I assured them that I was *Mrs.* Kraus and that I didn't need a wheelchair; they must have thought that being a Holocaust survivor meant that I was an invalid. The group turned out to be film people. They made me step back to the end of the plane and filmed me walking toward them, with the cameraman walking backward, pulled by a helper. It was very awkward, and I didn't know where to look. I was glad that at least I had thought to comb my hair and put on some lipstick before we landed. At last we arrived in the airport hall, where Michiko and her daughter Aki welcomed us with hugs and kisses and big smiles.

Each day, from early morning till late into the night, I visited museums, attended governors' and mayors' receptions, answered questions, and explained, talking and talking as never before in my life. Mrs. Bartošová was of little help; she did not understand the questions and was unable to answer in English. We were driven from town to town and slept every night at a different hotel. When I went to bed at last, I couldn't utter another word but felt satisfaction that I could tell the large Japanese audiences about our life in the Terezín ghetto and Auschwitz, about the gas chambers and the suffering. I was glad that I became the voice of those children whose pictures remained the only proof they had ever lived.

After a night at the luxurious Fujiya Hotel, we traveled with Michiko and Aki to Osaka. We took the famous Shinkansen "bullet" train, which levitates over a magnetic field at speeds of up to two hundred miles per hour.

Three hours later, we arrived at Osaka. Like Tokyo, Osaka didn't seem remarkable: skyscrapers, just like in any other metropolis.

But hold on! I thought. There was a beautiful castle surrounded by a park. It stood on a high hill, and each of its five floors had a green roof with corners pointing upward like fingers.

Next was a festive dinner. The food was traditional Japanese, and it came in tiny bowls, each containing two or three bites, beautifully disguised as flowers or leaves, in pink, yellow, green, red, or black. Things that looked like sweets were in reality sour pickles, the tea tasted like soup, and noodles turned out to be thin strips of radish. The meal was full of surprises, and I tried to use the chopsticks, to the hilarity of the company.

There were speeches of welcome, and I was asked many questions, of course. Like many times before and many times since, people there had an incorrect conception of what a ghetto was like; most didn't know what happened afterward. I tried my best to elucidate, explaining that the children whose pictures were exhibited didn't know what was going to happen to them, and their drawings were not acts of heroism. They were kids just being kids. At the same time, I was careful not to minimize the horror of their situation. My audience was filled with very attentive listeners.

Next morning we slept in due to exhaustion from the previous day and were rushed to Saty Shopping Center in Izumi City. On the second floor was the hall where our exhibition was being displayed. In the foyer were rows of chairs and a piano. On the walls were four large frames with photographs of Helga Hošková, Raja Žádníková, Willy Groag, and me, with samples of our paintings and explanations in Japanese. The main hall contained the exhibition itself, and I had to pose under my picture for the press photographers. The next day, the photos appeared in several newspapers.

Next there was a press conference. There were questions and answers for several hours, with translations back and forth. Later the audience was replaced by people who had visited the exhibition in the past. Their faces expressed deep concern and attention; some were wiping away tears.

Exhausted, our little company then went to have coffee downstairs. Suddenly we were joined by a red-faced schoolgirl. Michiko explained that she had been so impressed by the ghetto children's drawings that she wanted to meet me. Her name was Yuriko, and she had come running all the way from school with her satchel. She was so excited that she burst into tears. I offered to show her my family photos if she stopped crying.

In the evening we experienced one of the highlights of our visit to Japan. A member of the committee lived in a traditional house, and we were invited for dinner. I felt as if we were in a scene from a film. We left our shoes under the three wooden stairs and stepped onto fine mats. The rooms were small, with thin sliding doors, and contained only a few pieces of furniture. In the center of the main room there was a low, round table; the cedarwood ceiling was believed to be one thousand years old. Anděla and I sat with our legs stretched under the table, while the natives sat cross-legged. We were offered a truly traditional meal: sukiyaki, green tea, and many things that were cooked in the middle of the table in a large dish. A number of women in beautiful kimonos served us. Some were members of the family; others just neighbors. The atmosphere was serene, with a lot of bowing and smiling.

Alongside the house was a mini garden with cropped trees and shrubs and stepping-stones, and above all, the full moon hung in the sky like a lantern.

On Thursday we visited a very unusual museum. It contained the paintings of Mr. and Mrs. Maruki, who were in Hiroshima immediately after the atomic bomb. They helped bury the dead and were themselves exposed to radiation. Mr. Maruki continued to paint even into his nineties. There were four huge canvases in black and white at the museum, each depicting one of the four catastrophes of our century: Hiroshima, Auschwitz, Okinawa, and Nanking. They made a strong impact, and I was glad when we moved to the other room, where there were more cheerful pictures.

Someone told Michiko that the old couple would like to meet us. We were very excited; it was a great honor.

The Maruki house stood opposite the museum, and there was a kind of wooden stage in front of the entrance. We were invited to sit there on pillows, and Mr. and Mrs. Maruki joined us. The husband sat with his legs on the floor, but the old lady sat on her heels, Japanese fashion. Her face was like a porcelain doll's, with lively, shining eyes.

Mr. Maruki was sitting somewhat hunched and didn't seem to be listening. He didn't speak to us. We felt we must drink some orange juice and taste the cookies, which were brought out by a bowing and smiling relative or servant. Soon we were saying goodbye; I also bowed from the waist down, Japanese-style. As we were walking to the car, I heard a bell pealing. When I turned around, I saw a most wonderful sight. Mr. Maruki was standing on his bowed legs, with his white beard and dark glasses partly hiding his bluish singed face, and slowly pulling the rope of a small bell, which was hanging over the door of the museum. It was his way of saying farewell. I was so deeply touched that I cried.

Another lovely encounter later occurred at Saitama Prefecture. Of course, first there was the official part, the reception and the showing of the building and explaining of its function. But afterward we were invited to a meal around a very long low table. The mood was set by the host's advice: "You had better stretch your legs under the table; we know that you—chair-sitting people—have difficulty sitting on your heels." The food was Japanese, and I tried my best once more to use the chopsticks. The tastiest item was the crabmeat, which was served in the crab's shell. (Jews aren't allowed to eat this, but I don't keep kosher.)

After the meal came a long poem in Japanese. I told them I would like to hear a song, and at that, the honorable officials started clapping their hands and singing with gusto, swaying from side to side in rhythm. Then I offered a song in Hebrew: "*Heveinu shalom Aleichem.*" They caught the rhythm and helped by clapping hands. After this they requested a song in Czech. Anděla shook her head—she was shy—but when I started "*Na tom pražském mostě,*" she joined in. It was a lovely, informal feast, and it is my second-best memory from Japan.

There were other striking features of the landscape that we passed: rice paddies. Every little piece of land in Japan is cultivated; the shortage of arable land is very evident. Even a small patch between one industrial building and the next becomes a field. I had read about rice, how it is planted in water, and I had seen the bent backs and large hats of the planters in films. But I did not know that the blue of the sky is reflected in the water and that the clouds swim among the green seedlings.

Another new sight for me were the dark-green rows that looked like paint squeezed out of a tube in parallel lines, climbing up slopes or following the rounded hills. These were tea plantations. For some time the landscape consisted of small mounds entirely covered with trees, mainly bamboo. The cone-shaped hills might have been a hundred meters high and looked like a child's drawing. Very few of the houses we saw were traditional Japanese; they stood very close together and many had blue roofs. Sometimes the passage between them was so narrow that just one person could squeeze through.

We were once more in Tokyo, with its tall corporate buildings, but the grandest of them all seemed to be the former Yasuda headquarters, where the Seiji Togo Memorial Sompo Japan Nipponkoa Museum of Art is located. We went up by fast elevator to the forty-second floor, which was still not the top.

After a reception in the luxurious offices, we were escorted through the exhibition halls. Apart from the great European painters, two artists were the main stars of the collection: the American Grandma Moses and the famous Seiji Togo.

His are large paintings, but my attention was caught by a few pencil drawings of girls' heads. They turned out to be of one Czech and one Israeli; what a coincidence.

There are strict security measures at the fine art museum, and for good reason. It owns one of Van Gogh's famous sunflower paintings, which it purchased for a huge sum a few years before my trip. I stood in front of the glorious original and was reminded of the first time I had seen the painting.

Again I remember Friedl and the lesson she taught us three girls in her tiny room. The scene comes back, how she guided us to look at those sunflowers, at the colors and the bold brushstrokes. It was Friedl who not only encouraged me to continue painting but also to appreciate art.

Saturday was the last day before our departure. A taxi took us from the hotel to Urawa, where we were to meet Michiko. It took a long time in the permanently congested traffic, but finally we arrived and on time, too.

Then followed a two-and-a-half-hour-long session. We sat with the large group of officials around tables arranged in a square. Michiko gave a lengthy introduction about the Terezín ghetto and the children's drawings, and I thought also about how she happened to learn about them. I told my interpreter, Norie, she need not translate, as I could imagine what Michiko was describing. This made it easier for both of us.

After that, as in previous meetings, came many questions. How could the children, who knew they were going to die, paint such cheerful pictures? How is it possible that the pictures remained? To what do you attribute your own survival? What did you do to be able to smile again? Can you describe the saddest and the happiest moments you had in the ghetto?

The saddest I do know; I have told it several times before. It has become the symbol—the essence—of the grief for all I lost. It was the death of Marta Pereles, my friend and sharer of the bunk in room 23. Her father, a hunchback, continued to visit our room even when his daughter was no longer alive. We girls would fall silent, unable to look at him. He would sit by the window, quietly immersed in his sorrow. . . .

But it took me a while to recall a happy moment. Then I remembered the strange thing that happened soon after we arrived in Terezín: I told of the incident with the thermometer in that bare room in the Magdeburg barracks. When they looked at the thermometer and it showed I had a high temperature of 40 degrees Celcius, they crossed off our names from the transport list, and Mother and I stayed in the ghetto, which made me very happy. Even today I have no logical explanation for how it could have happened.

Later that afternoon, on our way back to Tokyo, we had a few free hours, and Michiko took advantage of them to show us her "headquarters" in Omyia City. It was in a rented flat, and I was surprised at its small size. It consisted of two rooms plus conveniences, squeezed into no more than some twenty-five square meters. We were told that this was the usual size for a family with two children. It gave me an idea of what was meant when I was told that the country was not big enough for its huge population.

Five or six female volunteers had been waiting for us with tea and cake. We sat on mats, feeling very hot. Two of the ladies stood near us with paper fans to create some ventilation. They were so sweet, those helpful ladies, that I became quite enamored of them. During our whole stay, they were always somewhere in the background, quietly taking care of our comfort and the smooth running of affairs, smiling and nodding all the time in lieu of English conversation.

The taxi arrived, which took the three of us back to Tokyo. We were on the way to the last appointment of our itinerary: the Japanese NHK television, the national channel; those that had covered us till this point were regional ones. The journey took a very long time, although it was the weekend and traffic was supposed to flow away from the city. Instead of one hour, it took two and a half hours. At a public phone booth, Michiko stopped the car to make a call to the TV station.

At eight o'clock we finally arrived, all disheveled and hungry. *How am I going to talk coherently in front of the cameras in this state?* I wondered. They promised us a meal immediately after the broadcast; Anděla and I had just enough time to comb our hair and powder our shining noses. The producer's name was

Mr. Toda, a good omen. (In Hebrew *toda* means "thanks.") Our interviewer was a stunningly beautiful Japanese girl who spoke English like a born American. She held a sheet with prepared questions and allowed us a few minutes to go over them.

But alas! They were all wrong questions, based again on the mistaken presumption that the children in Terezín knew of their approaching deaths and their drawings were therefore their last expressions of heroism. But our talented interviewer assured me that she would alter the questions. She composed new ones as we were walking upstairs to the studio. Within seconds she had grasped the correct approach, and, when we were seated, the cameras and lights centered on us, she conducted the conversation with absolute professionalism.

I pulled myself together, knowing that this was the most important moment of the entire Japanese sojourn. I spoke not only of Terezín but also of Auschwitz, of the Germans' ingenious deception at the inspection of Red Cross commission at Terezín and the rationale for the family camp, where men, women, and children were kept alive as an alibi and then exterminated in the gas chambers when they were no longer needed. . . .

Oh, this was exhausting! I felt the tremor of my hands and legs. In the office they gave us coffee and a two-tiered lunchbox filled with Japanese goodies and tied in a huge violet napkin.

It was over, and I felt that I had fulfilled a mission.

I noticed two other useful and polite traditions in Japan. One is the exchange of calling cards. Whenever strangers meet, they pull out their wallets and hand the other person their card. In this manner, I received thirty-one cards; on some the names are also in English, and a few of them even have a small photo of the bearer. The last night, before falling asleep after the demanding day, I tried to sum up the significance of this journey to Japan. I wondered why those childish pictures from a faraway country and a time long past should find such a wide interest and response in Japan.

Most of the people I met were young: the journalists, the executive committee, Michiko herself and her kind ladies, even the officials. They all must have been born after the war or been too young to remember it. What was it that accounted for the sympathy of the Japanese with our fate? The role that Japan played during World War II must still trouble their minds. I was asked a few times: What is your attitude toward Japan today in the light of it having been the ally of Germany?

Maybe the answer lies in the fact that both peoples were exposed to great traumas, Hiroshima and Auschwitz. As a lady from Sapporo said to me, "I can feel with you, because I am your age, and I know what suffering is. It is possible that living through catastrophe makes for brotherhood among people."

Sunday morning at Narita International Airport, there was Michiko with all her kind ladies. Each of them had a farewell gift for us. So many gifts, so many souvenirs! We smiled; we bowed. We also shook hands. They were all so lovely, it was difficult to take leave.

They waved to us past customs, past passport control; they even found another window to wave from when we were already on the escalator.

Goodbye. Goodbye, Japan. *Arigato!*

On one of my sojourns in Prague, I felt a longing to take a walk in the Old Town again. The day was windy and cool, though when the sun came out from under the bloated clouds, the weather became quite pleasant. I walked along the river and then over the centuries-old Charles Bridge with its black, weatherworn statues of suffering saints.

In Malostranské náměstí I took tram number 22, knowing that it passed the Náměstí Míru station, from which I could change to my usual number 10 or 16. As I was entering, I heard a recorded announcement that this tram was being rerouted. Several people got off and rushed toward the Metro entrance. Although I didn't understand exactly what the loudspeaker said, I recognized the name Vinohradská street, so I stayed on the tram. *Never mind*, I thought, *it will take longer, but I am in no hurry.*

I didn't know what a nostalgic trip into the past I was undertaking.

The tram now traveled through the district of Nusle and along the long street once called SNB Avenue. On my left was the old Koh-i-noor factory that produced the pencils for generations of schoolchildren in the Republic. And soon I glimpsed the little side street where Otto and I lived as a young couple. Our flat was in the last house of the unpaved alley; behind it lay the tiny gardens enclosed by wooden fences, each with a small toolshed in the corner, called *Schrebergärten* in German. The townspeople rented them to grow some vegetables and flowers or even a fruit tree or two. Soon after the end of the war, there was still a serious shortage of food, so the vegetable gardens were more a necessity than a hobby. Beyond them began the neighboring borough of Vinohrady with the huge barracks, where Otto did his military duty in the months before our marriage. I would see him walking home among the gardens from the window when he got leave.

The gardens are gone now; in their stead there are the impersonal apartment buildings of the Communist era, called *paneláks* because they were built of prefabricated panels.

Two stops farther on, the tram stopped near v Olšanech Street, where Otto's childhood friend Mirek lived. Under the Nazi occupation, contact between Christians and Jews was strictly forbidden, but Mirek didn't drop his Jewish friend. The two had an emotional reunion after they hadn't seen each other for forty years. Mirek was still living in the same villa on v Olšanech Street where he was born and where he raised his own children and grandchildren.

Around the corner stood the villa of the Kraus family. There is no trace of it now, no gatekeeper's lodge and no driveway with the proud sign over it: RICHARD KRAUS TOVÁRNA DÁMSKEHO PRÁDLA (Richard Kraus Ladies Lingerie Factory). In its place stands a five-story apartment building with two entrances.

Just opposite, on the other side of the street, lived the doctor who did the emergency surgery on my infected breast. Of course his nameplate is no longer on the house. He must have died long ago.

Toward the end of the street, before the tram turned left, there used to be Cinema Vesna. Otto used to go there on Sunday mornings, together with Mirek and other neighborhood boys, to see Westerns. At that time, films were still silent; the sound was provided by a man who sat under the screen and accompanied the action on the piano. He played marches or gallops when there was a chase and romantic schmaltz music when the lovers kissed. His repertoire was limited, and the boys knew exactly what melody he would play next.

Where the tram end-station depot used to be, there is now a modern office building. Not far from there was the baby-wellness clinic where I used to take baby Peter every week to be weighed and examined. Dr. Březovská would give him special attention, both because I was an eighteen-year-old mother and also because her husband, Bohuslav, the well-known writer, was a member of the same circle of authors to which Otto also belonged.

When the tram rounded the corner, I saw a low building with a gable and a wide wooden door. Before the war this was a movers' business, which belonged to a Jewish family whose daughter Hana was a classmate of Otto's. In those times moving was still done by horses and carts, and the wide door led into the yard with stables and sheds for the vehicles. The owners perished in the concentration camps.

After the war, when there was a catastrophic shortage of housing, the house with the gable is where we found the small attic room for my grandmother. The room could be reached only from the yard by a rickety staircase, but the landlady, Mrs. Adamová, was a very kind soul and made Grandmother as comfortable as she could. Every day Grandmother would climb down the stairs and walk to the Kraus house to help me with the baby. For her the little great-grandson was a consolation for the loss of her entire family.

Each time I had visited Prague after the Velvet Revolution, I passed the house and was sad to see it neglected and peeling. But this time I found it quite nicely renovated, with a new restaurant on the ground floor.

The next tram stop was near the Hagibor sports ground. The little iron gate is hidden by bushes, and from the tram window one can barely discern the name Hagibor over it. In the years of the Nazi occupation, it was the only place where the Jewish youths and children could gather to play and do sports. In the summer before our deportation, a kind of summer camp was held there. We children would walk to Hagibor from all over the town, as we were already forbidden to use public transportation, and some, like myself, had to walk an hour each way. But it was a wonderful and unforgettable time. We were divided into groups, each with a trainer or instructor. There were tents one could rest in; there were games and shows. Borghini the magician appeared and entertained the several hundred kids. The legendary Fredy Hirsch organized races and competitions. But at seven in the evening we had to start walking home, because the curfew was at eight and we wore the yellow Star of David identifying us as Jews. Hagibor was a world in itself, and we few who returned from the Holocaust remember it with fondness.

Almost adjoining the sports ground is the new Jewish cemetery. After the war my grandmother had the names of my parents and my grandfather engraved on the gravestone of my father's brother, Fritz. I always visit the place to honor my family and grandmother, who herself is interred in her hometown, Brno.

By now I was almost at the end of my detour. I got off the tram and started walking, leaving the past behind and starting to make plans for tomorrow.

The weather forecast had said it wouldn't rain, so I would be able to take another walk, but hopefully only in the present.

CHAPTER FORTY-SEVEN

Peter/Shimon

Each of our three children was born while we were living in a different place. Peter Martin (Shimon) in Prague, Michaela in Kibbutz Givat Chaim, and Ronny in Hadassim, though Ronny and Michaela were born in the same hospital. Ronny was to be our solace when we learned that Michaela would not live. Indeed, he gave us only joy; there was never any problem with him. He was a cheerful and charming child and has remained perhaps a bit less cheerful but certainly just as charming in his adulthood.

Unfortunately things did not go so well for Shimon. At school he was a good student and joined the army like all boys and girls in Israel. At that time Otto and I already started noticing some unusual behavior patterns. He would tell us how his commander persecuted him; he had bouts of paranoia or hyperactivity. But he did finish his army service and then moved to Jerusalem to study sociology at the Hebrew University.

Shimon was an exceptionally good-looking young man. Tall, with a well-proportioned body like a classical Greek statue. Indeed, one of our friends called him "a real Adonis." He himself didn't seem to be aware of his looks. He was intelligent, amusing, and friendly. He chose his friends among boys with some misfortune: one had a withered arm; another had just lost his father.

Shimon was already fourteen years old when his little brother, Ronny, was born. At that time I was taking driving lessons in the nearby town of Netanya. Otto would drive me there at six in the morning so that I would be back in time for school. Shimon was a competent and willing babysitter. He even didn't mind changing the baby's diapers when he cried.

Michaela was sick, and as the disease worsened, she often needed to be hospitalized. Watching her suffering became unbearable, and one day Otto had a heart attack. (Incidentally, President Gamal Abdel Nasser of Egypt had his heart attack the same night. Later Otto would joke: "Nasser came out feet first, and I came out on my feet.")

In Jerusalem Shimon studied during the day and worked nights in a psychiatric hospital. There he met Miriam, a nurse who became his girlfriend. Their relationship was very unbalanced; he told us that he wasn't in love with her, but Miriam was very much in love with him. When she discovered that she was pregnant, he agreed to marry her. But he begged us not to come to the wedding. We were puzzled and insulted, but we respected his wish.

It was not until eleven months later that she gave birth. They named the sweet little boy Ehud. Shimon stopped studying sociology and switched to a two-year hotel management course. He found employment in a youth hostel, where he was successful and well liked. But he had personal problems with the staff and after some time was fired. The same happened at the next hotel. Time after time, he was readily accepted, only to find himself unemployed again. It was as if he were driven to sabotage his position, not letting himself succeed. The young family was constantly overdrawn, couldn't pay the rent, and owed at the grocer's. We kept saving them from catastrophe.

It was clear that Shimon needed psychiatric help. He started treatment with a very expensive professor of psychiatry, which went on for many years. Fortunately, at that time, Otto and I began receiving an allowance from the Germans as compensation for the years we spent in their concentration camps. With that we could pay the professor, who worked so hard that he would usually fall asleep while Shimon was talking. The professor was of no help. Nor was the next psychiatrist, to whom Shimon had to travel twice a week from Jerusalem to Tel Aviv. Psychology didn't help; what he needed was medication. Meanwhile they had a second child, again a boy, named Assaf.

The marriage was growing unbearable, the atmosphere explosive. Shimon wanted a divorce. It was a bad time, full of hatred and accusations. They both claimed that we were inciting one against the other, and we had sleepless nights with worry.

After the separation Shimon left Jerusalem and moved to our vacation house in Rosh Pina. The boys stayed with their mother. To do her justice, it must be said that she was an exemplary mother. She worked two shifts, took night work with private patients, did all she could to provide for her children. Shimon tried to find work here and there and, in the end, landed in Netanya. We were able to buy him an apartment just a short walk from our place. For a number of years he worked as a caregiver for elderly men. Yet from time to time he had to be hospitalized in a psychiatric ward. He stopped working when he was about sixty, lived on a minuscule invalid allowance, and actually was almost completely dependent on us. He was taking a great amount of medication, which I would prepare weekly for him.

When Ehud was getting married, he came to Netanya to buy Shimon an elegant suit. He wanted him to look his best at the wedding. In the photo both parents are present, one on each side of the couple.

Then came the time when not only Shimon's mental but also his physical health deteriorated. He was unable to care for himself, too weak to walk, his back bent, his mind befuddled. He no longer enjoyed music, showed no happiness, even when his first grandchild was born.

I was glad that Otto was no longer alive to see Shimon's sad deterioration. I found a caregiver who lived with him, cooked, washed him, and took him out in a wheelchair. His sons were by now grown men. They loved him, and each in turn came to visit him from Jerusalem as often as he could. Of course they would also drop in to say hello to me, but after seeing Shimon, they would feel sad and depressed.

In July 2016, Shimon fell into a coma. At first he was in the Netanya hospital, where I visited him daily, although he didn't know it. Later his sons had him moved to a special facility in Jerusalem to have him closer to them. Ehud came almost daily to sit with him, talk to him, and stroke his hand, believing he could feel and hear him. Assaf also came, but for him the sight of his father's body without a sign of life was unbearable. Miriam, who had overcome her anger at Shimon long ago, was also helpful and kind. Being a nurse herself, she knew the doctors in Jerusalem, and through her connections Shimon was made as comfortable as possible in the hospice. After being in a coma for almost half a year, Shimon died on December 8, 2016, at 8:15 P.M., just a few days short of his sixty-ninth birthday. He is buried in Har HaMenuchot Cemetery in Jerusalem.

A year later, Assaf's daughter was born. It was December 8, 2017, at 8:15 P.M. in the same hospital where Shimon died.

CHAPTER FORTY-EIGHT

Ronny

Ronny, my youngest and only remaining child, lives with his family just a few minutes' walk from my place. He is thirteen years younger than Shimon. He and Michaela were both born in the same hospital and, in fact, on the same bed, but ten years apart. He was a lovely, happy child. When he walked to the kindergarten in the morning, he would sing aloud to himself. It was safe to let him go alone, because on the Hadassim campus, there was no traffic or other danger.

Our friend Pata, the former actor turned psychologist, would ask in later years, "What teenage symptoms did you observe in Ronny?" And Otto and I would look at each other and shake our heads. "None."

Actually, while Ronny avoided a phase of teenage rebellion, a rebellion of sorts came much later. When he finished the army, he bought himself a motorcycle, despite the protests of his father. Neither persuasion nor threats could change his mind. He himself claimed, "If I don't have the expected stage of teenage rebellion against my parents now, when will I?"

Otto was desperate; he was in a panic whenever Ronny returned late. In the end he solved it, at least partially, by buying Ronny a secondhand car. Even then Otto couldn't fall asleep until he heard the car returning.

Ronny served in the army for three years, becoming an officer and tank commander. He participated in the war of Lebanon and fortunately survived it without harm. Here is his description:

> The war started on June 6, 1982. Two days before that, I was recalled back to base from my vacation. We organized during Friday night and drove to the border Saturday night, June 5. On Sunday, June 6, we crossed the border into Lebanon north of Nahariya.
>
> We advanced on the Lebanese coastal road through the cities Tsor, Sidon, and Damour. Truce was declared at noon on Thursday, but we were still targeted and bombed with Katyusha rockets a few more times, until calm came at around 1:30.
>
> We took positions on the hills southeast of Beirut, allowed hundreds of thousands to flee the sieged city, and prepared to invade, but fortunately the order never came. We returned to base twenty-eight days after the war started.

Since boyhood he wanted to study psychology. His school friends used to discuss their personal problems with him, and he felt that this was his calling. First he studied sociology and practiced for two years. He had a girlfriend, Orna, and he would visit her kibbutz every weekend. But then he went to the United States to continue his studies in psychology, and they separated. A year later, he came home for the summer vacation and decided to meet Orna. She was studying dance in Jerusalem. Otto was giving a lecture in Jerusalem on that day, so we traveled together. Since Otto would be busy for several hours, I was free to drive

Ronny to the university. He went to find the dance department, and I stayed on a bench under a tree. After a while I saw them walking toward me with arms around each other, smiling happily.

That was almost thirty years ago, but they are still as tightly attached now as on that day.

That same year Orna joined him in New Jersey in the States. She switched from dance and studied physiotherapy instead. Both of them are now doctors, she in her profession, and he in his.

Ronny started playing the trumpet as a youth in Hadassim. For several years, he was a member of the Tel Aviv Youth Orchestra. In America he joined a group of retired doctors who played jazz for their own pleasure. After some time he decided, "It's a waste to play without an audience," and together with them, he founded a real jazz band. They called themselves the Jazz Doctors and played for many years, several evenings a week, at Café Angelique in Tenafly.

Ronny and his family lived in America for twenty-five years, and their children, Gabriella—nicknamed Gabby—and Daniel, were born there.

A few years ago, they moved back to Israel. Ronny felt obliged to be near me in my old age and also wanted his children to know their grandparents: Orna's parents and me. Sadly, Grandpa Otto saw only his two-year-old granddaughter, Gabby; Daniel had not yet been born when Otto passed away in 2000.

CHAPTER FORTY-NINE

Michaela

When Otto and I were new lovers, he told me, "I dream of having a daughter who would be like you."

Michaela came into the world a year after we joined the kibbutz. I had an easy pregnancy and felt almost no discomfort. Of course, this was at a time when mothers did not know if the baby they were carrying was a boy or a girl.

I had to register in advance at the hospital, which was in Hadera, about fifteen kilometers from Givat Chaim. No one owned a car in the kibbutz. To call an expensive ambulance just to convey a healthy mother to the maternity ward in order to give birth was inconceivable.

When my time came on September 17, 1951, at about four o'clock in the morning, Otto went to wake up the truck driver who had agreed to take me to the hospital. His name was Arnošt, a Czech from Náchod—a lovely man who had become our good friend. I climbed the tall step into the cabin and sat down next to him, and we were on our way. It was not yet the custom for fathers to be present at the birth of their babies. All the way, Arnošt was only concerned

I should not give birth in the truck. Every few minutes, he glanced at me and asked, "Can you still hold on?"

The nurse at the delivery room looked at me doubtfully. "Are you sure?" she asked. "You don't look ready to me."

But I was, and at noon that day, Michaela slipped out with one push. She was small, weighing 2.6 kilograms, but was fully developed and quite pretty. Otto arrived in the afternoon and they let him have a look through the glass door to see the daughter he had been longing for.

Three days later, we were released from the hospital. Next to the exit was a little registry office where they asked me, "What will your daughter be called?"

Without hesitation, I told them, "Michaela." It was the name I had chosen for my future daughter when I was thirteen years old.

It was in the Terezín ghetto, where my mother and I had lived for a short time in a room full of other women, one of whom had a girl of about five, Michaela, a sweet child whom she called Misha. *If ever I have a daughter, I will name her Michaela*, I'd decided then.

My little Misha had a special quality. She was so soft and cuddly and silky smooth that when I held her, she somehow got fused to my body as if she were a part of it. She was extremely pliant, no elbows or knees that would get stuck in sleeves or trousers.

Misha was the favorite of Rachel, the nurse in charge of the six babies in the room. She was an enormously fat woman who loved children, and whenever I came to fetch the baby, she would be holding her and would not want to release her. She herself had two older children, but one day when she was absent, the nurse who substituted for her told us that Rachel had just given birth. No one had noticed that she was pregnant, and she was as obese after the birth as before it.

I nursed Misha for only six weeks; afterward I had no more milk. It was exactly what the surgeon had predicted after Shimon's birth. He'd told me then that the ducts in my infected breast had been damaged by the surgery and that even the other breast would not produce enough milk for the next children.

But Misha thrived on the bottle, and the advantage was that Otto could replace me when I was too tired or when the weather was bad. He quite welcomed the opportunity to hold the baby while the other mothers suckled their babies with their backs to him. They liked him to be there, because he amused them with his jokes and funny stories.

From the baby house, Misha graduated to the toddlers' home, again six to a room with one nursery teacher and a helper. There Misha fell in love with Amalia, the blond daughter of a dark-skinned Syrian mother and Hungarian father. The two little girls were constantly together, usually walking with arms around each other. Poor Amalia; some two or three years later, she had a bad accident, which left her face with terrible burn scars. Multiple operations improved her looks, but a few lesions were left for life.

Misha was a warmhearted child, and this became apparent when she was still very young. She loved to give presents to her friends. When she was older, she drew or made little gifts with much imagination and talent. She was heartbroken over her beloved Amalia's accident.

Michaela was six years old when we left the kibbutz. On a truck provided by the kibbutz, we loaded our belongings, including our cat, Tonda, and drove to our new home: Hadassim Youth Village. The children were delighted; they kept running in and out of our three rooms, kitchen, veranda, and garden. They were only sad because in the middle of the journey, our cat had jumped off the truck. To our surprise, he found his way back to the kibbutz, and a few days later Otto brought him to us.

That September, Michaela—she was now called by her full name—started first grade. There were too few six-year-olds in Hadassim, so the first and second grades were merged and taught by one teacher and her assistant. Only very few pupils of such a young age were being sent to the boarding school, so most kids in the class were children of the staff. They had an excellent teacher, Hadassa, who was more than a teacher; she was an inspired educator whom the children adored and who, I believe, had an influence on them that lasted for life.

Our children also became friends with the Meyer boys, Shimon with Dany and Michaela with Gaby. Their father was the handicraft and drawing teacher, his wife a housemother in one of the dormitories.

Hadassim was, in a way, not much different from the kibbutz. The students and staff ate in a communal dining room, and the dormitories were much like those in the kibbutz. Our children had the additional advantage of having a private home as well. We used the dining room only for the midday meal; mornings and evenings, we ate at home.

Every week there was a film. One day they screened *Swan Lake*. Michaela was entranced by the marvelous ballet. For some reason, the small children were allowed to watch only till eight o'clock and had to leave although the film was not over. She couldn't take her eyes off the screen, walking backward as I was leading her out. To this day, I feel her pain as she wept that she couldn't stay till the end.

A year later, we heard that there was a circus in Tel Aviv. I took the children to see the show. As we were traveling back by bus, I noticed two ticks on Michaela's left earlobe. I had experienced ticks before and knew how to take them off. I removed them and thought no more about it.

Three days later, Michaela became ill. Our doctor, Dr. Matatias, came and examined her. The diagnosis was unequivocal: typhus. Otto and I became terribly frightened; we had seen hundreds of prisoners die of typhus in the concentration camps. But Dr. Matatias reassured us, "Nowadays typhus is being treated with penicillin and can be cured." He didn't even send Michaela to the hospital. It took just a few days, and she recovered.

On a Shabbat a few weeks later, we went to Caesarea to see the archaeological excavations. But Michaela became so weak she couldn't walk, and Otto had to carry her on his shoulders all the way back. Dr. Matatias suspected some ear infection and sent us to an ear and nose specialist.

We took Michaela to Ramat Gan to see Dr. Kraus, a friend and campmate of Otto's. He also treated Shimon's frequent ear infections. The first thing he asked to do was a blood test. The result was very alarming; she had an extremely low sedimentation rate. A thorough examination was necessary to find out what was wrong. We brought her to Tel HaShomer Hospital. For the next six weeks, the renowned Dr. Rotem tried to diagnose Michaela's disease. The poor child underwent painful examinations. They pricked her veins for blood samples almost daily, and she had no appetite and lost weight. She was shocked when an Arab boy with a heart disease died on her ward. One night she soiled herself in bed, and this broke her spirit.

Then came a consulting specialist from America, who concluded that Michaela was suffering from juvenile cirrhosis. In his experience the symptoms were usually evident early on. So much for the initial medical advice.

There is no cure for this disease. When we came home that evening from our daily visit, we broke down and cried. When Shimon saw his parents crying, he too cried. Trying to console him, we said that it was easier for him to accept than for us, Mother and Father. He never forgave us, blaming us for excluding him from sharing the pain.

The American specialist suggested giving Michaela a large dose of cortisone in an effort to stop the progress of the disease. She was allowed to go home and returned to school. The side effect of the treatment was a swelling of her face, the well-known "moonface." But she seemed better, was stronger, regained her appetite, and apart from the regular checkups at Tel HaShomer Hospital, led a normal life.

Nevertheless, we continued searching for a cure locally and abroad, knowing that her present state was only a reprieve. We took her to Haifa to a specialist who treated many young Arab patients with the disease and had a lot of experience. We contacted hospitals in the US and in Switzerland. Everywhere they experimented, but no one had found a cure.

Otto decided we should have another child, and one day I found myself pregnant. We didn't tell the children until the fifth month of my pregnancy to shorten their anticipation. The morning when I told them about the coming baby, they were so happy they just couldn't stop clapping their hands, jumping up and down, and shouting for joy. When Ronny was born, Michaela was ten and Shimon thirteen. It was a few months after his bar mitzvah.

For the next few years, there was no worsening of Michaela's disease; the tests showed even a slight improvement. She went to school regularly and learned well and even participated in end-of-school-year trips. Her best friends were her classmates Bettina and Zehava, who often stayed overnight. Each of them came from problem families, like the majority of the children who were sent to Hadassim. One year I made identical costumes for Zehava and Michaela for Purim: they wore dartboards with circles in black and white in front, on the back, and on their heads. They were a great success.

When Michaela was sixteen, Aunt Ella invited us to London. It was a very successful vacation. Ella sent us on day tours to Oxford, Hampton Court, Berkeley Castle, Blenheim Palace, the Cotswolds, and other tourist attractions. Of course we went with her to Kew Gardens, the Tower of London, Kenwood Park, and the open-air theater in Regent's Park, where we saw *Cyrano de Bergerac* and *A Midsummer Night's Dream*.

Ella was a very generous and loving person, but she had to be obeyed and did not suffer contradiction. One day, when Michaela did not get up in time for some trip, Ella pulled off her blanket and exclaimed in a loud voice, "Up! Up! Up!" Michaela burst into tears and rolled herself into the fetal position. Ella was stunned. She had not expected such a reaction, and I could see the pain in her face. But after that, she was much gentler with Michaela and bought her many presents.

When we returned from London, though, there was a sudden change. Michaela's next blood test was alarmingly bad. I remember the moment when the laboratory secretary handed me the results. From her worried stare, I understood that my face must have been white. I felt my heart pounding hard but hoped that my expression stayed calm. I was gripped by the anxiety that I would lose control and show my fear in front of the child.

This had been my greatest fear throughout the years of Michaela's illness. I dreaded the moment she would become aware of what her father and mother knew: that she would die. Not that we would tell her, heaven forbid, but that she would read it in our faces, in our gestures. When I bought her new shoes or when I sewed a new dress or blouse for her, I could not banish the thought that this could be her last dress or her last pair of shoes. *Will she live long enough to wear them? Can she read the anxiety in my eyes?* I forced myself to seem cheerful or at least composed, to smile when my heart contracted with fear for her young life. I did not know how long her disease might last. I did not, as Otto did, look for information about cirrhosis patients' average life expectancy and the manner of their death. On the contrary, I avoided finding out the details and possible complications of the disease. I felt that it was better so; it gave me more strength to pretend to her that soon she would get better.

After our return from London, there was no more respite. Michaela became irritable, and there were constant conflicts between her and Otto. She was moody and often unpleasant and nagging. Otto didn't have patience with her. She wanted to go away and live in a kibbutz.

Otto consulted with a friend named Ephraim in Ein HaHoresh, and he proposed that Michaela come to the kibbutz as an "outside" student. She would join the group of kibbutz children of her age, live with them in their dormitory, and study with them. Ephraim and his wife would become her foster parents and look after her. It was a generous offer; they both knew of Michaela's disease and her difficulties, yet they were ready to take the responsibility. Michaela was enthusiastic. She had been a kibbutz child till age six, and for her it meant a kind of return to better times. Ein HaHoresh is next to Kibbutz Givat Chaim and is not very far from Hadassim.

The plan did not work out. Michaela moved to a room with three other girls in the dormitory of her age group. The school year began; she was in grade ten. But soon there were problems. She didn't feel well, and her foster parents began to worry. We visited her once or twice a week. It soon became apparent that she could not stay there. Her relationship with the roommates also didn't add to the situation; kibbutz children are known to be a close-knit group that does not easily integrate outsiders.

After less than three months, we brought her home again. She could not join her former class; she had lost many days due to spells when she had stayed in bed feeling unwell and didn't go to school. It was therefore decided to have her repeat grade nine. She was not too upset by this because she also had friends in that class, and the teachers were the same. They all knew of her illness and treated her with consideration, although she did not demand any privileges.

The cortisone treatment had been long abandoned, since it had not brought any improvement. She now only got medication for her symptoms, and when her blood count went down, she got blood transfusions, which rapidly improved her strength, although not for long. What bothered her most were the painful cramps in her legs, which she got frequently, especially in bed.

We got advice that organic foods could improve her state, and a specialist in organic diet, Yitzhak Ben-Uri, was recommended to us. He lived in the outskirts of Netanya, where he grew many kinds of organic vegetables and herbs. He had built an annex where a few patients could stay and be under his constant super-vision. He tested Michaela by examining the irises in her eyes. He had a chart with explanations, and amazingly, even we could see where the damaged liver was indicated. He was aware that he could not cure her and told us so, but he promised she would feel much better if she followed the diet he prescribed.

Michaela was eager to cooperate and agreed to stay in the little hut in the yard but often joined the family in their house, where she was welcome and treated kindly. For the first days she had to fast, but Ben-Uri did not dare leave her completely without food. In just a few days Michaela was feeling better; there was no doubt that the diet was beneficial. In a week she returned home much improved; her skin had a healthy look, and she was cheerful.

However, to keep the diet was a complicated task. First of all, she was not allowed to eat anything that contained salt, which meant I had to travel to a health shop to buy unsalted bread and other items that, until then, I never thought contained salt. No animal products were allowed, neither milk nor cheese, and no eggs or baked goods made with eggs. Only unsprayed vegetables and fruit, which we bought from a farmer near Netanya or in a health shop in Tel Aviv. Many kinds of vegetables and fruit were also forbidden, such as tomatoes, eggplants, and oranges. It became a very time-consuming—not to mention expensive—task, but of course I did it all to the best of my ability.

Yet it turned out that Michaela was cheating. She would sneak into the fridge and take a piece of cheese or a pickle. She developed an obsessive craving for salt and did not hesitate to open other people's kitchen cabinets and help herself to things she was forbidden from eating. Neighbors told me secretly, not that they minded, but they worried for her, because they knew that she was on this strict diet.

In those years, when she was sixteen, seventeen, and eighteen, she loved new clothes, and I would sew dresses and skirts and blouses and knit her sweaters and pullovers. She was impatient and moaned at me when I needed her to try them on, which caused family conflicts. Otto became angry when she raised her voice at me, and he shouted at her that she should be grateful that I sewed for her; at me he shouted that I should stop making dresses for her when she was only abusive and didn't appreciate it. I had a hard time keeping them apart.

Michaela was about eighteen when her childhood friend Gaby reappeared. He was already in the army, serving at a base not far from Hadassim, and he started visiting quite often. She liked his visits. When he and Michaela were together in her room, I could hear her giggling; he was funny and amusing. In time I understood that they had become lovers. She confided it to me when she realized that she might become pregnant without knowing it. For several years, she had not had her monthly periods.

I made an appointment with the gynecologist Dr. Gross in Netanya. She examined her and then looked at me with a worried expression. "I cannot find her uterus; it is completely undeveloped," she said. I told her of Michaela's disease, which explained the situation. On the one hand, I was relieved that there was no danger of her becoming pregnant; on the other, I mourned the fact that she would never become a mother. As improbable as it was, my heart still hurt at the certainty.

Michaela was in the last class of high school. It was clear she would not be able to take all the matriculation exams; her attendance had been irregular, and her mental capacity was also affected. I didn't know it then, but later I understood that her brain was not receiving enough oxygen because of her low blood count. The school principal, Zeev Alon, spoke to her and gently explained that instead of a matriculation certificate, she would get a school-end certificate, which proved that she completed eight years of high school.

The question now was what she would do. Her classmates all went to the army, so she no longer had friends in the village. We thought she could learn some handicraft. She was talented in that field; she produced very pretty batik hangings and ceramic objects, and she also drew tasteful fashion designs. There was a handicraft workshop in Hadassim, led by Fili, the artistic wife of the school principal. She encouraged Michaela and paid special attention to her. In those years enamel jewelry came into fashion, and Michaela decided that this was what she would like to learn.

There was a shop that sold all the necessary tools and materials for enamel jewelry on Sheinkin Street in Tel Aviv. The owners, a husband-and-wife team, imported the materials from a German firm, and the wife also taught a course for beginners. Michaela started to learn there twice a week.

I drove with her to Tel Aviv. Sometimes I would stay with her and watch, helping her to understand the instructions and so learning them myself; other times I waited for her in a café. She loved the work, and we decided to establish a small work corner in her room, so she could start making things at home. I bought a sturdy worktable (the metal bases of the pieces had to be hammered into shape), a firing oven, tools and dies, clasps and chains and pins, and a lot more. But after a few weeks, traveling to Tel Aviv tired Michaela, and we stopped the course. She was also unable to grasp the more complicated procedures; her memory did not retain what she learned. From then on, she only worked at home.

Michaela did not suffer pains from her disease; the liver itself does not hurt. As I said before, she would get very painful cramps in her legs, which could last as long as half an hour. It helped a little when I massaged her leg muscles. Another problem was that her arms and legs, and even her abdomen, would become swollen, and she would gain several kilos. Against this (and without my knowing) she took diuretic pills, which expelled the water but made her skin dry and peel. She also suffered from dryness of her mouth, and there was a kind of alcoholic smell in her breath.

Nevertheless, she had a new boyfriend, Avi. He was a good-looking boy from Kfar Netter, a neighboring village. A nice, regular, down-to-earth, friendly fellow, doing his army service. On his free days he borrowed his parents' car and came to visit Michaela and sometimes took her out. When she was with him, she somehow revived, dressed up, put on makeup, and looked charming. Avi probably wasn't aware of the seriousness of her illness.

The disease had been dormant between her tenth and sixteenth years, but following our London trip, it progressed slowly but steadily, and the necessity for blood transfusions became more frequent. Each of us donated blood to the blood bank so that she had an ensured supply. After age twelve, Michaela was no longer treated at the Tel HaShomer children's department but in the department for internal diseases at Meir Medical Center in Kfar Saba.

One evening in September 1970, Otto suffered a heart attack. He was put in the cardiology department, where he had to lie without moving for twenty-one days. At the same time, Michaela was hospitalized two floors below, being treated for her edemas and getting a blood transfusion.

The stress I was under was almost unbearable. Here was my husband, his life in acute danger; there my daughter with her suffering. Moreover, this time she was more confused than ever, repeating endlessly some silly phrase and giggling uncontrollably. I became frantic with worry. Little nine-year-old Ronny was at home, being cared for by our friend Lea and by neighbors. Shimon was already in the army.

After a few days, Michaela was well enough to be released home. The blood transfusion had helped. Otto returned three weeks later. He was not allowed to go back to work and had to take it easy. But he felt well and soon became his old self again.

Keeping the saltless diet was all the time a great problem for Michaela. I would cook all kinds of appetizing food without salt, using dried celery leaves, which seem to taste salty but do no harm. She had a craving that made her seek the most salted foods she could lay her hands on. No warnings, no talking to her helped. Her legs and feet were constantly swollen. She tested them herself, pressing a finger into the flesh, creating a depression that did not disappear after she removed her finger. Somehow she managed to get hold of diuretic pills, which she hid in her bedside table drawer. I was discreet and never opened her private hiding places, but Otto did. He saw the pills and confiscated them. But after a time she had new ones. It was clear that she bought them frequently without a prescription at a pharmacy in Netanya, when she occasionally went for a haircut or just for an outing with Avi.

Summer came, the beginning of the school vacations. We used to go swimming in the pool, which was free for all Hadassim residents. Sometimes Michaela came, too, but she was becoming increasingly tired. Nevertheless, she went with Otto to Netanya to buy a present for my approaching birthday. Otto chose a picnic hamper, and Michaela a small cooking pot with a lid.

Our flat needed redecoration, and I arranged with a house painter to do Michaela's room first. Since she wanted to lie down during the morning, Ora Goren, the village nurse, invited her to come and rest in her guest room. In the afternoon Ora came to say that Michaela had not got up since morning and she was unable to wake her.

I went with her, and together we made Michaela sit up. She was unnaturally drowsy, and we had to hold her up to lead her the short distance to our house. Her room had not been finished yet; all the furniture was still outside. We laid Michaela on her bed on the lawn and covered her with a thin sheet, and she immediately fell asleep again. In the evening, when the room was finished and the furniture returned, Otto and I managed to bring her back in. But she was almost unconscious. During the night, Otto and I checked several times, but she did not wake and had not moved. She also had not passed water since the previous morning.

At a very early hour, I asked Ami, our next-door neighbor, to help me lift her into the car, as Otto was not allowed to do any lifting. I folded the back seat and made a kind of bed for her to lie on comfortably, and we drove to Meir hospital. Otto, who had examined her drawer and found an empty bottle of the diuretic pills, reported it to the doctor. On her chart was written *Suicide?*

A few evenings before, I had had a long talk with Michaela. She had been dejected, complaining about her swollen legs and abdomen. I'd sat on her bed and tried to help her overcome the black mood, speaking about food. If she would return to keeping her strict diet, she would not have these swellings. "Don't you remember how good you felt at Ben-Uri's, when you ate only what he allowed? You could feel well again if you kept the saltless diet."

She'd looked at me with hope in her eyes and had said, "You think even now . . . ?"

Her words had scared me. Was she aware that her disease was incurable? I'd wondered. All those years of her illness, my deepest fear was that she would somehow learn there was no hope. With my greatest efforts, I had kept up the pretense that she would get well again. It needed extreme strength. Often I wished to let go and cry, to embrace her and mourn for her young lost life. But it was imperative never to let her suspect my fears. Moreover, I also had to hold up the morale for Otto, who leaned on me for support. His rage at his inability to enforce a cure for her drove him crazy; sometimes he even behaved quite irrationally.

I could not allow her to give up. "Of course," I'd said. "Just try to overcome your craving for salt. You will see how good you will feel." It had seemed to convince her, and she'd gone to sleep with a renewed determination.

In the hospital, Michaela never woke up again. They put her opposite the nurses' station, to keep an eye on the monitor to which she was attached. I sat with her and watched her beautiful, serene face, the outline of her young feminine body under the sheet, and followed her breathing. The hours passed, and she did not move. I stopped a young woman doctor in the corridor and asked her if there was a chance that Michaela would come out of her coma. She answered curtly, "I have seen such cases," then she walked on briskly. When I left late in the evening, there was no change.

Next day was Thursday. On that day Avi was to return from America, where he had visited his brother. He had been absent for many weeks, and Michaela had been expecting him eagerly. He arrived in his car and honked the horn under her window, as he used to do, his face all smiles. Shoshana, our neighbor on the left, came out immediately and asked him not to make a noise. She told him that Michaela was in hospital and her condition was very serious. He was crestfallen and left quietly.

I saw and heard him from the window but did not speak to him. We were at home at the time, since Otto had to rest after we had been sitting with Michaela the whole morning.

A while later, Shoshana came to tell us that there was a call from the hospital. In those days, we still didn't have a phone. The message was that Michaela had stopped breathing. A member of the family had to come to the hospital to identify the body.

Neither Otto nor I had the strength to do that. We summoned Shimon, who was in Eilat, working in a children's summer camp. He arrived a few hours later and, together with my cousin Doron, drove straight to the hospital. The doctors asked us to allow a postmortem on Michaela's diseased liver for medical purposes. We agreed.

Ronny, then ten years old, was playing somewhere outside when the message arrived. He heard the news from one of the neighbors.

The funeral took place the next day at noon. The cemetery is in Even Yehuda, the village next to Hadassim. Friends and relatives gathered on our front lawn, where Michaela had slept only three days before. The ritual washing of the body was done by Shulamit, a Yemenite woman from the neighboring village of Ein Yaacov, our longtime babysitter. I asked her later how the autopsy scar looked, and she showed me on her finger how small the incision was. She said Michaela looked beautiful and peaceful.

I still wonder: Was Michaela aware of what she was doing when she swallowed the whole bottle of pills? Did she do it in the hope of getting rid of the edema before Avi came back from America? Was her mind muddled, or could she still think rationally? As it is, she was spared years of suffering, which inevitably would have ended in death anyway. I wish I could be sure that she only wanted to look slim for Avi's sake and that she did not intend to die.

CHAPTER FIFTY

Stolperstein

Not long ago, I received the news from Heiner Schultz that a memorial plaque with my mother's name—called a *Stolperstein* in German—would be placed on Falkenbergsweg, a street in Hamburg, on September 29, 2010.

As I was in Prague at the time, I decided to fly to Hamburg to participate in the ceremony. There are already twenty thousand such memorial stones in Germany, and over three thousand in Hamburg alone. The artist Gunter Demnig produces them and places each of them himself.

I arrived early in the morning, a day before the ceremony, and was met by Heiner and his daughter. On the way we passed well-to-do villages on the outskirts of Hamburg. I tried to recognize spots where we did forced labor, but everything looked totally unlike the war-damaged places of the past.

After breakfast Heiner took me by bus to see the place where our camp used to stand. Now there is only a grassy clearing in the wood. The only reminders of our camp are two concrete foundations where the barracks stood. On a large rock in one corner, an attached bronze plaque commemorated the camp of the

Jewish women. Heiner tells me that vandals ripped it off several times. Instead of the plaque, the text is now chiseled directly into the rock, paid for by a private sponsor.

Not far from there is Falkenbergsweg, which is actually a narrow road with houses on one side and the foot of the wooded Falkenberg on the other. Here is the spot where one *Stolperstein* has already been inserted, and the next one will be my mother's.

In the morning we retrace our steps together with Karin, Heiner's wife. A lady with a video camera has already come and polished the existing plaque, preceding Heiner, who had wanted to do it with utensils he brought in his knapsack. In a short time a small crowd gathers around, some journalists, a few students with their history teacher, and some members of the voluntary organization that started this commemorative project.

The artist sculptor arrives with a few workmen and a trailer containing the tools. While he kneels down to remove a few paving stones to make room for the *Stolperstein*, a few reporters interview me. They ask me to hold the stone with the bronze plaque. The concrete cube is heavy, the polished bronze top smooth and shiny. They take pictures while I read the name of my mother, Elisabeth Polach, and the dates of her birth and her death. I don't want to be photographed crying and create a cheap drama, but my eyes do sting and are surely red.

The artist is now ready, and he inserts the cube into the hole, pouring water over it to make it set, and the workers then fill the gaps with sand. The remaining sand is swept away and then Karin and another person each place two red roses next to the stone.

The ceremony ends. I stay a while to answer questions from the students, who are visibly moved, and then we disperse.

Now we have to hurry because there is a meeting with the members of the organization in Harburg. One of the ladies takes us in her car. Together with many more members, we attend a lecture in a hall, hear some explanations about a Jewish family who owned a shop on the busy street below. Then the large group descends to view the three stones in their memory and also lay red roses there. But not all passersby are aware of what the gathering is about. A young woman with a baby pram rushes by and scatters the roses.

The next day I get a guided tour of the city by my friendly hosts. It's a lot of walking, but the weather is pleasant, and the city beautiful with its multiple rivers, channels, and parks. My flight back to Prague, where I lived at the time, leaves at half past seven, and in just three hours I am magically back in my own bed.

CHAPTER FIFTY-ONE

Where Do I Feel at Home?

Otto and I started visiting Prague every year from 1990, until he became too ill to travel any longer. When he died, I used the money he had received as compensation for his father's property and bought a small apartment in Prague. Twice a year, in spring and in autumn, I spend several weeks there. I meet my old friends and have also found new ones. Although I speak Hebrew well enough, the Czech language and culture are still closer to my heart.

When people ask me, "Where are you really at home?" I don't know what to answer. My roots are no longer in the Czech Republic, but at the same time, I cannot say that I feel rooted in Israel. I enjoy the charm of Prague and the Czech landscape, but in Israel I love Lake Kinneret and the Mediterranean, where I go swimming every morning. My loved ones are buried in Israel, but the names of my parents and my grandfather, who perished in the Shoah and have no graves, are engraved on a marble headstone in the New Jewish Cemetery in Prague. When I am in Prague, I am relaxed and feel at home. But when I return to Netanya, it too is my home. . . .

And when I die, I will be buried next to Otto in Kibbutz Givat Chaim.

CHAPTER FIFTY-TWO

I Need Not Delay Anymore

One of my activities is giving talks about my personal Holocaust to students in Israel and also abroad. After the lecture I usually answer questions from the audience. For the youngsters, it's a harrowing experience, and often they ask with hope in their voice, "But after the war, was your life a happy one?" Can I disappoint them and say no? I make some funny comment to avoid a direct answer. But I think to myself, *If only it were. . . .*

Dear reader, I cannot stop here, leaving you feeling sorry for my life's sorrows and losses. Miraculous things happen to everyone and to me, too, of course. Here they come.

I have been lucky to reach the respectable age of eighty-nine (at the time of writing this). I am still reasonably healthy, despite being half deaf. I can travel, listen to music, drive my car, read books, paint flowers, play bridge, swim in the Mediterranean, meet old friends, and make new ones. I have recently even become the heroine of a book named *The Librarian of Auschwitz.*

My son Ronny is happily married and has two lovely children, my pretty granddaughter, Gabby, who recently finished her army service and enrolled at university, and handsome Daniel, who finished the last grade of high school and will soon start army service. Ronny's wife, Orna, is like a daughter to me.

Shimon's sons, Ehud and Assaf, have become wonderful men. Both are tall and good-looking, friendly and loving. They are successful in their work and are raising a new generation of smart kids. My relations with them and their mother, Miriam, couldn't be better. (Old bitter memories are forgotten.) I love to spend weekends with them and play with the little ones. It makes me happy that, despite Hitler's efforts to exterminate us, there are now fourteen Kraus descendants—the last one, my great-granddaughter, Michelle, is just ten months old.

No longer do I wait till . . . till the war ends, till we are liberated, till I marry, till the child is born, till we have more money, till the school year ends, till peace comes . . .

I need not delay anymore; I have caught up with my life.

ACKNOWLEDGMENTS

I AM INDEBTED to the publisher of Akropolis, Filip Tomaš. It was his idea to turn my reminiscences into a book. I wish my close friend, Dana Lieblová, had lived to see the book published. She had just completed the translation to Czech when she suddenly died. I am also grateful to Hana Hříbková, the gifted editor, for merging the separate parts into a whole. These three people became the midwives of my *Delayed Life*.

ABOUT THE AUTHOR

DITA KRAUS was born in Prague in 1929. In 1942, when Dita was thirteen years old, she and her parents were deported to Ghetto Theresienstadt, later to Auschwitz, where Dita's father died. She and her mother were sent to forced labour in Germany and finally to the concentration camp of Bergen-Belsen. Shortly after liberation, Dita's mother died.

After the war Dita married the author Otto B. Kraus, who was a fellow prisoner at Auschwitz and a teacher in the camp. They emigrated to Israel in 1949, where they both worked as teachers. They had three children. Since Otto's death in 2000, Dita has lived alone in Netanya. She has four grandchildren and four great-grandchildren.

Dita was the subject of Antonio Iturbe's internationally bestselling novel *The Librarian of Auschwitz*, published by Macmillan in 2017. Otto wrote a novel about his experiences, *The Children's Block*. Despite the horrors of the concentration camps, Dita has kept her positive approach to life. She paints delicate watercolors of the colourful wildflowers that grow in Israel.